MW00653016

manhood: the bare reality

Inspirational

Inspirational: A mixture of 'Inspire' and 'Rational', the thing about that is; once inspired, rational thinking goes out the window so with that in mind:

Can I cause you to follow a dream you had, to make you into a 'better' version of your dad?
Will I make you take stock of your life to be a 'better' wife?
What if my words lingered in your mind and in days you find yourself doing the 'right thing'?
That you pick up that dusty instrument and start (again) to sing?
What if old passions were inflamed by my words and how they were framed?
Let's say I painted pictures with my words and you saw a farmer with a herd.
Are you going to leave your nine to five, pack your car, drive, drive and drive until you reach the countryside and when you get to somewhere quaint, unpack your car and paint?
Should what I say remind you of a time when you were free, will you quit your life as it is shouting 'I'M NOT BEING ME!'?
What if, in this little verse I said 'There is nothing worse than not following your dream.'? Would your heart give a little scream at the memories of your youth, that halcyon summer spent in the DJ's booth?
Would a flashback come to mind of when you used to write in rhyme?
That instrument you played, how did it get waylaid?
Did you invent a thing but didn't get a patent?
What dreams are in you but unfortunately latent?
I want to bring your passion to the fore so when you get home and go through your bathroom door, stand in front of the mirror, stare at your own face, smile and think about your place in this humdrum world, think about the universe through which you're being hurled, realise your strengths, confidence and slightly selfish part, notice the swelling of the good bit of your heart, focus all your energy on the best bits of you and really understand that you can be SUPERYOU!

Carl Chamberlain, Poet
One of the 100 men in *Manhood: The Bare Reality*

manhood: the bare reality

Laura Dodsworth

pinter & martin

Manhood: the Bare Reality

First published in 2017 by Pinter & Martin Ltd, reprinted 2017, 2021
Text and images copyright © Laura Dodsworth 2017

Laura Dodsworth has asserted her moral right to be identified as the author of this work in accordance with the copyright, designs and patents act of 1988.

All rights reserved.
ISBN 978-1-78066-425-5

Editor: Susan Last
Design: Blok Graphic, London

A catalogue record for this book is available from the British library.

This book is sold subject to the condition that it shall not, by way of trade and otherwise, be lent, resold, hired out, or otherwise circulated without the publisher's prior consent in any form or binding or cover other than that in which it is published and without a similar condition being imposed on the subsequent purchaser. The author and publisher disclaim, as far as the law allows, any liability arising directly or indirectly from the use, or misuse, of the information contained in this book.

Printed and bound in the EU by Hussar

Pinter & Martin Ltd
6 Effra Parade
London SW2 1PS

www.pinterandmartin.com
www.barereality.net

Contents

Please note that all the stories in *Manhood* are personal opinion. The views expressed are those of the contributors and are not endorsed by the creator or publisher. No book can replace the diagnostic expertise and medical advice of a trusted physician. Please consult your doctor before making any decisions that may affect your health, particularly if you suffer from any medical condition or have any symptom that may require treatment.

Foreword

Laura Dodsworth has photographed 100 penises and published them. It makes a lovely addition to the coffee table for when company drops by. Perhaps the kids would like a look?

And there you have it. Our nearly universal anxiety when confronted with what Dodsworth describes as something completely taboo. Namely, the male reproductive organ. But Dodsworth's images aren't the central focus of this book. The central focus of Dodsworth's book is men's personal stories. Which brings us to more taboos of a different sort.

Men are are all the same, right? This idea underlies every story we have about men in bars, men at work, men on the street, men in marriages, men in love. Describe the fellow at the office who won't stop making awkward jokes about women, and we all nod our heads in agreement. Yeah, him.

But here's the challenge. The often ugly stereotypes we have about men flourish in the absence of more personal stories; in what is a near vacuum of any intimate understanding of actual men's lives. What do we ever hear of men's anxieties, fears, challenges, and secret joys? Men are daily policed and bullied to hide these stories because our culture enforces a version of manhood that is emotionally stoic, self reliant and unrelentingly self assured. We live in a culture where "real" men don't fail or cry and they sure as hell don't need any damn help.

Telling our stories is an act of giving and receiving help at the most basic human level. When we tell our stories of living, of our struggles, our joys and losses; healing and affirmation are granted to the teller and the listener, equally. But when generations of men are taught from a very early age to hide their private selves, their intimate stories, a narrative vacuum ensues. And as we all know, nature abhors a vacuum. So, men's stories are told for them, by the red headlines of rape and war, blood thirsty CEO's and power mad politicians; themes that rush in to take over the narrative, declaring men, in the collective silence, to be this or that, or the other.

We rightfully honor women's stories about their bodies, their journeys, their lives. The challenges women face in our garishly photoshopped world of unyielding abuse, violence and murder are spirit crushing. Women bravely telling their stories are acts of defiance and liberation.

But what of men? It turns out that images of penises are the perfect metaphor for men's most private selves, walled off from our collective awareness by shaming, held in check by our collective uncertainty about why we should give them our attention and for what possible purpose?

Refreshingly, you hold a book full of men's stories and men's bodies, their appetites, their joys, their insecurities and the path their lives take. One would have to assume that having your penis photographed keeps it top of mind. As such, these are quite surprising stories, refreshingly frank and honest observations, funny and sad.

By constructing her book in the way Dodsworth has, balancing straight forward images of men's penises against their winding complex stories, Dodsworth dares us to look. Which is an important pattern breaking moment, both personally and culturally. And when we do take that risk, when we do look, we discover not only the refreshing courage of each man's choice to be visible, but also the importance of acknowledging how vastly diverse men actually are.

Mark Greene
Senior Editor, *The Good Men Project*
Author, *Remaking Manhood*

Introduction

For two years I photographed and interviewed women about their breasts and in May 2015 *Bare Reality: 100 women, their breasts, their stories* was published. As I undertook this project I assumed my next project would continue to explore women's stories. Instead, after the book came out, I found myself drawn, perhaps compelled, to create an inner psychological and creative balance, and explore men's stories.

In recent years, *Bare Reality* and many more books, plays, films and art projects have allowed women to share their stories and reclaim their bodies, but penises remain the last taboo. Subject of exaggeration, source of pleasure, means to reproduce, cause of emotional anxiety, why don't men talk more about their penises? It's time to reveal men's thoughts and feelings and celebrate this important body part. It's time for *Bare Reality* with balls!

Discussions about masculinity, boys in crisis, male suicide rates, male body image, men's rights activists and a backlash to feminism are on the rise. While women may have suffered from their breasts being appropriated, packaged and sold back as an idealised aesthetic currency, men's penises are almost completely taboo. In the age of both internet porn and the ubiquitous airbrush, it's never been as important to dispel myths and ease anxieties.

In a similar style to *Bare Reality*, 100 men were photographed and interviewed. The photographs are educational, sensitive and honest, presenting the normal spectrum of size and shape, hopefully helping men with body image anxiety. There are no digitally-expanded 'packages' in underwear advertising, no huge jackhammer porn penises, just real-life men in all their diversity and glory. Many more men than I could have imagined have suffered from the feeling that they are too small, too inadequate in some way, and this belief has bled into different aspects of their life. Why should these notions about size blight lives and perpetuate shame?

Breasts and penises are not direct counterparts but both embody ideas of femininity and masculinity, womanhood and manhood, and offer intimate windows into our emotional and psychological worlds. Feminism has helped women to re-interpret womanhood and break down feminine stereotypes. I don't feel this has happened enough yet for men. I don't claim to hold the answers but instead offer 100 men's thoughts, feelings and stories.

In some ways, *Bare Reality* was a response to the men in my life and the male stories all around me in society and the media. I became more comfortable with my own womanhood and redefined being a woman on my own, fresh terms. But I didn't feel I knew enough about men. What stories would men tell?

These days we are all less bound by gender and traditional roles, but is there more confusion about what being a man means? In a world where men's magazines can feature moisturisers and face scrubs, but honest, heartfelt emotional confessions are rare, it's time to hear from men themselves. If we're moving past the old definitions of masculinity, who better to talk about where we are now and where we're going than men.

From veteran to vicar, from porn addict to prostate cancer survivor, men from all walks of life, aged from 20 to 92, share honest reflections about their bodies, sexuality, relationships, fatherhood, work and health in *Manhood*.

One of the stereotypes about men is that they don't talk about their feelings. Masculinity is equated with 'strong and silent' and the 'stiff upper lip'. Undertaking this project was a risk - would men talk? Would they talk to me, a woman? I found they stepped into the conversation with hunger, and a surprising honesty. This project exists because 100 men did talk frankly about their feelings. What a privilege, and how fascinating, these exchanges were.

I hope that *Manhood* will open up conversations about what it is to be a man. Young men may recognise their own aspirations and anxieties. Women will find *Manhood* enlightening and moving - I don't think many will have ever heard men talk like this. I hope that awareness of male cancers and men's mental health will be advanced by this book. Mainly, I hope we can all understand each other a little better and find more kindness for ourselves and the men we know in every day life.

Manhood: The Bare Reality is not a manifesto for men, nor my world view. 100 men simply give you their stories, how they think and feel. They reveal their manhood in both senses, with grace, humour, courage, and sensitivity. I fell in love with Men. Perhaps you will fall a little bit in love too.

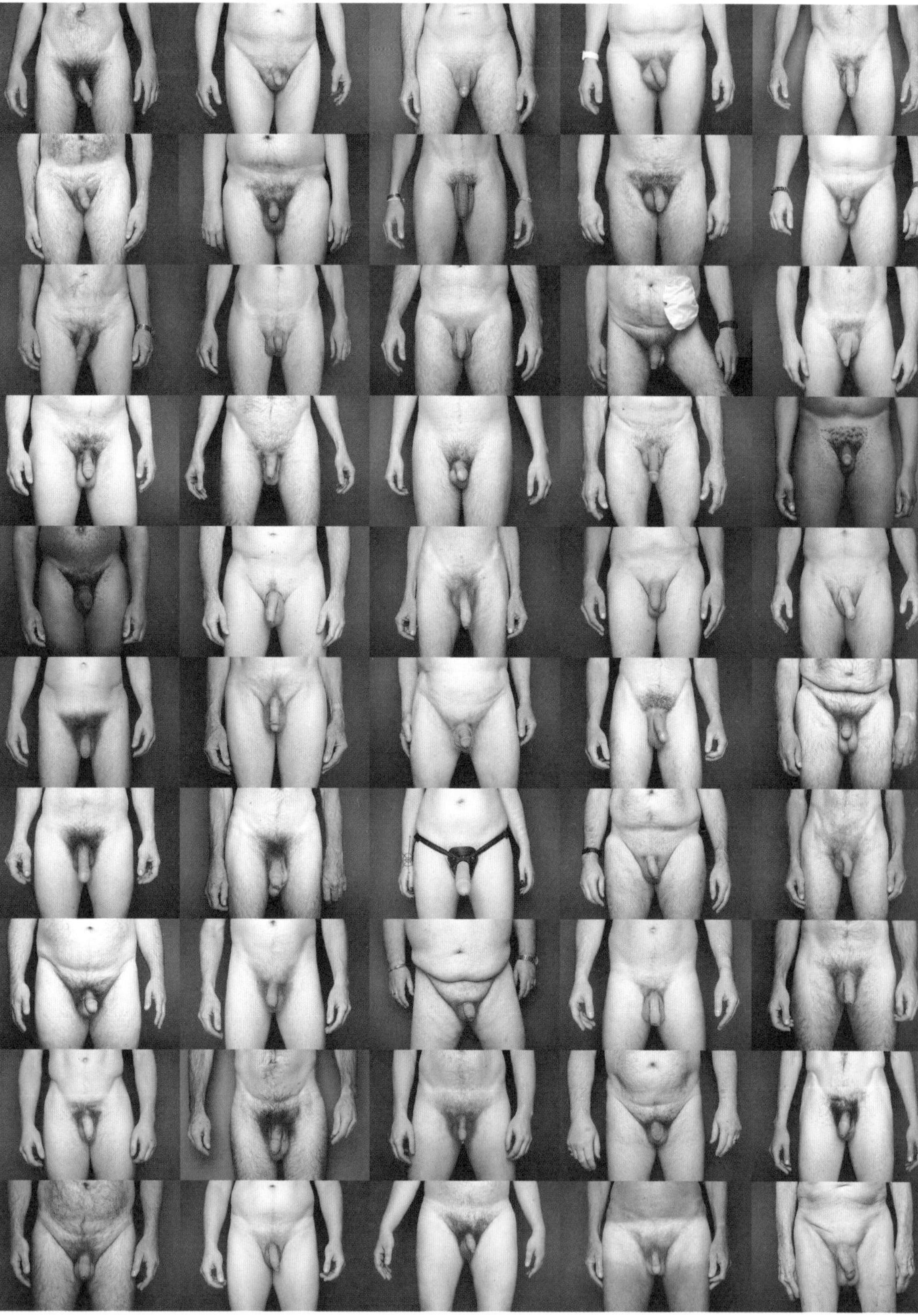

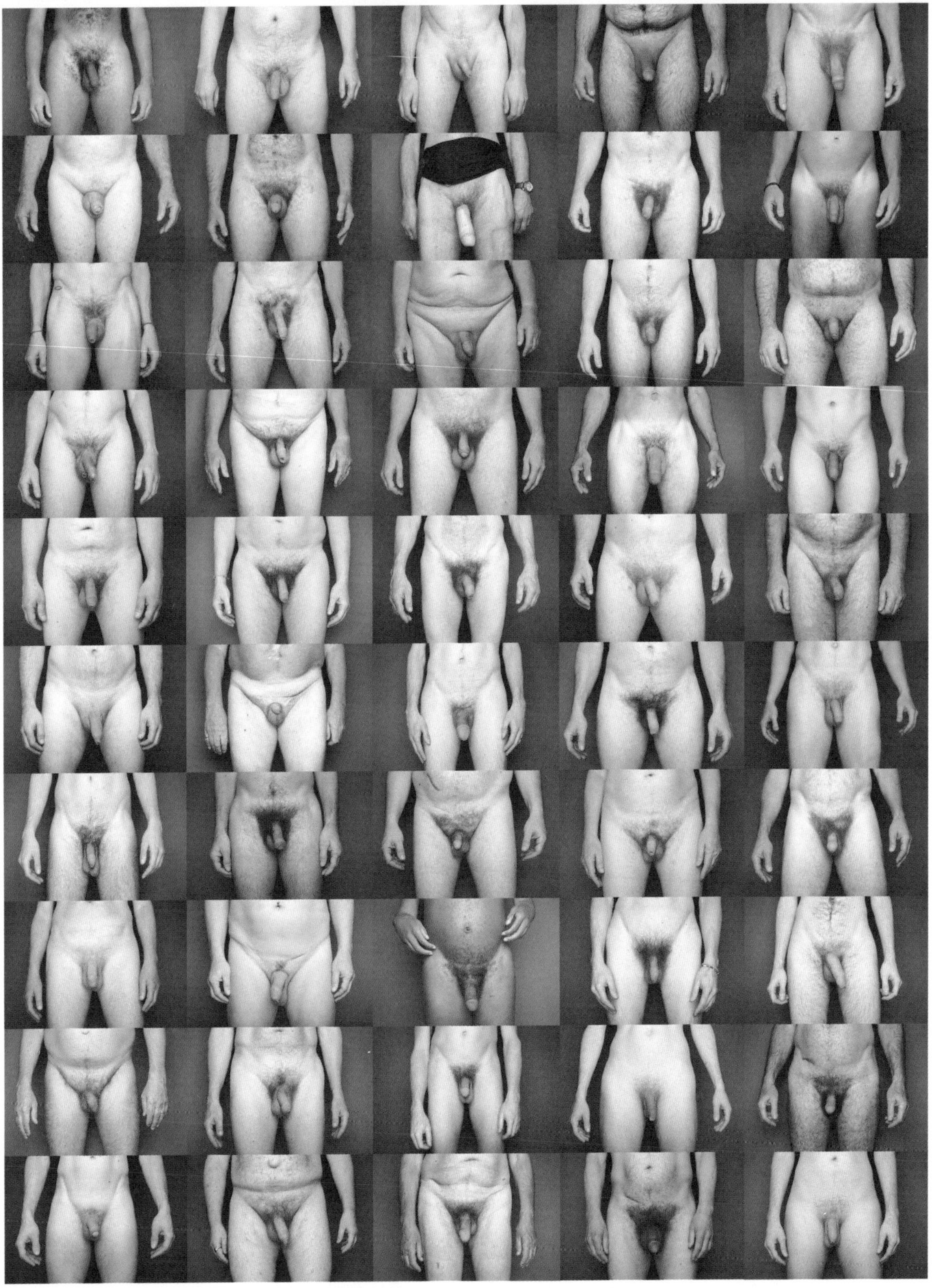

"I lost my virginity to the wife of my school teacher"

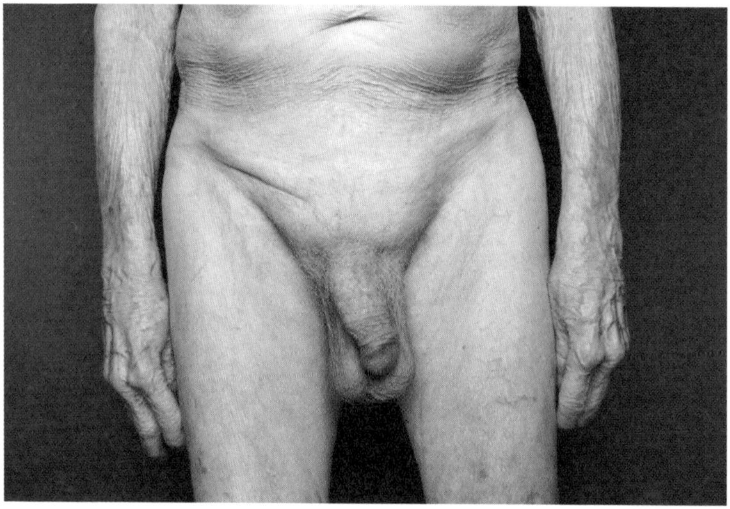

I lost my virginity to the wife of my grammar school teacher. He was sent to France as a spy and resistance fighter. They had made an arrangement that while he was in France and there was no way they could keep in touch, that if they were sexually interested in someone else, they could have a relationship. They were both in love and would remain that way throughout the war, but it was an arrangement. I was 18 and went to stay with her when I had my embarkation leave. I knew them both and was fond of them both.

I was in a single bedroom. In the morning, the door opens, and in comes this woman, in her robe. She took it off and kneeled beside the bed. And there was this 18-year-old naïve boy. Man? Boy. Not sexually experienced at all. I'd never had sexual intercourse. It was an act of kindness. I immediately fell in love with her, of course.

I loved her. I'd loved her before. I'd had great feeling for her, but this was incredible. I left with an enormous pleasure. On the other hand, I was in the army. War wasn't something I'd chosen, I was called up.

I had an easy war. I was a driver and a wireless operator. I didn't come in contact with the enemy. I didn't have difficult tasks, I just operated a radio. I didn't like being conscripted, but I didn't object. It was a justifiable war and I expected to be conscripted.

After my school teacher's wife, my next time with a woman was with a prostitute in a Naples brothel. I stayed all night. That's unusual in brothels. When I woke up and looked at her, I thought she was lovely.

I no longer have an attitude towards masculinity. I am affected by dementia now. A psychiatrist said I have dementia and prescribed drugs. It affects the way you think as well as your memory. Up until the age of 87 I still had normal feelings about sex and attraction, but these completely cut off and disappeared with my dementia. If I look at a pornographic image I have no sexual feeling. I am physically incapable, I couldn't get an erection now. I occasionally masturbated until a few years ago, but it's not there for me now, it has disappeared completely.

The absence of sexual feeling doesn't matter to me at all. When I was younger it would have been disastrous. You know, if a man can't get an erection, he'd go and see a doctor and get it sorted. Like all men, it was a major interest, but I have no interest in it now. I have been married twice and had a number of affairs that mattered to me a great deal.

Life has changed for women and men during my life. There is a more liberal partnership between men and women and an improvement. Although when I was young there were plenty of men who weren't sexist individuals.

Longevity is increasing. My grandparents died in their 70s, but they were more like people in their 90s now. Ageing happens later now. Up until I was 87 I felt normal in most ways. OK, I couldn't ride a bike as well as a young man.

I would claim I am a male feminist. What's the word that covers all the different problems? This dementia... There are other forms of oppression, like class oppression. That's it, I remember, I'm an intersectional feminist. I believe very much in that.

Ninety-two years old

“I told cancer to fuck off”

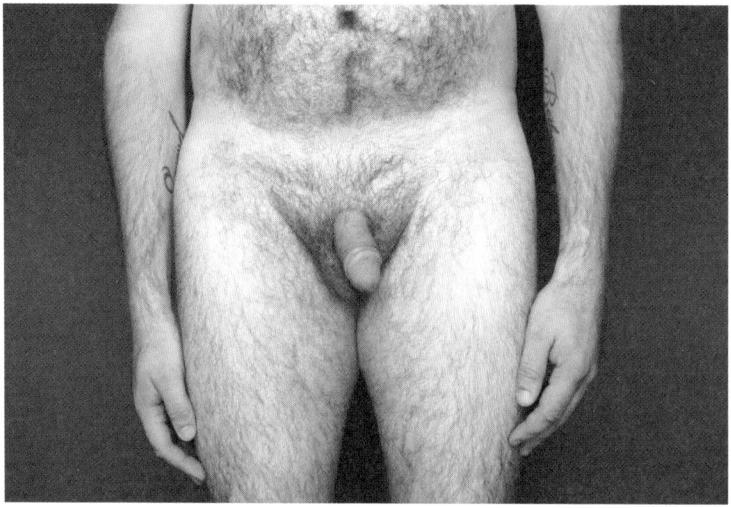

I’ve had testicular cancer twice. First when I was 22, and the second time a couple of years ago when I was 34. Shit happens.

I was lying in bed, having a scratch down there, masturbating, as you do, when I felt a lump on my left testicle, about the size of a pea. I was too embarrassed at the time to tell anyone about it. If I’d told my mum she would have made me go to the doctor, and he would have felt me down there, which I really didn’t want to happen.

I ignored it for a good nine months until it was the size of two fingers put together. I bit the bullet and told my mum I had a lump on my bollocks.

She looked it up in a medical book, which said it could be a cyst or testicular cancer. So I went to the doctor the next day.

The doctor said it was very unusual and sent me to the hospital. The urologist felt my bollock. By this time I was very scared. He said he couldn't be sure till after the biopsy, but he was 99 per cent sure it was testicular cancer. I thought I might die. The nine months I'd ignored the lump flashed by me like I was a drowning man. I fainted.

It was cancer, but it was in the early stages. I had three weeks of radiotherapy as well as having the testicle removed.

I felt lonely afterwards. I knew I wasn't on my own, but this was before the days of Facebook and Twitter. There weren't support groups in those days. There are shitloads now. I helped to form some of them!

One of the first things I did after the operation was get a porn magazine out and masturbate. I had to make sure it worked! *(laughs)* One testicle is fine, it doesn't affect the ability to have sex.

I met my fiancée four years later. We tried for kids, but it didn't happen. I had a sperm test. The swimmers were doing their thing, but there were hardly any of them. In a normal ejaculation there are close to a million swimmers. I only had a hundred. I'd frozen sperm before the radiotherapy, just in case. My mum talked me into it. She said, 'I won't be deprived of being a grandmother just because you're embarrassed. Besides, you do it every night anyway.' So my fiancée and I had IVF and we had twins, a boy and a girl.

After the kids were born I found myself feeling really tired and low. I had trouble concentrating. I wasn't as up for sex as I should have been. One day I felt like killing myself. I got very scared. I remembered hearing about another testicular cancer survivor who had felt the same and it had been due to hormones. The doctors tried to fob me off, said it was in my head, told me to grow up basically. It was shit. I had to go back about three times. In the end the doctor gave up and I had a blood test. He said my hormones were low but not that low. I went for a second opinion. When I saw an endocrinologist he said if I had seen him in the first place I would have already been on HRT.

I was 31 when I started taking HRT, a synthetic gel I rubbed on my arms. It worked straight away and I felt like normal again, like being really tired and then having a coffee and Red Bull. I had to shower the gel off before bed, otherwise it could rub it on to my fiancée and turn her into a bearded lady!

A few months later I found another lump in the shower. I thought, 'Shit, here we go again.' The GP tried to tell me it was a cyst, but I asked for an ultrasound for peace of mind. I could see the shadowy lump on the scan. I asked if it was cancer and the radiographer said he couldn't say. I said, 'Come on, there's just the two of us in the room. Is it cancer?' 'Yes.' Shit happens.

Cancer was no problem second time round. I knew what was coming. There was better support than 14 years before. I knew I would survive it. Both times I had cancer I told it to fuck off. I went to the shops the day after I was diagnosed the first time, and walked past a Cancer Research poster that said one in three of us would have it in our lifetimes. I thought, 'Shit, that's me.' And I said out loud, 'Well, I don't know what the fuck you're doing in me, but you can fuck off.' It felt like an invasion. My body was the battleground. For the first time in my life I felt confident, like 'This is me.'

Instead of the gel I now have an injection every ten weeks. That's for life. After the operation I waited till everyone was out, looked at some porn and had a wank. Everything worked. I was told that the first orgasm would hurt, which it did. Sperm is made in the testicles, semen is made in the prostate, so you can still come but there's no sperm. The missus couldn't wait to have a go on me. That was good!

I've had tattoos since having cancer. I'd seen pink ribbons for breast cancer, so I had an orchid one for testicular cancer. I've got toy soldiers holding a banner for testicular cancer. I have a tattoo that says 'Strong' in Japanese. At least, I hope it does! This tattoo says 'Survivor.' That's one for the testicular cancer group I'm involved with. This one says 'My brothers' and it's is dedicated to the testicular cancer brothers we've lost, the ones going through it and the ones who've come out the other side. This one here – 'The storm inside of us' – that's because the day before I was rediagnosed I watched a film called Lone Survivor and a character says, 'There's a storm inside of us. The deepest, darkest place we go to fight our biggest battles.' I thought that sounded good.

My mum died of cancer two years ago. She had skin cancer and it was everywhere. It was treated, but it came back in a big way, in her bones, liver, kidneys, you name it – and eventually the brain. The last time I saw her before the cancer took complete control of her was a chance meeting in a cancer centre. We were both there for a check-up. I got a 'Well done, the chemo's worked, you're alright.' Mum was there to see what else they could do. She was dead in a month. She died of cancer and I hated myself for surviving. I really, really hated myself. I tried to kill myself. I took an overdose. My fiancée came back from school and found me on the kitchen floor. I got referred to a shrink.

I started feeling low last week. It was the anniversary of trying to kill myself. I decided to see it as the anniversary of living instead. My mum would want me to be alive.

You can see something like this as a curse or a blessing. I see it as a blessing. It's changed my outlook on life. I found confidence for the first time in my life. I'd always been self-conscious before cancer. I wore glasses, I didn't have much success with girls, I felt useless. I told cancer to fuck off, and now I live in the moment.

It's one thing losing a bollock or two, but it could be far worse.

Thirty-six years old

"I've had more than my share of sex"

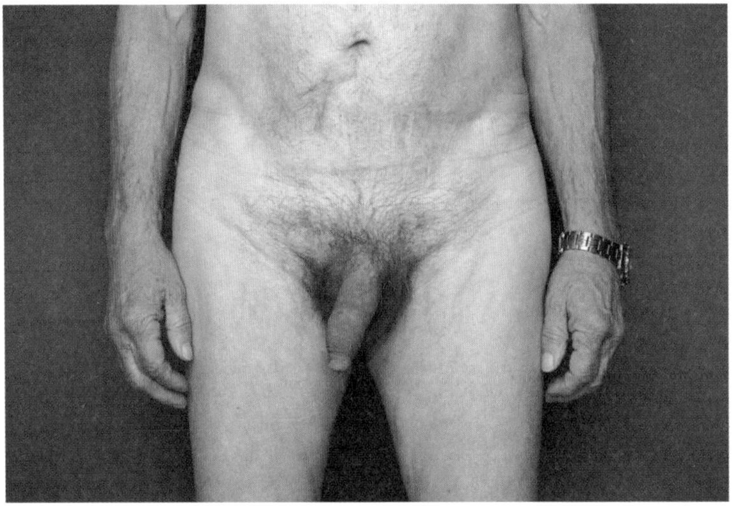

I don't have children. My father was a very cruel man and I didn't want to be like him. He was a nasty man. He was very successful, what they used to call a financier. He was at all the flash clubs in London. He couldn't relate to his family. My sister and I used to have nightmares about him. He was jealous of my relationship with my mother. By the time I left home when I was 16 he had done such a good job on me that I had the biggest insecurity complex you can imagine. I didn't think I was fit to walk under the carpet let alone on it. When something good has happened to me, I have had to make myself believe, 'Well, I am as good as anyone else.'

I went to boarding school when I was six. When I came home in the summer term I walked into the drawing room. I hadn't seen my father for three months. I had slightly muddy shoes. I said, 'Hello Daddy.' He threw the teapot at my head. I was such a nervous wreck by that age, my reactions were so fast, that I dodged it and it smashed on the wall beside me. When I was six he also threw a little toy dog I loved on the fire. He did it to annoy me. I pulled it out and sewed it all up with big stitches.

My mother was brought up in India. Her family lived like kings. They had their own private railway carriages. She rode elephants and played with the maharaja's children. She came to England and met my dad, who was a bit of a scallywag. He spent all her money. She only stayed with him because of the children. In those days, in the 1950s, what could she do?

He used to hit her. When I was about 13 I tried to throw him out the window. He was hanging on by his fingernails. I pushed with all my fibre, every last bit, to push him out and kill him. I wasn't strong enough. But had I been strong enough, I would have killed him and life would have been very different.

I used to hero-worship other boys' fathers. I'd think they were wonderful. I knew the difference. My maternal grandfather, the one who'd been in India, was an idol to me. He had great moral fibre and values. I tried to model myself on these better people.

I can see my father right now, lying in the hospital when he died. I was thinking, 'Phew. We're free.' They stuck a rose and Bible in his hands.

When we got his ashes I said to my pal, 'We've got to get rid of these.' It was pouring with rain and we saw a skip by the side of the road, with a load of shit inside it, and I thought 'Perfect.' I dumped the ashes. I drove off and felt better. It's not nice. But we had tried to love him so many times, and forgive him over and over.

I don't like hurting people at all. I know what it's like to be hurt. When my father did it I covered it up, I never showed it. Never. That is part of self-preservation. I'm alright now. I'm OK.

At boarding school I was thrashed with a cane and bullied by other boys. I tell you what, when you're beaten with a really thin cane when you're little it hurts like shit. After three days the stripes all go red. Five days later they're black, like they've been painted on you. Today it would be called mutilation. There's no one to go home to, you're in a dormitory with other boys, your back is against the wall. We didn't know any different. But you come away from that and no one can do anything to you that you can't recover from.

Some people fold in life. Problems come their way and they fold. People with cancer, they fold. Some people said to me, how do you cope with having cancer four times? They talk about boarding school giving you backbone, and I suppose to some extent that is true.

I've had cancer four times, all completely independent of each other. The first time was the throat. Then bladder, and that involved the genitals and so on and so forth. That was pretty nasty. And nose cancer, inside and out. Then I got prostate cancer too.

There were all sorts of therapies available for the prostate cancer. I asked the surgeon about the survival rates for different procedures and the only one that was 99 per cent was surgery, so I said, 'Take it out.'

They don't tell you the consequences at all. Firstly, you are quite badly incontinent for a while. But for someone as sexually active as myself, erectile dysfunction was a terrible thing. It's pretty common. I'm on the national helpline now and I speak to men all the time about it. You can go on Viagra, but it didn't really work for me. There is a suction pump thing, which worked, but frankly by the time you've gone through that kind of nonsense, everyone has gone cold, you've lost it. I avoided the injections to start with. Eventually I got round to it. You inject into the penis, it's only a hairline needle, but it doesn't always work, and it's more paraphernalia. The final option is an implant. That involves putting a reservoir of fluid in the abdomen which connects via a tube to a pump in the scrotum. When you want to have an erection you squeeze this bulb. You can do that very surreptitiously. It lasts forever. It's very popular!

My girlfriend and I are probably going to get married. We have sex every day. Sometimes more than once a day. I think I'm a bit unusual. I suppose I have a high sex drive.

She has terminal cancer herself, but she's on chemo and providing she stays on the regime she'll keep going forever. I've made a lot of mistakes in my life. I've had a lot of girlfriends, I've been married before. Maybe I'm short on commitment, I don't know – but my philosophy is that as long as you get it right in the end it really doesn't matter.

When my partner and I couldn't have sex we pleasured each other. You can still have an orgasm without an erection, there's no difference. Sometimes it's better. The only reason for an erect penis is for penetration. You can masturbate and orgasm without an erection, and people don't realise that.

I've had more than my share of sex, and I still am even now. Fantastic. I don't have much to complain about.

Seventy-five years old

"I've chased an idea of what being a man is all my life"

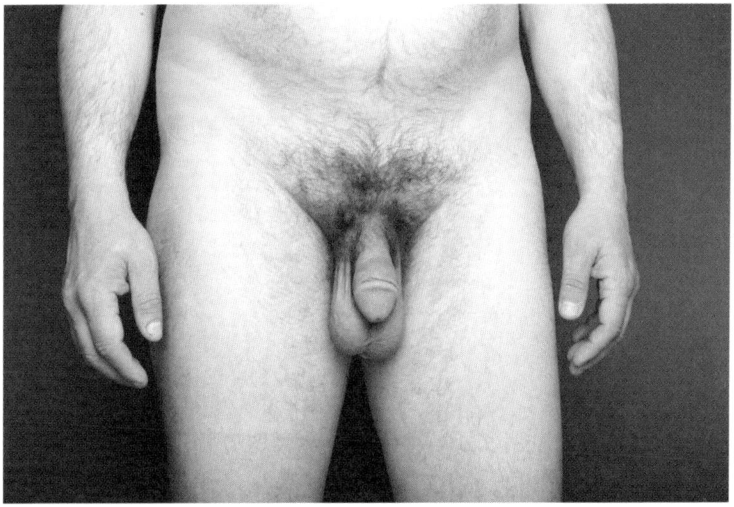

My relationship with my penis is the longest and most successful I've had. I'm impotent these days. It's funny, it should bother me more than it does.

I haven't had a drink for about nine months now. I am a recovering alcoholic and cocaine addict. It's one day at a time at the moment. For the last five years I was just doing coke, booze and, frankly, wanking myself stupid. Wanking was an addiction too.

Coke and booze together – fuck me, that gets you horny. In the end, it was the only way I could get the horn. And that was one of the things that I was really scared of when I came into recovery. I thought, 'That's it, you're never going to fuck again and your life's going to be boring.' I've always wanted to be the rock star. As Lennon said when the Beatles split up, *(adopts Liverpudlian accent)* 'Nobody wanted to admit the party was over, but it was over.'

Towards the end, it'd be two half bottles of vodka and a couple of grams a night. Not that much actually, compared to some people, but it's not about the amount, it's about what it does to you and where it takes you.

I've chased an idea of what being a man is all my life, since I was 13 or 14. What did being a man mean? A drink, a drug and a girl in your hand. I was the eternal adolescent.

I'm very much in limbo at the moment, it's been a funny six months. The first six months of recovery were a real stretch. I still wank, but mainly if I feel too tense. It's almost divorced from the sexual. It's not because I get the horn anymore. I used to have a drink or a line if I was tense; now it's the occasional wank. I wouldn't say it's an addiction because it's a lot less than it used to be.

Before, on a night on cocaine and vodka, I could wank for three and a half hours without fucking coming. I'd fantasise about bored housewives, older women, granny fucking. Not grannies but, yeah, 60-year-olds. I've always liked older women. My mum had big tits and a big arse and I don't do anything under a size 12, 36DD. I was at loggerheads with my father; it was a classic Oedipus thing.

My father was a very strict, upstanding, quite religious member of the conservative Jewish community. He doesn't drink, doesn't take drugs, maybe he had one affair in his whole life. He would always say about my music, 'Turn that rubbish off that you're listening to.' It's the classic father-son story, as old as time.

I didn't want to turn into my father. I chased the idea of cool. I wanted to be everybody from Humphrey Bogart to Fonzie. My generation has chased a myth of what a man is. It was sold to us through the idiot box and the silver screen: keep drinking, keep puffing, keep chasing the birds and it will all be all right. Then you wake up at 49 and your liver is fucking hurting, your heart is hurting and you think, 'Oh yeah, you'll be cool, you'll be very cool – you'll be cold, because you'll be dead soon.'

I don't give a fuck about what being a man is now. It's not about being best, the worst, the nihilist, or the most cool, there's just 'be', and that's it. Be and behave. I've got stuff to get on with and I'm so thankful that I'm not obsessed with women anymore. It's really weird, the big head gets it, but the little head doesn't react. I can look at women and know that they're attractive, you know, but there's no stirring in the loins. But I'm alright with that because I had a great time before it turned into a car crash.

I remember measuring my penis with a ruler when I was a kid, about 12. It was four and a half inches. I wanted it to be bigger, of course. I remember wondering why it was so small in a flaccid state. My sister told me that women like it fat rather than long and thin. That made me feel better, but I wonder if it contributed to the fact that I did become very good at eating pussy and overcompensating in foreplay.

I have to say, when I put my mind to it, when I'm not drunk, I'm a bloody good lover. Obviously I'd really fucking try the first few times, because I wanted to impress her. But once I was ensconced on her sofa with her internet, watching her telly, I got lazy, you know? There were times when I would sneak into the bog for a wank. I couldn't leave if I was in a relationship I didn't want to be in, I couldn't be the bad guy. I had to manipulate it in a passive-aggressive way so she threw me out. I've seen how my sister has been hurt. I have to be the good guy. It goes back to Humphrey Bogart and Fonzie – I want to be the tragic, but noble hero.

I used to do stand-up and I'd say that when your first memory is of a bearded man coming to your cock with a knife you tend to be a bit neurotic for the rest of your life. Surely God could have created men with circumcised cocks if that's what he wanted? If I ever had a kid I would never circumcise it. I would say, 'It's your decision. Later, if you want to join any faith, you can do it.' I suppose I hated religion because I was forced to go to synagogue and I hated all the fear and the guilt.

I actually really enjoyed my life, you know? I'm pretty much the rake when it comes down to it, chasing the senses. Look, I've got no kids, no wife, never been married, no career, I'm a fucking trustafarian.

Everybody in life is dissatisfied with what they've got. It's really strange at 49 to be learning to be grateful for what I have. I'm alone, but I don't feel lonely, you know? It frightens me, but if my penis is never inside a woman again I'm alright.

Forty-nine years old

“I think sex needs to be put back on its fucking pedestal”

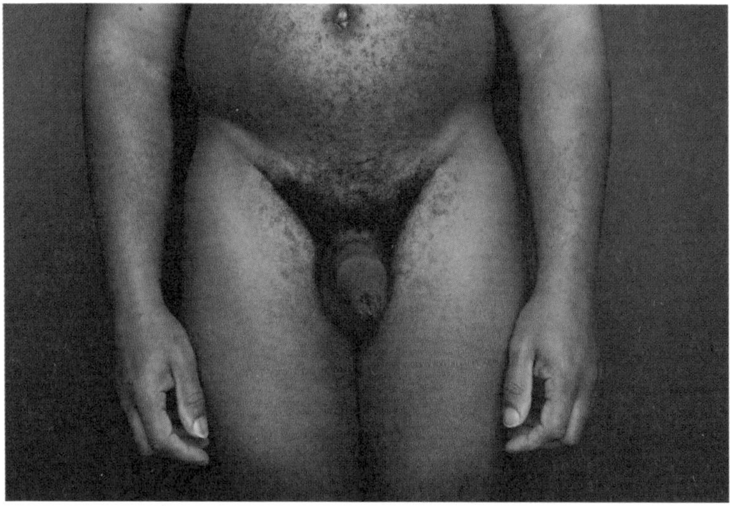

I’m kind of intrigued about this opportunity to talk about my relationship to... I don’t want to say penis and I don’t really like saying cock... Rufus, yeah, Rufus. *(laughs)* My penis, Rufus, is kind of a barometer of my health, my happiness and my fitness. My sense of my wellbeing is related to my sexual energy.

I’ve always felt most in communion with my body and with another person’s body when I feel that my overall fitness, health and energy are high. Ironically, the only time I’ve ever worried about Rufus is when I went through a period a couple of years ago where Rufus wasn’t rising and it was a sign of another health condition. I'd never even thought about how stress can affect your body and your sexuality. If it wasn't for that I would probably never have realised I had high blood pressure or that stress can have a negative effect on your desire to have sex.

I knew there was something wrong because the desire was there, but Rufus just wasn't. I was like, 'Man, what are you doing? You don't seem that bothered. I'm bothered, the whole team is bothered, what's up with you? Come on, man.'

I've got quite an active mind and I'm often juggling stuff which is to do with deadlines, work, writing and different projects, and the only time my mind is completely silent is during sex. A partner once said to me, 'Well, what do you think about when we have sex?' and I said, 'What do you mean, what do I think about? I'm just like... I'm here with you. You're naked, we're making love and what else is there? There are no thoughts!' And then I thought, 'Oh, you fantasise about other things? Other people? Really?' For me sex is almost about vacancy. It is a moment of complete embodiment, of being totally calm in the world, do you know what I mean? It is about being fully present.

The penis is a tool of communication. It's a kind of a gateway to losing who you are and your ego, to actually be fully absorbed into the beingness of another person, as well as into a different you, a more primal you. I think there is nothing greater than being fully present in sex. It is a spiritual journey. We can play with power and sex, but bear in mind that it's play. I think there's an opportunity for a creative and renewing exchange. And Rufus, whatever you want to call it, is part of your gateway to that.

I'm the first black man in the project? Where do I start? That's such a head-fuck. When you're a young black man you experience inordinate attention and focus on you as a sexual being, especially in the club sphere. Men are men, and we like an easy time; we're insecure, we don't want to be rejected. And it's intoxicating to have people give you attention in a very sexual way. It's like a simple vocabulary. 'I don't have to do any work, I don't even have to buy any drinks, I don't even have to be handsome.' *(laughs)* Fuck! It's intoxicating, but, like any addiction, it has its downside. It's not necessarily a very individual attention. This is not really about me, this is about a persona of black men, you know: penis size, greater sexuality, up for it. It's a thrill ride and I've participated in it, but with a degree of self-loathing afterwards, because I think, 'What the fuck? I've just been someone's Mandingo fantasy.' And I've done it, not because I'm black, but because I'm a bloke and an advance was made and I know that there's not much expected of me. As a man you can compartmentalise all that stuff, but there's a part of you that wants people to want more from you, to be curious about you. It's not that black men are more hyper-sexual, it's just that men, given the opportunity, would want to be as sexual as possible, to have their cake and eat it.

I grew up in a working-class environment and would sometimes go to down-home black clubs and I would be approached by white women who said, 'I don't date white men, I just date black men.' The side of me that is postgraduate-educated, goes 'Woah! Why? A man's a man. What's that about? This is a fetish that makes no sense.' Sometimes these women end up as victims of it because they're looking for hyper-masculinity and they pick out certain kinds of men.

I think it has a damaging effect on some black men I know who accept and internalise that sense of themselves. When you're a minority in a society you internalise how a majority society sees you. You begin to create your identity partly out of response to the projection. And also the projection can become the tool of solidarity. The projection can be a means of bolstering our sense of self or our self-esteem.

Women and men both enjoy sex, are curious about sex, and boast about sex in different ways, but I think men are more afraid and less understanding of the emotional nature of sex and compartmentalise it. In compartmentalising there is a sort of self-brutalisation that goes on, because sexual exchange is always more than just a conversation and a cup of tea. There is something of yourself that you pass over. I think in some ways women are perhaps more in tune with the emotional investment that comes with sex, the sense that there is a boundary that is being crossed that is more than mechanistic and more than just pleasure. That doesn't mean to say that all women want to stick with every man they sleep with, but I think that there is a different quality of understanding of that exchange for some women. Sorry, it's really hard to talk in these bold terms because all the time I'm thinking that's bullshit because of all the exceptions. So I'm just using these broad brush strokes with these massive caveats.

I think maybe we're just afraid to be idealistic. We're all afraid, we don't know how to name what it is that we're doing. In ancient societies we worshipped the phallus and the vagina and there was a reason for that. If we acknowledged that sex isn't just about gratification, there is a broader communication, I think we'd be more respectful. I think sex needs to be put back on its fucking pedestal.

Forty-six years old

"A brain haemorrhage was the best thing that ever happened to me"

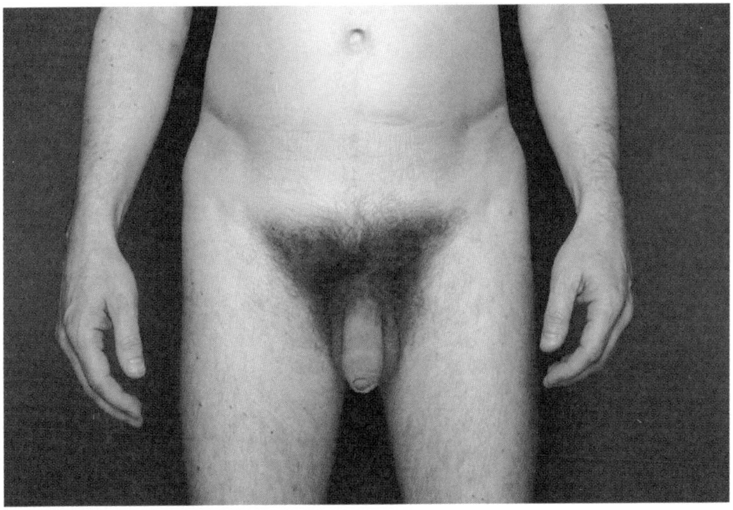

I am generally happy to get my clothes off and yet this feels edgy. Last night at dinner I said, 'I'm having my bits taken tomorrow.' I didn't even say 'having a photograph of my bits taken', I said, 'I'm having my bits taken.' Why did I call them my bits? It's like a middle-class English cloaking of nicety.

What is going on behind that? I don't know... It's like I want to impress people – if I'm happy for my bits to be photographed, it means I'm brave and fearless. So it probably means that this is pushing the envelope a bit for me.

I'll tell you what it actually comes back to. I believe that behind this sense of shame around my dick is the worry: 'Is it big enough? And what are other people going to think when they see how small my dick is?'

Whenever I'm somewhere where men are naked I'm always looking at other dicks and thinking, 'Ooh, I wish mine was as big as yours.' Or, 'I'm glad mine isn't as small as yours.' So I put myself in a pecking order of men and their dicks and I believe that there is an importance to the size of my dick and that if it's not big enough, then... I don't know, I think it probably comes straight back to, will I be loved? So I draw this correlation between dick size and love.

Recently, my sexuality has begun to feel more fluid. In the past, I've boxed myself: 'I'm a gay man.' I thought I couldn't find women attractive, so I wouldn't go there. Actually that's changed. A few months ago I was single and I said clearly to the Universe that I was ready for the next person, rather than the next man. I knocked down the walls of my box, this box that I'm a gay man, only to find that the next person who came along was still a man.

I have noticed that when I have got involved with women, on rare occasions, that I don't feel the same 'Grrr.' I really, really feel it with men – some men – and only extremely rarely with women. I'm trying to push myself to have intimacy with a woman because I think I should, or there's something unresolved around it.

I'm more than happy to say that my highest purpose is peace in the world and the happiness of all humanity. I want to be in a world where people respect other people, where there is no killing of other people.

Some time ago I thought that the way to fulfil my mission in this life would be to become a politician, or to be on a much bigger stage than being a writer. That kind of fitted in with some ideas of grandiosity that I have had run through my life. I thought world peace was a problem I had to sort out, just me alone: there was no sense of connection with anyone else. I was going to be the one and everyone else was going to love me because I'd sorted everything out. So that was where it came from, this need to be loved.

What I have come to realise is that I want to open my heart to loving whoever is sitting in front of me. Because unless I'm peaceable with the person in front of me, whoever that person might be, how is world peace ever possible? So, for me, it's actually a whole series of what can appear to be really tiny acts that will change humanity.

Talking is more the edge for me, rather than showing you my dick. Sitting here as a former journalist, I realise that I never felt bold enough to ask questions that were going to get to the truth of something. I was a very middle-class English type of interviewer, very polite and respectful.

I had a brain haemorrhage and that stopped me in my journalistic tracks. I was part of this whole 'buy more, consume stuff that's going to fall apart, so buy some more stuff that's also going to fall apart and, yeah, then buy more and, oh, how about buying some more and look at this lovely shiny new toy, this will make you happy' culture. It finally took a brain haemorrhage for me to realise I wasn't happy. I was like a dog chasing its tail and it wasn't a very nice tail. It was a bit stumpy and bitten because I'd been chasing it for so long.

I collapsed at home, was taken to hospital, had a brain haemorrhage, was in hospital for two weeks, then came out. Six months later, when the blood had been reabsorbed, I had a scan. The bleed was on the left side and they found an aneurism on the right side. It was not connected with the haemorrhage at all. I had brain surgery to clip off the aneurism. Between the haemorrhage and the surgery I had my first episode of mania. I was depressed, then manic, depressed, manic. I was diagnosed bipolar. I didn't agree with the diagnosis so I kept stopping my medication and I kept ending up back in hospital, often sectioned.

Eventually I found two things that helped me. I found Scottish country dancing and started a gay Scottish country dancing club in London with some other people called The Gay Gordons. And I found Nichiren Buddhism. With those two things in my life I once again stopped taking medication and I have not been back in hospital since.

I don't consider myself bipolar, I consider I have tendencies: I see things at the poles, good, bad, happy, sad. The Buddhism and my chanting practice enabled me to see that I needed to leave London. I was so aligned with my highest selves, it was like the road just unrolled itself in front of me. And my life is sweet now.

I was living totally in my head and I was not connecting my head with my heart, and I believe that is why the Universe said, 'Right, we'll show him.' So I had the bleed in my head and was on one level unable to use my head. I had no choice but to go down into my heart, and I very quickly saw that the haemorrhage was the best thing that ever happened to me. And I later came to see that the mental health diagnosis was fantastic too. It was such a massive thing to be told that if I didn't take medication for the rest of my life I would be in and out of hospital forever. And I just thought, 'No, you have no idea.' So part of my quest has been to prove that this is not who I am. It's not the essence of me, which I call my Buddha nature, my highest selves. My Buddha natures are pure and loving and glorious and joyful and all this other stuff is just like sprinklings of something just all drifting past me.

Forty-six years old

“My penis enters the room before me”

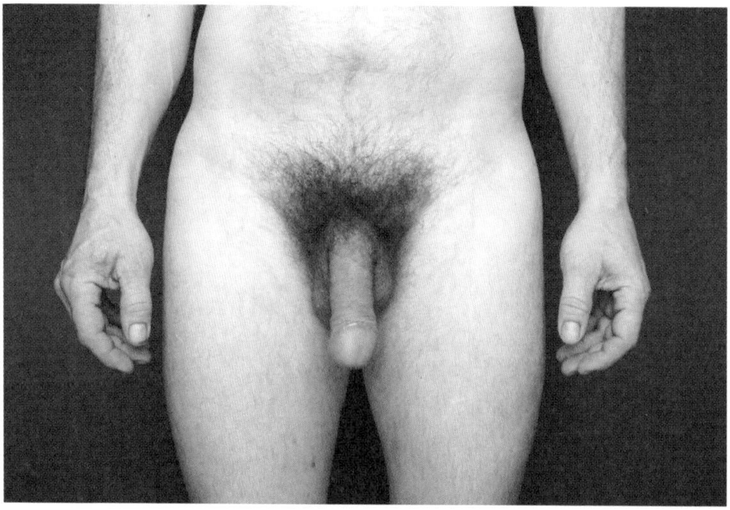

When I was in my early twenties, there was a knock on the door one day. It was a policeman. He said my brother wanted to contact me. I said that couldn’t be true, because I didn’t have a brother. It turned out my father had died. He had been a bigamist, and he had another family. I have a half-brother and a half-sister, and she has a half-sister who isn’t related to me.

My half-sister is ten years older than me. I first met her when I was 22. I met her a second time 22 years after that. Why was there such a long gap? Well, we got on really well, there was a deep connection, but there is no shared history. And time just goes by, you know. So, the other reason.

There was a deep connection, but there was also a strong attraction. One time, we were in a darkened hallway, we were very close to each other, and I honestly thought she was going to kiss me. It was so erotic. I kind of ducked out of the way. And that's the reason we haven't seen each other more.

My penis is, in some sense, a handle on to the deep core of my being, my whole sexuality. I'm very much aware in relationships when I feel attracted to someone, and sometimes it's purely from the genitals, and sometimes the heart, and sometimes both. I can clearly feel the difference between a heart connection and desire, and when they operate together.

I'm in a new relationship. There is a definitely a strong emotional connection. But I still have a heart connection to my last partner. That relationship ended suddenly. There are all these different connections from the heart to different people.

So, how we got together... I've just finished a course. About an hour before the end, a girl on the course told me she was in love with me. It was lovely to hear, and very flattering, and I really liked her. But although I knew I would really enjoy getting physically close to her, I also knew deep down there wouldn't be a relationship. I was driving away from the course and I thought about how I wished it had been this other girl on the course. I wondered why I hadn't had the courage to say anything to her. And then she texted me, saying some lovely things and that it was a shame nothing had happened. I pulled over and said, 'These are beautiful words, but they don't have to be spoken in the past tense!'

She's just stayed with me for a week. It was really intense and passionate, making love for hours... It's like that at the moment. Ah, it's wonderful.

My partner has been spontaneously referring to my penis as 'him'! Apparently because he enters the room before me. I'm slightly disturbed by this, although there is a hint of truth there somewhere.

Sexual abuse is rampant. I went to a boarding school where there was lots of sexual abuse going on, it was horrible. The police raided that school in the end. We had enforced prep every night, but there was one night a week you could take an hour to go to judo. Of course I went to judo. I was told you could stop off with this housemaster on the way back for a cup of tea and biscuits, and you would then get back and prep was finished. So, I go to him for the first time with a friend from judo and he started rubbing me here and here *(indicates lower belly and back)* and then his hands start moving down, and he goes 'Oooh, you lovely little man.' And then I totally got it, and knew what was going on. He was a pervert. I remember how disgusted and contaminated I felt after that.

I think most of the girls I have been with have been sexually abused in some way. My first girlfriend had been raped in an alley. All I could do was draw on my experience, how contaminated I had felt, just from that incident. I wouldn't pretend I could understand, but I had some empathy.

The energy that rapes and pillages women, and the world, and doesn't see the long term, is an unbalanced, penetrating, aggressive male energy. It's out of control. Male energy is a source of amazing creativity, a drive to learn and understand, but in the modern world it's led to reductive thinking and exploitation.

I feel it's important to balance the polarities of male and female. We have to look beyond the macho jerk, but still be fully male. Balance out our female and male qualities.

Forty-four years old

"Live, love and fuck in glorious shame-free technicolour"

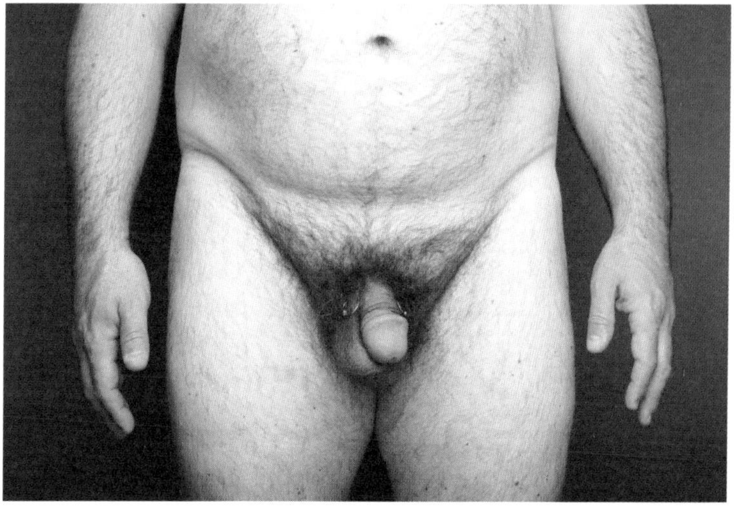

I didn't have a very safe childhood. My dad left my mum when I was three and my mum had a lot of issues. I felt hurt a lot as a child, and I became unwilling to let other people touch me. For a long time I was over-controlling of all connection. I would say no very quickly to anything that suggested emotional risk.

My dad and I maintained a relationship after he left me with my mum. I think he felt very ashamed about leaving. He visited every week, he paid for my schooling and he was very active in my life, he just wasn't physically there all the time. I went to boarding school when I was 13.

My dad was really pleased. He had this kind of ambivalent thing where he wanted me to get away from my mum, but didn't want to take me. It was problematic when I lived with him in the summer holidays because I was experimenting with drugs and having a wild time. I was out of control for a while. He's a pharmacist so it was obvious I was taking drugs. After I got married my dad and I settled into a better relationship. Then when I separated from my wife it was more problematic again. Everything for him was about settling down, getting married, having a good job, a roof over your head. There was a constant drive towards safety. He was Jewish so there was this background of wanting safety.

I really, really like that I am circumcised. I don't like the look of foreskins. I like the clean and tidy look of my penis. I have two piercings and when I am erect they sit on the side of my penis and look really nice. I understand that foreskins are a pleasure zone, but they just look odd to me.

I've had an argument with a love in the past about it. I said foreskins are absolutely ridiculous little things and I don't know why everybody doesn't get circumcised. She got really offended and went down the whole genital mutilation argument. Intellectually, I understand it could create a trauma in a person, and it's irreversible; I get that. Personally and emotionally I just don't feel it though. I guess I wish people could be old enough to make a choice, but it's too painful and traumatising when you are older.

I have a big relationship with sexuality, and my cock is a part of that, but not all of it. I would say I have a complex relationship with my cock. On one hand I really like the way it looks. It's a grower, not a shower. It looks small when it's flaccid, but it grows to a nice size and girth when it's erect. I've been told by a lot of women that it feels nice when we make love, it feels smooth.

I feel like men and cocks are thematic of the world: men and violence. Most sexual violence, but not all, is committed by a cock. Whether it's a woman or a man being raped, most of the time it's a cock doing the raping. So I have a troubled relationship with the act of penetration, although at the same time it is something I like very much.

For a long time I wasn't that interested in penetration, I liked other acts better. I'm really into BDSM. I was more interested in other ways you could get off that don't involve genitals. I was on antidepressants for a couple of years and I couldn't get an erection most of the time. That opened up a whole realm of what sex can be.

Over the last few years I have discovered for the first time how good penetration is, and the potential there is for intimacy. I run sex parties and workshops, I've explored lots of different things, but now I'm ironically coming back to the most intimate connection that can happen between two people, which is penetration. I am opening up now, at the age of 43, to the possibility that my cock is the vehicle for a really profound connection with another human being.

I've generally got myself into situations where there is less risk of emotional hurt. I was drawn to fetish and BDSM because they are forms of connection with varying degrees of intimacy and I have tended towards the ones where I've had more control and less heart risk.

I've been consistently dominant in the last ten years. I work as a dominant and I run my own business. I spend my whole life being dominant. In the last year I have let go and wanted to embrace vulnerability.

After I moved into teaching more about intimacy, it forced me to question my own relationship with intimacy. Fundamentally I have longed for it, while finding it hard. It's a big admission in my life.

I enable people to accept themselves more fully using sexuality and BDSM as a vehicle. I do that through running workshops and holding socials where people come together to explore these themes. I also run coaching and pleasure-based sessions. My mission is to enable everyone, including me, to live, love and fuck in glorious shame-free technicolour.

It took me a long time to get control. I used to come very soon after penetration. That's quite common among men. I would ejaculate quickly, and that's part of the reason I didn't like penetration. I like being erect and feeling the sexual energy move through my cock and body. So, knowing I would come quickly, I would leave it to the very end and then it would be the icing on the cake, not the main act. Through getting more experience, it now depends on the woman and the situation and I can last longer.

It still varies how good it feels. There have been two or three women where the penetration has felt extraordinary, and in all cases the relationship was a bit dysfunctional and it didn't feel so wholesome. In the connection I am in at the moment, penetration can go from really amazing to quite alright, but it never feels bad. When it feels amazing is when my heart feels very open. My tendency is to go a bit faster if I feel like I am losing sensation. When my heart is open we go very slow. It can also depend on how tired I am. I don't think it's very physical, I think it's more to do with emotion.

How our bodies fit together, how 'clean' that moment is between us, whether there is emotional baggage; there are lots of things that affect how penetration feels. It's true of all sex acts, but it feels more true of penetration than anything else.

Forty-three years old

"Sexuality is more complex when you are disabled"

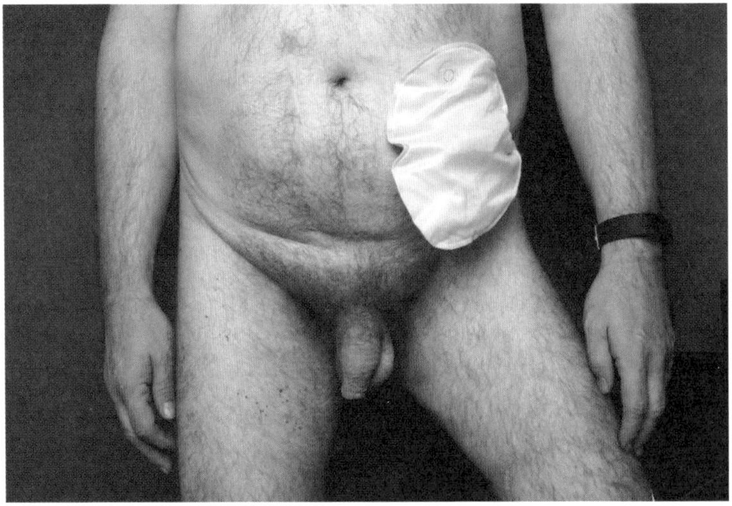

I have an impairment, which disables me when I interact with society. I was born with spina bifida. Luckily for me, the damage is very low down, so I can have an erection. It's also why I used to be able to walk fairly well.

I have an interesting relationship with my penis. One of the effects of my disability is my incontinence. I have to attach a lot of things to my penis. Since I was a child I've had something attached to my penis most of the time. I have visible scarring down the side of my penis from one of the continence devices I had as a child. Also, because of medical tests, I am exposed a lot. My penis is public property.

The reduced sensitivity means my erections aren't that reliable. It takes a little bit more effort and physical contact has to be more robust. I'm aware of touch, but less sensitive to the quality of touch. Although my erection isn't brilliant, it is long-lasting. Bizarrely, it will last after ejaculation. It's a fairly useful semi, hard enough for penetrative sex.

Sexuality is more complex when you are disabled. You have all the normal problems, like different levels of desire, but then there are other complications, like I might urinate when I ejaculate. So I'm not keen on receiving oral sex. The medication I'm on can affect my libido. Antidepressants affect desire. My stress levels can be high.

I have to empty my bladder just before sex. And afterwards I have to think, are we going to do anything else, or are we finished, in which case the continence device has to go back on. I get a month's supply of devices at a time from the chemist. So, if I need to use extra ones because of sexual activity, I have to make one last for longer the next week. It's awkward only getting a month's supply, but sexuality is seen as very tertiary. I think sexuality should be taken into account more.

For better or worse, I went to a school for disabled kids. Nowadays I would be in a normal, mainstream school. Back then there was no provision, no disabled access. My local disabled school wasn't very good, no one even sat exams. So I went to a disabled boarding school to get a proper education. That was an environment with virtually no privacy, because we shared bedrooms and bathrooms. A bathroom had two baths and two showers. Other lads needed a lot more physical assistance, so there were a lot of staff around too. I got used to seeing everyone else and being seen.

We were normal teenagers with raging hormones, but malfunctioning bodies. Half of us had stuff attached to our genitalia. It made a quick fumble quite tricky. One girl I was dating was semi-incontinent, so the catheter would have to come out. You are trying to explore each other and there's all this stuff, this extra layer to go through. Also, when you are incontinent there is leakage. If you fumble in a girl's knickers there may be pads. My early sexual experiences were coloured by the non-standard nature of it.

There was a lot more same-sex experimentation. You're with people in the same dorm, there are dirty stories and masturbation. I'm not ashamed of that, but some people now are very, very ashamed and deny it ever happened. But it did.

I would define myself as bisexual now. I think I had the opportunity to explore a side of myself I probably wouldn't have explored in a mainstream school. I would say I am sexually attracted to men and women equally, but more attracted to women emotionally.

Because of the spina bifida I can't feel my feet very well. I trod on a nail and got a bone infection, which was quite unpleasant. The antibiotics didn't work. They thought I would end up losing the foot anyway, so I had an elective amputation.

It was weird losing a foot. Signing the paper to have it done was strange. The foot was preventing me getting better and preventing me working. I was a freelancer and money was getting tight. I was about to lose the house. Losing the foot was a step on the way to getting back to work. What is important is functioning, not how I look. The range of movement in my prosthetic foot is as good as the movement in my old foot.

I get stared at far less in a wheelchair and I find that really interesting. I think I look less threatening. You know, you have the media trope of the killer with the limp, glimpsed through the fog. Also, because of my build, my hair cut and my general demeanour and accent, people think I am ex-military, which I think makes them more sympathetic. I am very sensitive about not portraying myself as something I am not though.

People never used to make eye contact before, now they smile at me in the wheelchair. Whether I am seen as more attractive or they are making an effort to cheer me up, I don't know. I was never asked out when walking, but I have been several times in a wheelchair. I've been asked to dance in a wheelchair at a few dinner dances, and I was never asked before. I find it interesting. Maybe it's because I've got fitter in the chair. I have broader shoulders and am more muscular and I hold myself differently. I used to be quite slight. I'm only short, so I look taller in a chair as well.

A girl I had a massive crush on gave me a metaphorical massive kick in the nuts. She said, 'What I love about you is that you aren't a threat.' I didn't want her to see me as a threat, and she meant it as a warm compliment, but it also meant she didn't see me as sexual.

Forty-eight years old

"I've quit porn"

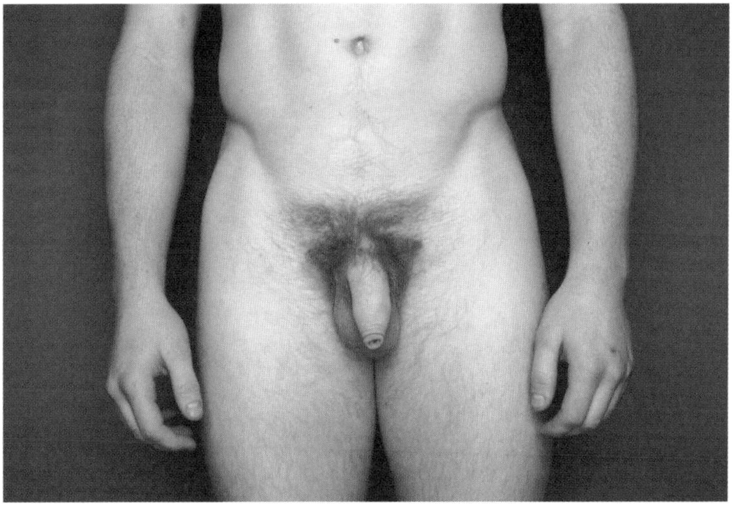

I'm really into sports, but I don't particularly care for appearance. I like to look good but I think of my appearance as more of a byproduct of sport. It's common for people to go to the gym, work out loads, but there's nothing useful about the muscles they're building. If I was in a bad situation I'd be able to get out of it comfortably because of my fitness level. Parkour is my main sport at the moment.

I know a couple of gym bunnies, but I can't really get along with those people. For some reason gyms all have these walls of mirrors, and people that obviously lift loads of weights stand there and take their picture for Instagram or Facebook or whatever. It's really narcissistic.

Loads of people use steroids. When I was in college, a couple of guys were taking steroids, injecting it into their butt cheeks, or getting their friends to, which is a bit weird. They had such bad anger issues. I don't know if it's the kind of person that does that sort of thing or if the steroids lead to the anger issues, but they were so prone to anger that if you made a joke that was slightly denigrating towards them they would flip. It was just banter, a joke. One guy literally started shoving me around the car park and I was like, 'You do realise if you hit me you'll get chucked out of college and you'll lose your job?' and he said, 'I don't care.' I was like, 'How can you not care?' It's just a bit worrying really.

I've quit porn. Actually I quit masturbation entirely for quite a long time.

I used to have issues ejaculating with my ex when having sex. Hand jobs and blow jobs were fine, but that was normally because they were on the rougher side. I think ejaculating became associated with my hand and watching porn. I had issues with being on top too. I think that's because when watching porn I would lie still, whereas when having sex I actually have to be up and mobile.

My new girlfriend did some research on it. There are a few issues. Watching porn is nothing like actually having sex. Also the feeling of the hand is nothing like actual sex or another person – there's this thing called the 'death grip.' What happens to a lot of people is they grip too tight when masturbating and they get used to it and then sex doesn't feel tight enough. I mean, some people are very tight, but they're not that tight. For me, a mixture of all of these led to my problem. My girlfriend and I are having sex perfectly fine now. Well, we're getting there.

Shall I tell you how we met? We met doing parkour and we were friends for a while. A few years ago she wrote up a sex contract as part of an art project but she never got the chance to use it. One night she asked me if I wanted to sign her sex contract with her.

I said no at first. Then I mulled it over and thought, 'What's the worst that could happen, really? Like, I'm friends with her, but what's wrong with sex? Why not?' I messaged her to ask if I could change my mind. And then she sent over the contract. It's a great idea, but it took me a while to get over how weird it felt at first.

The one we signed was called 'Three Mergers', as in having sex three times, and then you decide where you want to go from there. You can sign another contract, or you can just leave it and not do anything again. You can cut it off at any time, but the idea is you sign it like you would anything else. So you sign this contract and then you do the deed. Obviously it's not properly legal in the UK.

Our first kiss? OK, that was awkward. It was on this sofa. *(laughs)* It wasn't in the contract, but we decided beforehand it would be a bit weird if we didn't kiss while having sex, or building up to sex. We went to kiss each other and the first thing that happened was our teeth clashed and we both went 'Ow.' Then we went to try again and it flowed a lot better.

We got to the bedroom and I told her I had issues with staying hard and ejaculating. I didn't want to say beforehand, it felt really awkward. I wasn't undressed at that point and it's never too late to say no. She said it was fine and we'd work through it. I didn't lose my erection, but I didn't ejaculate having sex.

Porn is an addiction in the end. In the same way that gambling isn't a physical addiction, it's not actually in your blood, but it gets into your mind. I used to use porn every day. Quitting porn and quitting masturbation was like a reset. After several weeks I could orgasm during sex again. It had to be quite rough, fast sex to start with, but at that point I could. Then it changed from being kind of awkward and a bit annoying that it wasn't happening to, 'Oh, I can orgasm with sex now, this is good.' And then it kind of slowed down and got really good. I would like to be able to orgasm from more gentle sex. It still has to be a bit faster than I'd like. I still have issues with coming when I'm the one moving, and not lying down. That's getting better too, I'm very close.

A lot of older men who started watching porn later in their life actually don't have many issues because they've been with women, they know what sex is actually like. The problem is when people start young on the iPhone that their parents got them, they don't have to sneak to the computer or anything, they can just watch it, every single night, hardcore, softcore, they can watch people getting fisted, elbow-deep up the bum if they really want to, that kind of thing. They can watch anything they want and that's when it gets to be an issue. If you get brought up with things from a young age then they stick with you. If you hit puberty and get straight on to porn, which happened to me and to a lot of people my age, that's when it becomes a big issue and affects you later on.

Twenty years old

"Naturism is relaxing and freeing"

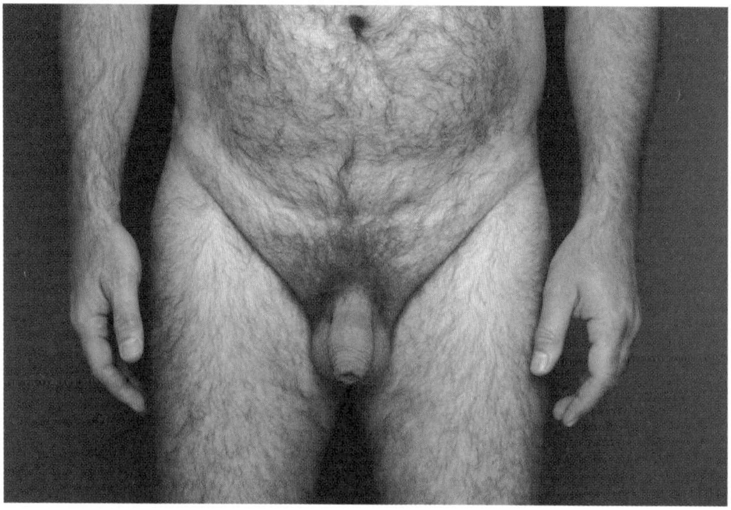

I don't think I have any particular anxieties around my penis. In naturist environments you realise there's a distribution of sizes so that anxiety goes away. I don't feel that my penis defines me as a man.

Naturism is an incredibly positive way of life. You're very often judged on how you dress, whether you've got smart clothes, grubby clothes, casual clothes, whatever. In a naturist environment all that is stripped away, so we're all equal here. You don't actually know if someone is a millionaire or on the dole, it doesn't make a difference. You're judged on the person you are, not how you look or how you dress or anything else. It removes a whole bunch of rubbish from conversations.

A couple of years ago we had a new neighbour and she was quite keen to make a big impression in the street and invited all the neighbours around to get to know them. She had a dinner party. Well, we'd never been to one, the circles we move in don't do dinner parties. It was all very pretentious, 'Here's my Mary Berry' and all of that stuff, and we felt really, really uncomfortable. The next day we were back at our naturist club, it was a sunny day and we walked in and one of the women came up and said, 'Oh hello, love, alright?' and gave us a big hug and we felt 'Oh, we're home.'

Naturism is relaxing and freeing. It completely de-stresses you. I don't think as a family we would be without it now. And actually I think all the people we're closest to are naturist people.

A naturist environment is a very safe, non-threatening environment. To be honest, I actually think you'll see more potential for sexual aggression and intimidation on the average High Street on a Friday night when the pubs turn out than you ever would in our naturist club. It wouldn't happen, it's just... yeah, it's unthinkable that that could happen.

I think we should be a hell of a lot more comfortable about socially nude environments. We're out of kilter with other countries on mainland Europe. We're so reserved here. This country is illogical and I think we cause all sorts of problems psychologically. We're almost talking children into hating their bodies and hating themselves, and from that flows eating disorders.

My youngest daughter went to school camp when she was eight and there was an instruction they had to take a swimsuit for the showers. Yeah, for the showers. We're talking about the same gender, the same age, the showers weren't mixed or anything like that. The idea was they'd go into the changing area or whatever, get undressed, put a swimsuit on, go and shower but not be able to shower properly because they've got a bloody swimsuit on, come out, presumably take the swimsuit off and dry and then get dressed again. My daughter was outraged by that because she's been born into naturism.

I think there's a problem with the way things are going now. They don't have showers after PE anymore because they can't see each other with no clothes on. We seem to be in a situation where we would rather have dirty, sweaty children, than let them see each other naked. I find that really perverse. That sort of attitude won't stop a single child being abused or coming to harm – presumably that's the pretext under which it's done. The secondary impact is that it's encouraging deeply troubling and unhealthy attitudes to the body. It's sad.

I'm really proud of my daughters because they have a healthy attitude to their own bodies. They're grounded and it leaves them free to enjoy friendships, and concentrate on things they should be concentrating on, rather than sitting there worrying and looking in mirrors trying to make things better, which aren't ever going to be better.

As a parent you want to protect your children from those who would harm them and actually through naturism they have learnt to differentiate. Because the human body isn't always indecent, it's about context, it's about behaviour. They would know the difference between a naked man hiking in the countryside and a man doing something indecent, whereas a lot of children are brought up to fear all aspects of the human body and that's not healthy.

My wife is a survivor and she basically grew up hating herself. She was sexually abused as a child. Through naturism she's got control back over herself, her body and what's done with her body. She did a lot of work and had counselling. So, yeah, that's been quite a journey for her.

When all the horrible Saville stuff came out, people in the media and keyboard warriors on the internet derided the survivors and said, 'Oh it's funny how they've only just decided to come forward after forty years.' Actually, that's complete bollocks, excuse my French. It takes a huge amount of courage to come forward. I know the tremendous damage that sexual abuse does. My wife will never, ever be the woman she should have been. She can't ever fulfil her full potential; all we can hope is to get her as close to it as she possibly can. It absolutely destroys… Sorry, I'm getting emotional, but it destroys and wrecks lives.

It's incredibly hard, sometimes it can feel like there's a third person in your relationship. It's almost like a cold, dead hand reaches through time and grabs her by the shoulder and pulls her back. It's horrible, really horrible. Nowadays she's in a good place, but every now and again you see her confidence go.

I've got a daughter who's fifteen next month and the thought of a man my age finding her attractive fills me with disgust and horror. It's grim.

I guess all people like to look at people they find attractive of the same or opposite gender, but there has to be a cut-off point at which you say, 'That's not appropriate.' It's down to you personally to be the arbiter, isn't it, of what's decent. Set your moral line in the sand.

Fifty years old

"When I send a dick pic, it's someone else's photograph"

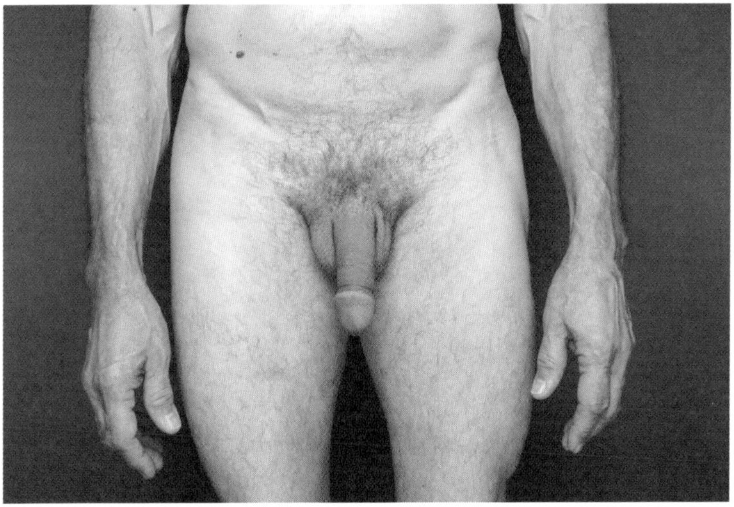

When I was younger, it was all about my penis and sex. I used to want sex with almost anything that moved!

Man plus man equals more sex, because men desire sex and it's easier to get gay sex than straight sex. With a woman you have to be nice to her, or whatever, but with a man it's just 'I'm horny, let's have sex.' Sometimes you don't even have to talk. I can be walking down the street, give a man the eye, and then be having sex in a public toilet. That doesn't happen much anymore, now it's all about the internet. You can go on the internet, message someone, and they can be round your house in an hour, having sex. Sometimes you don't even know their name. Then they're gone! Instant gratification. As I've got older I tend to want a little more. I want a relationship or for them to stay a little longer.

I had a few long-term girlfriends, until my late 20s, but at the same time I was sleeping with men. Sex flows easier with women, you don't have to roll them over and spit on their arse before you fuck them. *(laughs)* It's quite nice, much softer, gentle, more like 'making love.' It's more rough with a man. For me, the most intimate thing is kissing. I prefer to kiss a man; it's a lot more passionate for me than kissing a woman.

My first real sexual experience was when I was 12 or 13. I was coming home one day and this guy who was anything from 19 to 25 started walking next to me and chatting. We ended up going down a dark lane. He pulled out his penis which looked massive to me at that age, then he sucked me off. I don't think I could come. I remember being so shocked. 'Oh my God, I can never do that again.' But of course, that didn't last very long!

When I look back at it now, I realise he was a paedophile, but at the same time I was very consenting, I wanted it to happen. As an older person, he shouldn't have done it; it was wrong. I think he was an opportunist and he knew I'd be quite easy. I was very sexual when I was young. I thought about sex. We lived in the country, and I would watch rodeo riders and I would look at their crotch to see if I could see anything. I was aware there was something I wanted. If a child is sexual, it's a dangerous time.

I'm a top. There is versatility, but generally you are more top or bottom. Men ask how big you are online and want to see a picture before they agree to meet you. When I send a dick pic, it's someone else's photograph. I'm not sending a photo of my dick to someone! No one has ever spotted the difference when they've seen the real thing. I'm not interested in what someone's penis looks like, I want to see their face. I'm like, 'Can you send me a photo of your face?' I think it's more sexy not seeing a dick pic. For me the chasing and unveiling is more exciting.

For me, as a top, I am the aggressor, the one who's going to show you how good I am, so size matters. It doesn't matter if you are the bottom, you just get fucked. If you are a top you want a big penis to ram into the other person.

I'm not big on porn, I've never really liked it. I prefer the real thing. I met someone who wanted me to fuck him while he was watching porn of she-males. It put me off, I felt like a sex toy, like an aid. He wasn't 'with' me, he was with the porn stars. A lot of people these days put on porn if you go round. It feels disjointed to me. I want us to concentrate on each other, not porn. It's used much more than it used to be. I think there's a problem if you need porn to get yourself off while there's a real person with you to do the actual job. I don't want to watch a screen while having sex with a real person.

Both men and women are portrayed a certain way in the media. Sex sells. The media will always use images to seduce us. We like to think we're not influenced by it, but we are. I buy protein powder and I look at the pictures on the container. I think, 'OK, that's what I want to look like.' We are sexualised, men and women, and I don't think we can ever move away from that. But the pictures aren't realistic. I've worked in the health industry for a long time and I have a good idea of what it takes to look like that. Most people don't and never will. I see how hard triathletes and boxers work. They only look like that while they're training. As soon as they stop they lose it. No one has the time or inclination to train that hard, that long. Models might train hard for six months to look like that, then they're photoshopped anyway.

More young men are using steroids now, especially in gay society. In your 20s your body is still growing and you should be able to pump your body up easily, you shouldn't need steroids. Instead of training hard, they want instant gratification. They will destroy their insides. In one gym I know, I would say 50 per cent of the gay boys are on steroids. There's too much pressure these days to look a certain way.

If I could go back in time I'd tell myself to relax a bit more and enjoy being who I was. Between my 30s and 40s I literally ate chicken and protein shakes and did nothing else. I was a skinny child, and I grew up thinking I wasn't big enough. I still don't think I'm big enough; the skinny person is still inside my head and in the mirror.

When I was younger I thought being a man was about being buff and having a big cock. But you change as you grow up. Now it's about being a good person and giving to society. You should think about who you are, rather than what you can get from others. Whether you are wealthy or poor you can give back to society in some ways.

Men don't expose themselves emotionally and mentally. We need to express ourselves in different ways. I'm glad this was about exposing a soft penis, not a hard one, because it makes us more vulnerable. A hard cock is about 'grrrrr', being a man, but being able to expose your soft, natural cock is more about your soft side.

Sixty-three years old

"The little rascal gets me into trouble"

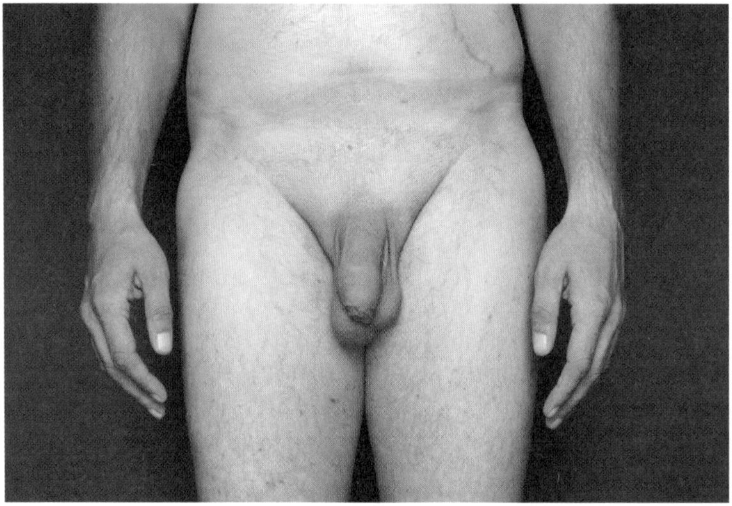

I see my penis as two different entities. There's your little thing you wee out of, and then there's the little rascal who gets you into a lot of trouble. I don't pay attention to one entity, but I do pay a lot of attention to the other one, the mini-me. I wouldn't say it has a personality, unless sometimes it looks up at me to say, 'How can I mess life up for you now?'

I'd normally call it dick or cock, and I think this is the first time I've ever called it a little rascal, to be honest. Whenever I'm messing around I always refer to it as cocking, dicking or knobbing about. It's always about a penis, isn't it?

It's definitely got me into trouble with girls I don't really want to be with. He goes, 'Let's have some fun, shall we?' There have been dearth periods where I've gone six months without... anything! At that stage anyone will do. I'm straight, but in those circumstances *(laughs)* I've not only had sex with people I shouldn't, but I've had relationships and lived with people I shouldn't. He gets me in trouble and then I have to deal with the consequences. I'm so one of those people who won't rock the boat.

I lived with a girl for two years and I didn't even like her. I couldn't stand her. I didn't even find her that attractive. I was afraid of being honest. It was immaturity. I didn't want to upset people. Now I would talk about it.

I used to have a really bad self-confidence issue. I felt dorky, ugly, lanky and stupid and 'out there.' I would concentrate on any fault I could find on my body. In my late teens I was out doing really well with my music but all I concentrated on was my belly. Pulling women was a reassurance thing – that I could get it. It reinforces what you think about your attractiveness. It was a need. I had a massive shift in confidence in my 20s. I did a lot of reading, thinking and learning, and studied philosophy.

I had a good relationship with my parents, open and honest. I had a body book and we talked about everything. That's what I try and be like with my children. That's a body, that's what it does, and there's nothing to be ashamed of.

I do treat my son and my daughter differently, but then they are biologically different. I probably put up with more boisterous behaviour from the boy than I would from the girl. The girl is a lot more affectionate, she will want to cuddle up and have her hair done, and the boy will just want to punch you. The boy used to want to play with dolls just as much as the girl did, although it soon occurred to me that she was dressing them and mothering them, and he was hurling them across the room at her. Playing with the same thing, but using them in different ways. It's just reacting to how they are really. I don't expect one to be better or more successful than the other though.

My dad thinks the girl should be locked up till she's 40 and not allowed to date! I'm not down with that, life is for living, and I want her to enjoy her life. The only thing I want for my children is to be happy and enjoy their lives.

I'm not averse to getting a vasectomy. I'd feel relieved to know I wasn't having any more children! It wouldn't affect my sense of manhood. I'm not sure when I could take a day to rest, when I have the kids to take to school though, otherwise I wouldn't have a problem with it.

My penis is a tool that comes out of the arsenal, it's a weapon. Oh, what a crap choice of words. I don't mean it's a weapon. What I mean is, I've got fingers, I've got a penis, I've got a tongue, and I use them – I think – very well. I've never seen sex as all about my penis. I use my hands for everything in life, so I gravitate to using them first. The penis is there for a purpose, but I can get better results for a woman with other things. My own satisfaction is secondary, sometimes even thirdly, or fourthly... I am almost entirely motivated by my partner's satisfaction. I can come at any point, but in a sexual situation I want to take full advantage of seeing her enjoy it. I really get off on it. The more I see her enjoy it, the more turned on I am. Maybe I want to be thought of as a better lover? Sometimes I make her come three or four times before I do.

Thirty-nine years old

"I had surgery to create a penis"

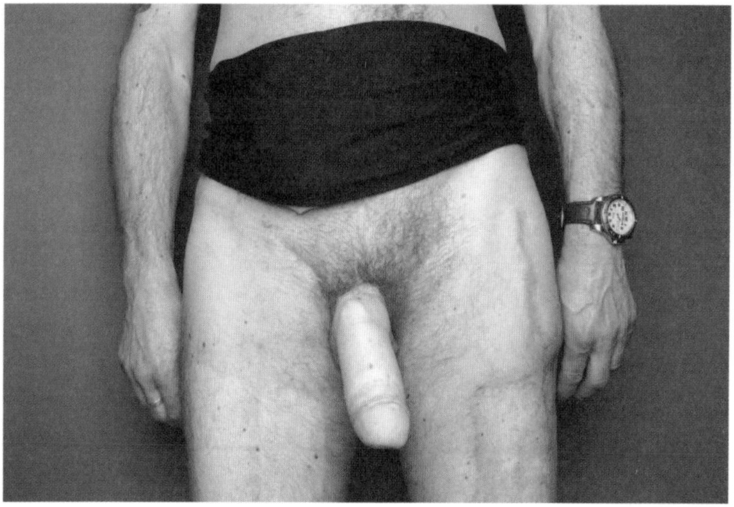

I was born in a female body, anatomically and biologically female, but I never felt a girl from at least the age of three. I felt completely male.

I can see it in early photographs of me, dressed up as a cowboy with holsters and in the way I stood. I felt like a boy and all my friends were male. When I reached puberty it started to dawn on me that I was different. I didn't feel comfortable in this body and knew there was something wrong about me when sexual feelings started. I fancied girls at school when I was nine and I knew that was wrong.

I went to a mixed school, then an all-girls school. On the plus side I was with lots of girls that I could fancy, but I hated it because I wanted to play with boys. I used to play football with my male friends at the mixed school, until the nuns banned me because they said it was too rough. I had all these messages when I was growing up that my behaviour was wrong.

At home my parents were pretty OK about me being a tomboy. I climbed trees, I was outdoors all the time, I was allowed to wear trousers. It only became painful and problematic when we were going to smart events where I was required to put on a dress. I threw tantrums – I felt a huge resistance to being feminised.

Sexuality felt massive, loaded with shame, because at the all-girls school if you were a lesbian, that's it, you'd be bullied. The problem was I didn't think I was a lesbian anyway. I was attracted to women, but I felt like a guy.

I changed my gender when I was 26. I was treated as male in public by the time I was 28. I was much more masculine by 30. I noticed changes in how I was treated, certainly in the business world. When I was female and in the company of men in any kind of professional context I was treated as 'less than', inferior, stereotyped. As soon as I was perceived as being male, men would assume that I was the one in charge. Always. *(laughs)*

There are very old-school belief systems around power. I think there is an immediate male privilege. I mean, I'm a small guy in height so I was surprised to feel that power, and actually didn't know what to do with it.

There is something about being a small man. I had friends who said to me, 'You're mad doing this because you'll be a small man, you don't want to have a Napoleon complex.' People were trying to put me off. I'm mostly over a lot of that stuff now but I carried it for a long time. 'Oh, he's too small. I can't fancy him.' I notice it a lot when I go to bars. I can almost guarantee that the taller, bigger bloke will get served before me, and I get quite angry about that. There are a lot of associations and assumptions with small men – either he's the victim or he's going to be a little annoying, aggressive person.

When I started taking hormones, wow. I felt a complete mix of fear and excitement. My periods stopped, which was an utter relief. I'd always had problems with my periods anyway, because I have Crohn's disease. Periods were like a burden I was carrying as well as a shameful, regular reminder I was a woman.

Then I started getting facial hair, which was wonderful. Of course, you're always checking the mirror. I've got loads now, I think it gets more as I get older. Obviously I'm losing it on my head as well, that's the pay-off. I don't mind that too much, in some ways it's validation.

During the process you focus on the new things, exciting changes. But then it's not enough, and you want more. The next thing was, 'I don't want breasts.' At the time you had to live in your gender identity for a year, then take hormones, before having your breasts removed.

I had 34B breasts. Getting rid of them was fantastic. Luckily I was able to keep my nipples. I don't really have scars actually. *(Shows me his chest)* They just peel off the nipple and then they take out all the mammary glands.

I spent about nine years researching surgery to create a penis. I went all round Europe because I wasn't happy about what was going on in the UK at the time. There were people having real problems with their surgery. Trans guys weren't talking about it because of the shame. The only stories I ever heard were bad. So I travelled around Europe and met other trans men. I finally settled on surgeons in Belgium. The reason I chose Belgium was because I was able to start meeting guys there who'd had the phalloplasty surgery, and they showed me the results.

In the UK they normally do a forearm phalloplasty where they take all the skin from the top of the arm to make the penis shaft. Now, I've got a tiny arm so it would have been a very small penis. I thought, 'Why the hell am I going to go through nine hours of surgery, when that's all I'm going to get?' *(laughs)* I thought I might as well get something of a decent size. So I had a thigh phalloplasty. Most surgeons are quite strict and won't give you something that's too big in length. Of course, size is the first thing most trans men ask about.

Bigger sizes can fail. It's all about blood flow. The longer length increases the risk of the blood not hitting the end. Then it dies off and you get necrosis – not something you want to have! I think that's partly why I left it for so long, because the surgery was constantly evolving.

My penis is just over five inches. It gets harder, but not bigger, when erect. I wanted a decent size, predominantly in order to satisfy a woman.

The surgeons take a couple of nerves from the arm and the inner thigh to hook up to the clitoral nerve to get you the erotic sensation. The clitoris is basically de-hooded and buried underneath, within the shaft at the base. That is connected via a nerve that runs down the penile shaft. The nerves are still growing, and changing. It won't be the same as a penis, but it is amazing.

I never had vaginal intercourse as a woman. I'd masturbated, but mainly my clitoris. I tried masturbating my vagina a few times, but I felt really uncomfortable. It felt almost like I was disassociating. It felt like rape. A couple of men did try and have sex with me, but I just couldn't do it. It was almost like an immediate kind of body shut-down.

I can still orgasm, but it's different. When I was masturbating my clitoris I could orgasm very quickly, now I think it takes a bit longer. But I can have an erection for as long as I want, because it's a mechanical pump. Part of the pump is in one of the testicles, you squeeze it, and saline fluid goes down a plastic tube that runs through the penis.

The first erectile device didn't work. It's quite common for it to get infected. I was gutted. My biggest fear was that the doctors would say to me, 'You can't do this again.' I waited three years because it was just such a hectic time in my life and I was too exhausted. The infection lowered my body's immune system. So I only had the new erectile device in April last year and luckily it's worked and hopefully it will stay working.

I still have a lot of confidence issues around using the penis. I haven't had a relationship that would allow me to build up the confidence, but I have been a little bit experimental. I climaxed with one woman.

I've also experienced lots of really unhealthy rejections. I won't go there anymore. I've just had enough. I hope for love. I want to be desired. I've had tastes of it, but I haven't properly had that experience.

Forty-seven years old

"I think my penis would like to tell me to have more sex"

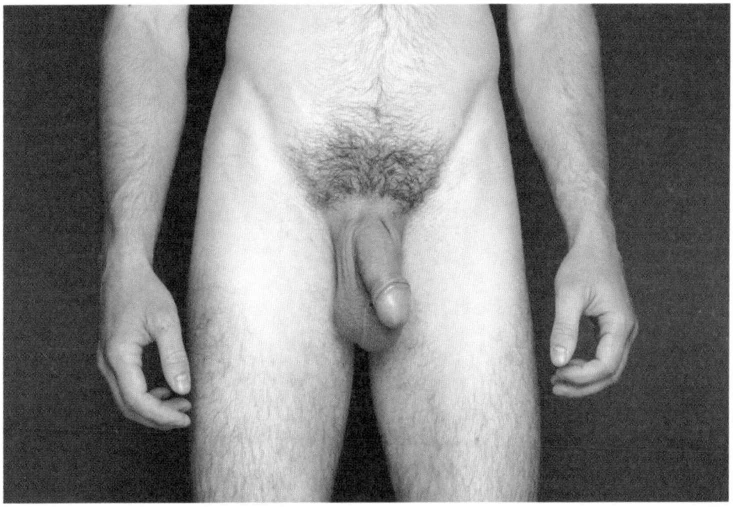

I'm quite an open person. It's easy to talk about how I am feeling, when traditionally men aren't supposed to. I love my penis. I'm not embarrassed about it, it's just a bit of skin. When they are flaccid they have that little bit of a jiggle. They don't look like anything else on the human body. They are a bit silly, aren't they? You can just fling it around. If you so choose!

When I was a teenager I was worried about being too small. I've spoken to women and gay men about size – I was probably drunk when I asked the gay men – and I don't think size is that big of a deal.

If I let it grow, I have a lot of pubic hair. I prefer to be cleaner. I like cycling, so if I let it grow it can get a bit warm down there. And the other practicality, I suppose, is whenever I've given oral sex to a woman, hair can get in your teeth and be a bit less pleasant. I don't mind if a bit of hair gets in my teeth, but if I can 'manscape' and be more presentable for women... I assume it's what they prefer. I don't think anyone wants it bald, but if you can show you care, it's good. At least, it makes me feel better about myself.

I like rock climbing. It's very adventurous, you have to walk up a cliff face, maybe through a forest. It's not dangerous, but there is an element of fear and danger. There's a lot of satisfaction when you get to the top. You have to sort of solve a problem with your body. It's therapeutic. You can't think of anything else while you're doing it. It's a way to be present. I'm not that present in the rest of my life, there's a smartphone, I'm juggling different things. When I rock climb it's just me, no phone signal, and a few mates. It's serene. Unless you fall, *then* it's scary. You don't get hurt, but it is scary. And you have to pick yourself up, have a biscuit and try again.

I live with three men. We do a lot of weightlifting. I want to get better at rock climbing. Sometimes when I look in the mirror I think I look good, but it's not, 'Must be bigger!' I want muscle mass, but a low fat ratio so I am lighter, to help the rock climbing. My American football player friend just wants to be bigger. I'm quite lucky because I have a good metabolism and I can eat what I want.

I think these days people realise there is still an imbalance between men and women, and it's upsetting to the people I know. Why is it still like this? It should be politically and economically balanced. Men and woman have to engage and work together to change. I'm interested in environment change and, in much of the world, women will suffer most from that. It's an inevitability that it will happen.

Some of my more timid female friends get interrupted a lot. I don't think the men really notice they do it. I notice it happen when I'm talking to a woman, and I'm like, 'Dude, that's disrespectful.' It bums me out. I think of my friends as the ones who understand, but there's still an unconscious thing.

I was fifteen the first time I had sex. Me and my girlfriend smoked a joint in the woods, then went back to mine and had sex. It was fun. We were high. It was very intimate. Lots of cuddling and kissing first. We went out with each other throughout the whole of sixth form.

If my penis had some advice for me he'd probably say 'Come on mate, talk to some more girls, you've got a job to do.' I'm busy at the moment so I've not had much time for partying or meeting girls. I think my penis would like to tell me to have more sex.

I've never done this before, but I'm now on Tinder. I'm winging it at the moment. I've messaged a few people, but I don't know what I'm doing. There's been a bit of banter. Hopefully it will lead to a coffee or a drink or something.

Without a doubt men make the first move. I've been approached once, and it was really, really cute. I had a girlfriend at the time, so I had to say no, but I was very flattered. I like trying to approach people too, it's fun. I think it's quite culturally ingrained that men make the first move, but I wouldn't mind being swept off my feet now and then!

Being a man means knowing there are things I can help people with. I'm taller and stronger than most women. Not that I go around protecting people! As an understanding male I feel I can talk with my female friends about anything. Maybe that's an extension of being a man; I want to solve problems. I feel like to be a man is about helping to solve problems.

I'm a vegan because of the environmental impact. Meat is the main driver of deforestation. It's the easiest thing you can do in your life which makes a difference. I think there is something shaming for men in particular about being vegetarian or vegan. It's not seen as masculine. There is definitely an element of laughter, a snigger, if it gets brought up outside the friendship group. I've been mocked for it by 'blokey blokes' when I've been eating out.

Twenty-two years old

"Eating, weight and depression are all tied up for me"

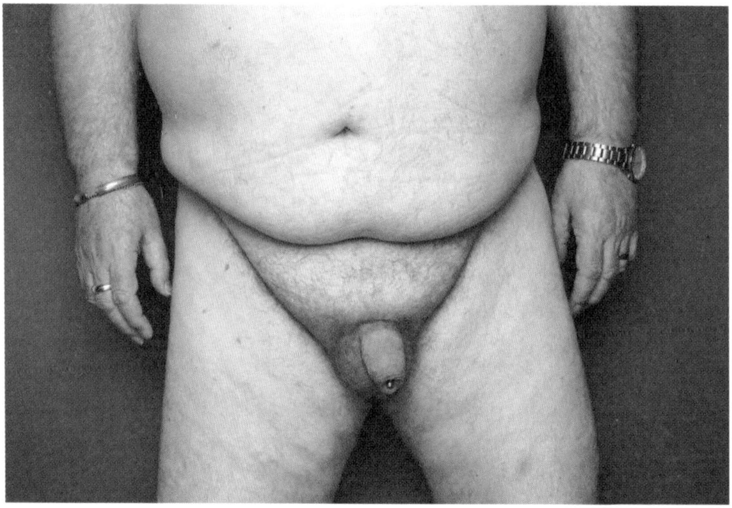

I've not thought about my penis greatly, until about eight years ago when the idea of a piercing, specifically a Prince Albert, popped into my head.

It doesn't bother me stripping off for the photo today. When some guy you don't know, and his young lady assistant who you also barely know, stick cold steel bars through your dick, there ain't much dignity left.

I thought I'd better not spring it on my wife! She was as intrigued by the idea as me. She's happy with it. I don't know it's there now, it's just part of me. It feels right, a bit like wearing glasses. It's odd, I wouldn't have expected that.

I think there's a bit of a rebel inside me and I was brought up to be comfortable with nudity. I had a pretty bohemian upbringing. My parents lived with each other just after the war, while my mother was waiting for a divorce. That was very unusual then. My father had been a conscientious objector during the war. He had a hard war, working a menial job in a hospital and working on the land, just not fighting. Yes, they were both rebels.

I've got type 2 diabetes. I've been on every combination of drugs and the problem isn't cracked. I'm on insulin now, and I don't think that's going to work either. Yes, I get moaned at, because I need to lose weight. I know everything I should be doing, I know I need to lose weight, but I can't. It's up here, it's mental. It's all tied up with depression, which I have had for many years.

I say this to every medic I meet: 'Accept me as I am, even though am I overweight and diabetic. This is who I am. You may make me lose weight, but you will end up treating me for much worse depression.' Eating, weight and depression are all tied up for me.

Originally I was a comfort eater. I know I still eat that little bit more than I should, but I've stopped putting weight on and, in fact, I've lost 15 kilos this year. I haven't noticed any effect on my health yet. I think I will if I lose another 10 kilos. It's always there in the back of my mind that I need to exercise, and even that depresses me. I have had therapy to change the relationship between eating and depression, but that hasn't worked. Hypnotherapy didn't work either.

I was first diagnosed and treated for depression not long after my wife and I got married, just over 30 years ago. Looking back, I think I was depressed as a kid. I was under a lot of covert pressure to succeed. I don't think my father knew he was doing it. I don't think I got enough hugs and praise. Although I spent lots of time with my bohemian parents, I think I was actually a bit lonely. I think something back there triggered depression and comfort eating.

The diabetes isn't as well-controlled as I'd like. I'm aware of all the things that could go wrong. I think I am still in denial. Depression keeps me in denial.

I am closed down by depression. I'd always been an introvert anyway, but depression makes it much more difficult to get out of my chair and do anything. Before leaving today I had to have a chat with myself: 'Come on, get out of the chair, have a shower and get on with it!'

Sixty-five years old

“As a gay you are a sexual outlaw”

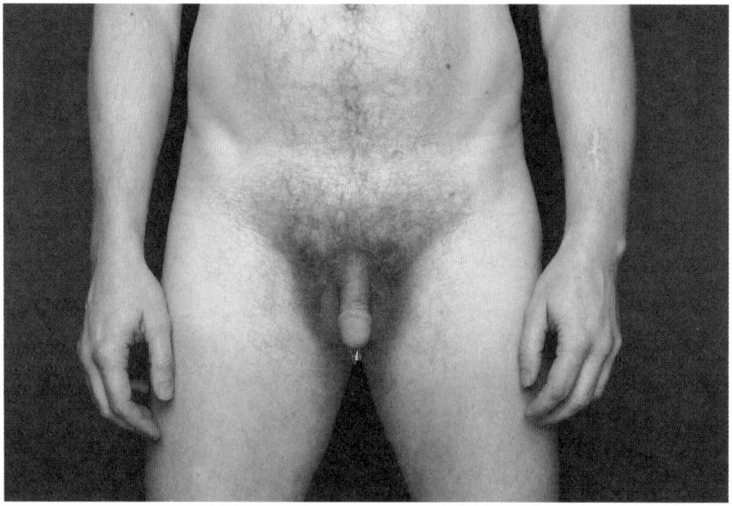

I do love my willy. It always behaves as it should, it gets hard in seconds, and I’ve never had trouble coming. I call it different things at different times. In a sex situation, it’s a cock. Otherwise, dick or willy. ‘Suck my willy’ doesn’t sound very sexy.

A few years ago I was quite drunk at a party and missed the last Tube home. It would have been a long walk. A minicab pulled up and asked if I needed a taxi. I said I didn’t have any money so I couldn’t pay for one! He said he could give me a lift as far as Soho. We chatted away and it soon became pretty clear what the jig was! He ended up saying he’d drive me all the way home if I had sex with him. I thought I might as well, otherwise how else would I get home? I think he thought all his Christmases had come at once! He was quite a good-looking Asian guy.

It was probably the quickest sex I'd ever had. He didn't want to take his clothes off, he just pulled his pants and trousers down. I didn't even have to suck his cock: I just put my hand and mouth near it and he came. That was easy! 'Can I come back later? I've got to get some fares, otherwise my wife will wonder where I've been,' he said. 'No, sorry honey, that's it!'

It's sad he can't come out and express his sexuality. And it's sad for his wife she's at home not knowing he gets his cock sucked. It's a funny anecdote for me.

Sex is generally much more open and on the agenda for gay men. Whether it's real or perceived, men don't have to skirt around some of the emotional issues, or social or physical foreplay, like they do with a woman. Also, by coming out you have to declare, in a way, that the social and sexual norms are not for you. As a gay you are a sexual outlaw. A lot of the value judgements about sex are just a load of bullshit. Sex doesn't have to lead to marriage, or anything, it can just be sex.

Before I came out I'd had sex with women. I enjoyed it at the time. I grew up in a small town where there was no gay outlet, but I was a horny teenager and I had to do something. I wanted to explore my sexuality and relationships. I don't think I would be able to have sex with a woman now, I'd struggle to get it up. Certainly, the first time I had sex with a man, I thought, 'That is what people write poetry about, or kill themselves over.' The second I kissed a man any doubts completely vanished. It felt right in a way kissing a woman didn't feel right.

I had a medical circumcision when I was about one year old. My foreskin was too tight and sometimes it would bleed. My mum always says how upset she was when I was put to sleep with gas. I suppose if I had a choice I would rather I hadn't been circumcised. Having had sex with uncircumcised and circumcised men I can tell the difference. Uncircumcised cocks look better, and the helmet is more sensitive. I accept mine was needed, and it is what it is. Generally, I think it's better not to cut bits off babies. Foreskins evolved for a reason, they don't do any harm. There are religious reasons, which I don't really agree with. Sometimes religious circumcisions aren't even done in hospital, or with anaesthetic. And there's the idea that it's more hygienic, but you can always wash it. We wash other parts of the body rather than cut them off. I find it strange that someone can cut a bit of their newborn baby off.

I had a piercing about 10 years ago. I was sat in a chair, very nervous, my cock in a man's hand, with a big needle about to go through the urethra. There's no anaesthetic, but it's not as painful as you might imagine. The cock ring aids sex for me. I can feel it rotate, or push against the side of the head. I like the way it looks too. It can be hard to suck someone off when they have a piercing though. Luckily I don't have any fillings, or it would be like eating a KitKat with the wrapper on. My partner would probably find it easier to suck my cock without a piercing, but he doesn't have any strong feelings on it.

I don't think I'm a particularly camp or effeminate gay man. If you are, you're more of a target for criticism. Saying that, people must be able to identify me as gay, because I've been called 'queer' in the street. I usually just say, 'Thank you for noticing,' and trot on in my merry way.

I have experienced a bit of homophobia, but I don't care. I know it sounds trite, but I'm self-assured, and it doesn't hurt me. I truly believe there is nothing wrong with being gay. If someone didn't give me a job because I was gay, then yeah, I would be pissed off if I was the best person for the job.

Men do worry about their cock size. I would like mine to be bigger. I'd probably like my biceps to be bigger too though! If you're a straight man and you have insecurities about your cock, at least yours is the only one in the room. If you're holding your cock and someone else's then you can't help but compare and contrast. In my experience, once you start having sex, no one really cares. My cock's not massive, but it hasn't stopped anyone enjoying themselves.

I once had a fling with a man who had a tiny cock. Tiny. This one was probably about a centimetre long, both unerect and erect. It was thin too. A mini baby cock. Neither of us ever acknowledged it was that small. It made sex difficult. He couldn't fuck me, there wasn't enough. And I couldn't suck it, it was too small. He was hairy and masculine in other ways. I know it sounds patronising, but I felt sorry for him. Normally, if I split up with someone I'll tell them why, because if you don't they'll be forever wondering. But this time, I couldn't. Unfortunately for him, he wanted to be the active partner in sex, the top. Oh dear. Poor chap.

Sometimes cocks can be too big though. 'You're not sticking that up me! I'm going to have to lick both sides really quickly and pretend it's a blow job!' *(laughs)* That's problematic too. Some men like a big cock, but not me.

Forty-two years old

"My biggest sadness is the end of my marriage"

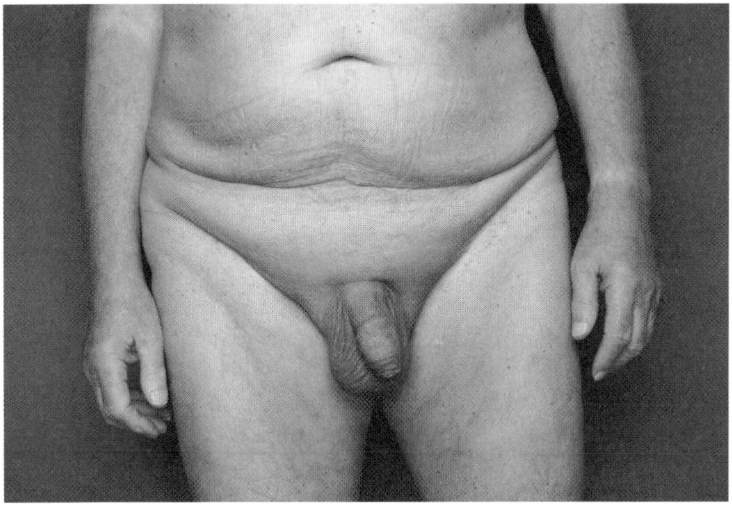

I'm very sad to be divorced after 42 years. I was 20 when we married and she was 17. We did quite well. We had a nice life for a long time. We just grew apart somehow. I find it difficult to feel a purpose now.

After I retired we went live in France. We'd been there for four years when we separated. If a couple have made the children and family the centre of life, when the children leave they find themselves looking at each other and thinking, 'Where do we go from here?'

I won't accept full blame for our separation but it was about 70–30 my fault. We grew apart. We never really talked about it, and that's my fault.

I think my wife had some difficulty with her menopause and that reduced our intimate life together. I found that difficult. We should have been able to pick it up again...

I didn't put enough effort in. Not too long after our 40th anniversary she told me she didn't care for me anymore and wanted a separation. I must say, she used the word separation and I was hopeful we could use the time apart to think. I didn't realise she was developing feelings for another man. On an emotional level I find it very difficult that my wife married someone I knew as a friend. She is apparently very happy now.

When we finally separated she told me we never talked. I have to accept that was true. My wife said that when she raised things with me I didn't talk about them. It is a matter of serious regret to me, still.

I think I have never been as committed as the ladies in my life would have liked. I haven't managed to work out how I could have done better. I've never been verbally or physically abusive, I'm quite a tidy person, I don't leave clothes lying around. On a day-to-day basis I'm a pretty reasonable sort of person. I'm not a serious drinker and I've never smoked. I think the lack of conversation was the issue.

I've had a relationship since then with a nice lady. We lived with each other for a while, but that didn't work. Sadly, she has contracted pancreatic cancer. She is projected to die fairly shortly, which is horrible. She stays very positive. I try and help her as much as I can.

At the moment my relationship with my penis is difficult. I sometimes have problems with erections and take prescription drugs. My girlfriend and I haven't had a physical relationship for a long time because of her illness. I have been seeing another lady secretly for a couple of months. I like sex, I enjoy sex, I think about sex. It's very important to me. The lady I see now is very pleasant, but I don't want my girlfriend to know. In that respect I am being unfaithful. I can't talk to her about it because she's ill.

My career was in banks. I have been distraught about the behaviour of banks in recent times. I believed in the bank, I thought the bank was doing the right thing. But banks got taken over by salesmen; spivs, frankly. One of the bad things Margaret Thatcher did was to create the casino-style arrangement we have now, where banks can do what they like. When I joined the bank as a young man I was interviewed by one of the seven joint chief general managers of my bank. They wanted that level of seniority to be sure you had the potential to be a branch manager. That sort of level of integrity was important, and I believe I followed it. But then they introduced sales targets. When you introduce targets you open the way for cheating. And frankly, we joined in. It ends up not being for the customer's benefit.

These days I try to be more considerate about other people. I temper my reactions more. I haven't intended to be aggressive in life, but maybe I have been. I've tried to be patient but sometimes I've snapped.

I consider myself to have been very lucky in life. I had two parents, four grandparents, a reasonable education, reasonable jobs. I'm not rich, but I'm not poor. My biggest sadness is the end of my marriage. I can't see myself ever marrying again.

I do look at young people getting married much more cynically now. I genuinely hope they will be fine. I see couples of my age doing things together, and I wish I could have achieved it. I don't think marriage let me down, I think I let marriage down.

Seventy-two years old

"It's easier to retreat into my own private space"

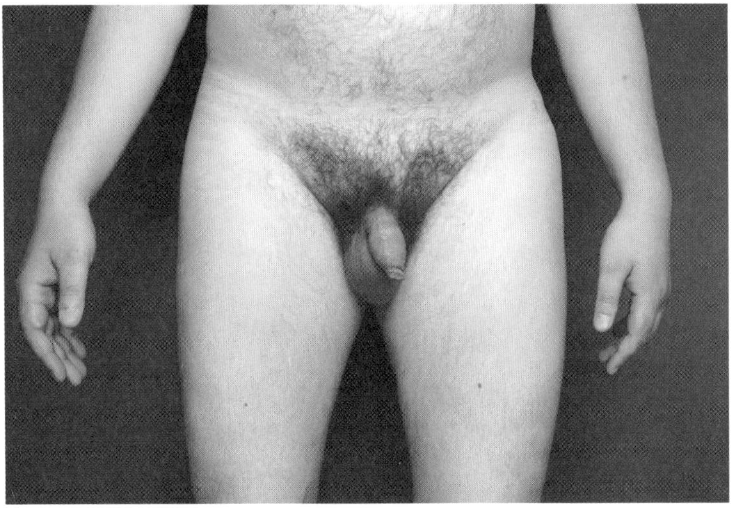

I'm mildly autistic, I have Asperger's syndrome. I found out when I was 19, and since then I have tried to be vigilant about my behaviour. It's exhausting a lot of the time; to a point it's rewarding as well. I feel better having interacted with people, I feel a lot less isolated, but I have to be aware of my boundaries. I'm always conscious of making a fool of myself and saying something stupid. This kind of anxiety follows me everywhere I go.

When I was younger I was quite self-conscious. There was a time when I used to get drunk and act the fool. I used to drop my pants a lot at parties when I'd got into the wrong state of mind. I was known for it. It became a little bit of a stigma for a time. Ridicule, ridicule. Mocking. I might have sabotaged myself socially, making a real big fool of myself. I have tried to learn not to make too big a fool of myself, not be too much of an exhibitionist. However, this in turn has made this a little bit... I'm more conscious of my behaviour now than anything else. What really matters now, I think, is people's behaviour as opposed to their body size or their body shape.

I was even recorded on videotape dropping my pants and flashing. Thankfully it was before the days of the internet. I'm glad it happened then and not now. This type of indiscretion, and the ridicule, can lead to online bullying.

I did kind of hate myself for the way I allowed myself to be carried away back then. I had a little bit of trouble getting through university after I left school, a lot of mental difficulties. I was a fool. What I take away from that in the long term is being mindful of my behaviour at all times.

I keep human contact at a certain level, interacting without being necessarily too intimate, because being too intimate is something that's going to be too imposing, either on yourself or on the people you're interacting with. I use distractions, I watch a lot of film series, box sets, and DVDs. I devote myself to acting and writing poetry. I develop my intellectual side and the social side through poetry and theatre. I think that is healthy. But occasionally I find social interaction exhausting and it's easier to retreat into my own private space, but even that private space has to be maintained in a kind of a healthy way.

Occasionally I experience spurts of frustration and I have used internet pornography. I think the pornography industry is designed to feed off sexual insecurity and sexual frustration. In one sense it can be a healthy exploration of sexuality and fantasy, but it does feed off low self-esteem. I think using it to excess can lead to a deepening of the sense of alienation and isolation that some people feel. I've certainly felt that on occasion. So, I don't have the internet in the house. I go out and use libraries or internet cafes. I'm cautious about being distracted on the internet. I try to limit my time when I'm using it.

It can be a difficult thing to talk about with people because if you start talking about this type of thing, people are like, 'Woah,' they always step back from it. I can't really talk about this type of thing to my GPs or my doctors or my psychiatrist.

Moving on the poetry circuit, I've listened to a lot of women poets and heard about their experiences, just talking about life, being objectified, being a lass, being viewed a certain way, being treated a certain way, sometimes in overtly sexist ways, but sometimes in more subtly sexist ways. The feeling I get is that they feel the need to break out, and I agree with this.

I've been involved in two relationships and my first relationship was actually with… well, it's kind of complicated. She was very young, she was 17. I was attracted to her and she to me. What drew us together was we both had the same issues. We'd been aware of each other for a couple of years, but then we got together in a pub one afternoon to read some poems. We started talking and at some point in the conversation she admitted that she self-harmed. I used to do that. I told her and we felt connected in that way. Although we were attracted to each other, because of her age I kept humming and hawing, humming and hawing like crazy. She was very fragile, very vulnerable and I didn't want to hurt her or take advantage of her. I was seriously questioning, 'What sort of a person are you to be attracted to someone this young? What are you, vile? Are you a kind of a predator?' However, her dad, who is a nice guy and who cares for her, actually gave his blessing to me. He said, 'She trusts you, I trust you, so if you want to develop your relationship that's OK by me.'

So we started going out. But when we were going to do it for the first time and she got naked in front of me, the penny dropped for me how young she was. It took the whole night for me to say so, but eventually I had to tell her that I couldn't fully go through with it, I couldn't have sex with her. I ended the relationship. She was in bits, complete bits.

We got ourselves on reasonably good terms again. She's in a long-term relationship with someone who's a little bit closer to her in age, who is also on the autistic spectrum. She thinks she may have a thing for people on the autistic spectrum.

My second relationship was with an older woman, about eight years older than me. We met at a poetry night. I felt completely relaxed in this relationship, there were no age issues because she was an older woman and intellectually we were on the same level. We could talk to each other about different things. However, my insecurities came to the fore. I slipped into a bit of depression and anxiety at that time. She eventually took me to dinner and said, 'Look, I don't see a future together. I'm not your mum. You need someone to look after you. I don't think this is going to go anywhere.'

I really don't know if I want another relationship at the minute. I've still got those yearnings, those attractions, but sometimes I just wonder if it's worth it.

Thirty-four years old

"Entering a woman is just exquisite"

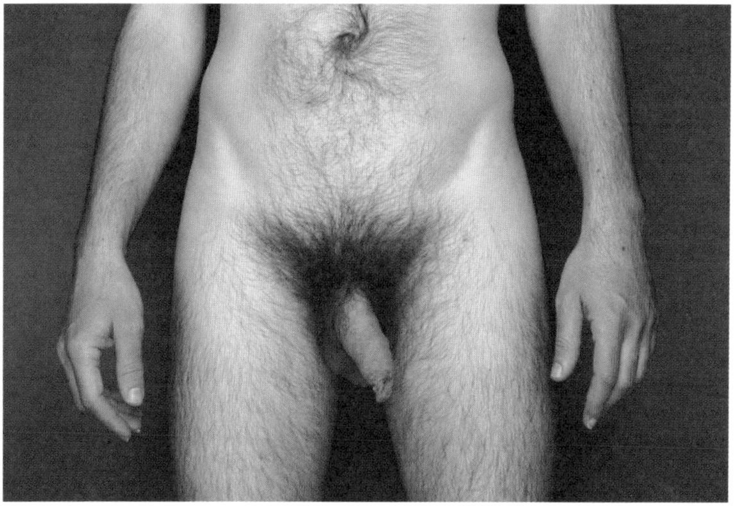

It's been through a lot of adventures. Yeah, I feel good about it. It takes me into a field of exploration: being big and erect, being small, masturbation, feeling the sensations when I watch a nude woman on the beach, or a movie. What arouses it, what doesn't arouse it.

The initial sensation of entering a woman is just exquisite. It feels like the world isn't there anymore and I feel more present; it's the most intimate, beautiful thing. Sometimes what comes after is even more extraordinary. There is no need to fantasise with a woman. I am fully present, fully into the sensation of being there with her. Thoughts subside.

Sometimes I fantasise when I masturbate, but never during sex. I used to worry that watching porn might affect me, but it never has. I used to watch a lot of porn, but I've also been through years when I don't watch it. Now if I feel like entertaining myself then I do. Mostly, I watch masturbation by women, or intercourse, or lesbian porn.

The most amazing time I made love was after I broke up with a woman and we met again without any 'story'. We had a clean slate. Making love to my woman after a difficult time, after hurt and pain, was beautiful. It magnifies the love. Having lost the love and it's still there... wonderful.

The penis can function on its own, but when the heart is also there it's not just physical, it's emotional too. There are times when it is without heart and more like a wild animal, when you just want to fuck. The penis is very much there then.

Good sexual experiences have to do with trust and not having labels. When there is no burden, no 'have to', no routine. It's better when it is free and in the moment and it doesn't have conditions. Then I can relax and be myself. When the world is heavy, when I am stressed, then it doesn't feel so good.

When I ejaculate there tends to be a feeling of loss and emptiness, and a loss of energy and passion. And sometimes it's not like that, it's exquisite. That is why I am exploring Tao and Tantra, where I don't have to ejaculate. I can bring the energy up and then not ejaculate. It's something I want to experience, but it's not a goal as such. If I don't ejaculate I have more energy in life, or for more lovemaking. There can be so much love, passion, and a desire to embrace, and somehow through ejaculation that subsides.

I've had two accidents with my penis in the course of 15 years. The first time it was because of the fucking condom, it was really tight, it kind of wounded me, and my string snapped. It heals on its own, given time. The other time was after anal sex.

Anal sex is more wild and raw, it brings out the animal more. It can be beautiful, but there is more lust in it. The anus is tighter, the constriction on your penis is very strong, so the sensation is stronger. I've only had it with one partner – she liked it too – but I think it drove us to a point where we were not so intimate anymore.

I like my penis, it serves me well and I really appreciate it. There was a point when I wondered if I was big enough, but it has never been a problem.

I grew up near a beach in Greece. I remember seeing my dad's penis when I was a little boy. A bee stung me, and I was in a lot of pain, and he peed on the sting. I saw my dad's penis and thought, 'Wow, that's big!'

My dad is a good guy, he has a really good heart. He is artistic, so I picked that up from him. He played with us and we had a lot of fun. But he could be very angry. We have issues with anger in the family still. There are expectations about money, status and family. My own family has broken up and he doesn't feel comfortable with that.

I have a two-year-old son. As a father I'm present, conscious, loving, attentive. I also have fear and hurt. I have experienced loss and now I can really live the gift of parenting. It guides me inside a lot. I see my edges, my ego, my longings, my anger. Everything is on the surface. I hope that my son can be himself. I hope he will be happy and at peace with who he is, whatever he chooses.

Masculine ideas about status and money have killed us. Masculinity has killed us. When I was back home most of the men at home in Greece were very macho. I felt like I was the sensitive guy, the artistic one, the exploring one, and I didn't fit in. Now I feel like my masculine side is out more, and I express it more through determination, presence, boundaries, being true, being strong, speaking my opinions, taking the initiative in groups. At the moment I perceive those qualities as more masculine. The feminine is more acceptance, embrace, compassion, allowing and receiving. In a woman, that sensitivity and openness to be with 'what is' really attracts me. If a woman sees you, including your darkness, even anger, and stays with you, that is an amazing blessing as a man.

I feel stronger and more confident when I express these masculine qualities. And in my life those qualities have attracted a woman more. I'm very sensitive and I do express my emotion; I am confident enough in my masculine side to do that. But it's always a dance. In me there is a lot of openness, emotion and understanding, but there is also that force of masculinity. When I can marry these qualities I am in my power.

For me, it is super-attractive when a woman is just feminine. When she has power I admire it and am attracted sometimes. If she is balanced then I can be more balanced too. The dynamics are beyond me!

I feel that lately there has been a lot about empowering women, and healing the feminine. I would like to see the same for men. Speaking for me, there is a longing to return home from war. A lot of it is an internal journey, to give up your weapons and stop fighting. It would be so great to be met by women who understand that, with acceptance and grace. To see beyond the anger and frustration and see the core of what it is to be a man. Maybe at the core we are all the same and we don't have to talk about men and women anymore.

Thirty-seven years old

"He's a better barometer of the situation than me"

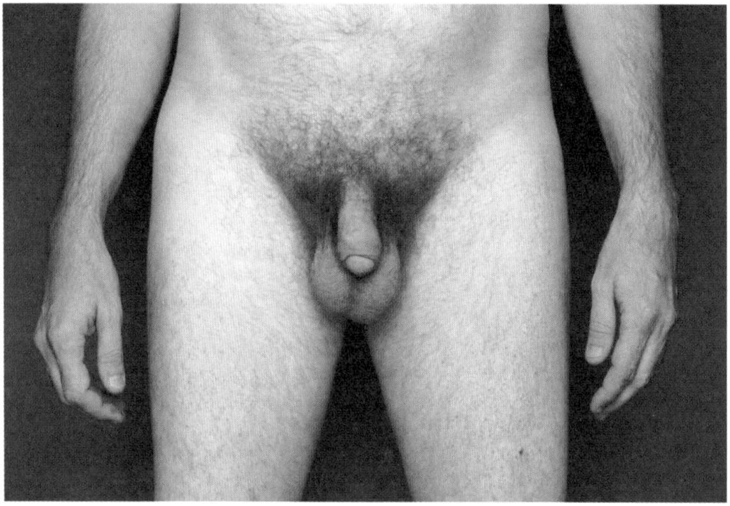

My relationship with my penis is pretty good, almost like a best mate. He's nearly always there for me. On the odd occasion he isn't, I've made a joke, and either the joke diffuses it, or maybe there's another reason why we shouldn't have sex. I think he's a better barometer of the situation than me. There is a concept that you shouldn't have sex without the three yeses: from your head, your heart and your sex. On occasion, my penis has said 'no' even when my head and my heart have said yes.

My job is very technical so when I get home it's better to do creative things. I write poetry and music and I paint. I fill my life with other interests because I don't have any kids.

I don't believe having kids is completely off the cards. I have five nephews and nieces, so from a genetic point of view I feel that it's covered. I do wonder whether I won't be able to pass on some parts of myself through children. It's partly why I write and paint and do other things, they are a legacy.

As a man you are expected to want to pass on your name. It's almost our responsibility to find a woman and bring her into the family, have some kids and pass on the family genes. I'd also like to pass on my philosophy of life, bring someone into the world and help them through it, so my life is not wasted. If I had a son or daughter, they could affect the world after I leave.

There have been phases in my life when I have really wanted children and I think it has been detrimental to some relationships with women – wanting children was more of an impetus than the relationship itself. As I get older it doesn't feel as central to my life anymore, but I still have a fear of the future and not having children.

I think if I don't have children by a certain point it might be too late. I'm meeting more people who are choosing to co-parent and have a baby together, but who don't intend to have a relationship. Obviously having the relationship as well is the dream! *(laughs)* I'd be open to it potentially, but the woman and I would have to have a good relationship. I wouldn't want to find someone on the internet; it feels disrespectful to the child, like chucking my seed off the side of a truck as I'm driving by and not caring where it lands.

I think my penis is pretty good. It's bigger than average and it's straight. If you hear anyone talking penises down, they talk about size and curvature, so I always assumed I had nothing to worry about.

People talk about growers and showers. I feel conscious that my flaccid penis is a bit small. I felt when I was standing there for the photo it was small. I'm small when I'm not excited, but relatively big when I am excited.

My first introduction to Tantra was by a guy at work. I didn't know what to expect but there were ten guys and ten women, all stood in front of each other naked. That was quite a nervous time for me as you can imagine, so there wasn't much on show! Afterwards he told people at work that I had a tiny penis. Why would he do that? It was even written up in the women's toilet for some reason. I never spoke to that guy again. It was super mean of him. The Tantra course was supposed to be confidential. And people aren't normally naked in Tantra either. I got unlucky. I'd suggest avoiding doing a Tantra course with someone you work with.

I've had one other criticism of my penis. It left me with an awkward feeling. One of my first girlfriends said that when my penis was erect, which is seven and a half inches (sorry, I didn't want to brag before!) it hurt her. She was a relatively small girl. I was young and inexperienced and hammering away like a jack rabbit. I've heard you can touch the cervix and have a cervical orgasm, but banging away at it is obviously uncomfortable. She broke up with me the day after we had sex. After that I didn't have sex for a while because I was afraid it would hurt a woman. I stayed away from women, sex and relationships for about ten years. I couldn't talk to anyone about it, I was too embarrassed. I purposely watched porn showing a man with a big dick, to encourage me that if a woman could take a dick that big, then I was alright.

I started to feel better when I took another Tantra course (without someone from work there!) and talked to women about penises, how they are used, sensitivity, and stuff like that. After ten years of worrying about it, I gained better insight into my own sexual nature and how to be with a woman. It sucks when you are going through it, but I'm OK now.

Good sex is a connection. Without a connection you are really just masturbating with a woman there. Pregnancy can come from sex, so there should be respect. Good sex is not about whether you ejaculate, whereas bad sex is pretty much only about that. The emotional leaving of good sex is connected with general disrespect for women. It's been going on for thousands of years. As soon as we took the feminine out of the deity, and when men took control of society, we lost a lot of our emotional history.

Forty-one years old

"My goal is to give every woman an orgasm"

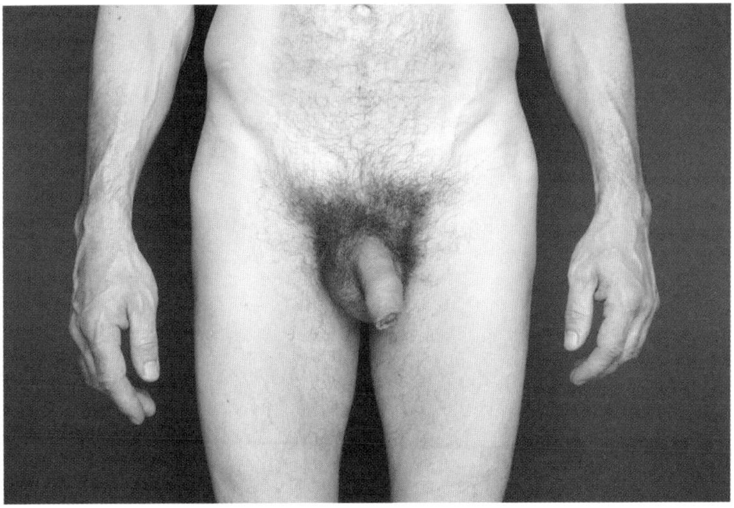

My penis is average, like the rest of me: average size, average height, average intelligence, average weight, average penis. It's less than six inches as far as I know. I haven't measured it myself, but I know what six inches looks like.

I lost my virginity when I was fourteen, kind of coldly. The girl was older than me, about sixteen, and she was standing with the door open, looking out for her mum and dad to come back from the pub. *(laughs)* That was the beginning of sexual intercourse for me, no buttercups in a field or anything like that.

My penis has always been about fulfilling women's desires, ever since I had a weird dalliance when I was 16, with a 34-year-old woman in the south of France. It was the first time anybody had ever come with me, and she shuddered and shook and exploded. My goal ever since has been to give every woman an orgasm. No complaints so far.

The older woman in France is a terrible story actually. I was going on holiday with family, and we were travelling to the south of France on a coach. We'd left Victoria and I still had a spare seat next to me. A beautiful woman got on with her two kids. They sat at the front and she came and sat next to me. After about an hour or two of the journey – it was night time – I put my hand between us, then I put my finger on her leg and then... Then she grabbed my hand and put it 'there' and I went, 'Cool...' She said to me, 'How old are you?' and I said, 'Sixteen,' and she said, 'I don't know whether to be flattered or disgusted,' and I said, 'Be flattered.' I was that stupid.

Then she joined in, she started touching me through my jeans. She slipped over and put her head down and went down on me, there on the coach. I was hiding her with my top. I turned around and my mum's ice cold blue eyes stared right at me and I said, 'My mum's watching you.' She wasn't that much younger than my mum. She got up, very embarrassed. I was mortified. She got off at the campsite before us. Her child came up and said, 'My mum said can I give you these,' and she gave me a sweet with a note in, which gave me the address of her campsite and her name. I put the note in my pocket and ate the sweet.

A woman came up to me in a nightclub on the campsite and said, 'Excuse me, are you English?' and I went 'Yes,' and she said, 'Is your name Carl?' and I went, 'Oh, it's you!' That was the night we went back to her caravan and she explained about touching her clitoris and moving slowly and she guided me through her orgasm and then she did the shuddering, exploding thing. And she was saying 'Thank you,' and 'Sorry,' and I was going, 'Don't be sorry.' And then, because I'm scum – or I was scum, I don't do it anymore, I don't steal or lie or cheat anymore – when she went to check on her kids I opened her purse and took 50 francs. She realised before I left that I'd done it. And she said, 'You can't do that, here, what are you doing?' and I just went, 'Oh, it's too late, I've done it. See you later.' Because that's what I was like. I was emotionally disconnected from everything at that point.

Love doesn't last. My mum was battered by my father. He put her through a plate glass window when they were recently married for waving at someone that she worked with. He hit my brother in the face with a cricket bat. He did lots of bad things, so we left him and stayed in the first battered wives' hostel in London. I thought we'd be there overnight but we were there for six months. I've grown up with quite a toxic vision of masculinity, but I have moved on.

Someone I know was trying to have a fight one night. I blocked his way, 'Stop trying to get past me. It's over. Stop trying to get past me.' If I hadn't been drinking I would have stepped out of his way, but when he tried to get past me I punched him in the throat. He's a really lovely guy. If I'd been sober I would have either have talked him out of it, or I would have walked out and left it to somebody else to deal with. So that's one thing I've changed. I don't drink now.

I've got three children. I've got a daughter I didn't find out about until she was 16, and I've got two children who were planned. They now live in Australia because my wife never forgave me for cheating on her before we were married. I drank to excess for a long time. I haven't drunk for a year and three months.

I would never hit them. At one point my wife asked me to hit one of them for what he'd done and I couldn't, because where does it go? If you give a tap on the back of the legs and they do the same thing again, then you've got to do something more. And that's when you end up being completely violent towards your children. So that's another way I've moved on, I won't be violent.

On one hand I am angry I wasn't told about my daughter till she was 16. On the other hand, maybe I wouldn't have been a very good father. While she was growing up I had ten years of raving, hedonism, shagging around, blackouts. I didn't respond to an invite to her 18th because I couldn't be sure that I was going to be there. I was still drinking at the time. But cuddling's hard now. It would have been a lot easier if I had known her for 16 years.

I couldn't tell my mates about a girlfriend I loved, because she weighed 13 stone, which was quite heavy. But she was lovely. She's lost five stone and seven pounds in the last 18 months. There are people that had a go at me for going out with her in the first place. Somebody said, 'Standards.' My violence is quick *(snaps fingers)* and I'd seen myself hit them when they said that. And then I realised what I should do is just carry on loving her and ignore them. She's exactly the same human, she's a little bit more confident, but not much. She dances a little bit more, but not much. She's still the same human being I fell in love with, the human who looks me in the eye and is honest. I don't fall in love with a cute arse or pert breasts.

My masculinity is better when I'm in a relationship, because there's a mirror and standard.

Forty-eight years old

“Almost all the men I know refer to God in the masculine”

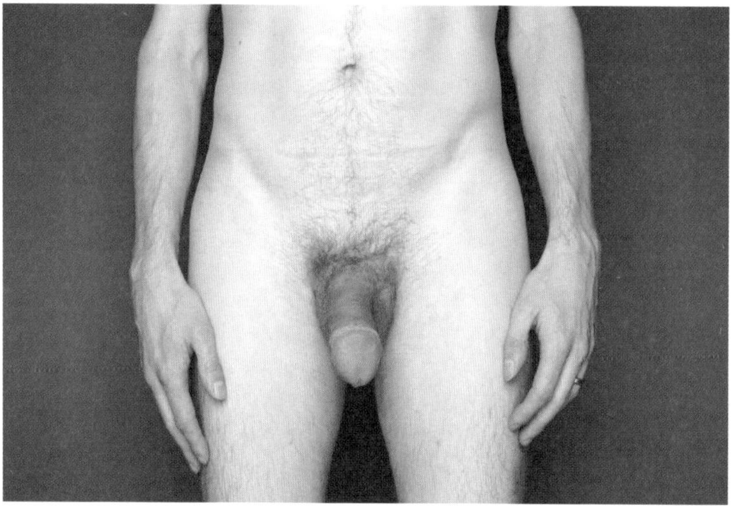

I’ve been ordained with the Church of England for three years. I trained for two years at theological college. During my course I read feminist theologists on spirituality and did some work on masculinity and spirituality.

Almost all the men I know refer to God in the masculine. They assume God is male in the way that they are male. Most men don’t think about how their bodies relate to their beliefs, yet a lot of the women I know are very conscious of the way their bodies relate to their beliefs. I think this is partly because women have historically been excluded from certain aspects of religion because of their bodies: things to do with menstruation, sex, and taboos around childbirth. Women couldn't go to the temple if they been menstruating or had recently given birth. They couldn't partake in religious rituals until they had been purified. Although that dates from thousands of years ago, I wonder how much of that is carried over into Christianity. The default body, the male body, is pure.

When young men and women were separated at church seminars, the men would be talked to about what to do and not do with their penises – you can't masturbate and you can't have sex before marriage. Young women were warned not to lead men astray by the way that they dressed. When I was growing up I didn't realise how toxic this was for men and women. What it does to young men is make you assume that your penis is powerful and you mustn't do the wrong thing with it. There is very little talk of what women might want – just don't touch them because you might get them pregnant and get into trouble.

It's taken me a long time to work though this cultural and religious baggage to the point where I am comfortable with my manhood in both senses of the word.

Part of me was nervous I might get into trouble by being in this. What would my fellow Christians think of their priest being willing to strip off and reveal himself? What would my bishop think? I was nervous about getting undressed. I was also worried about what my wife would think about other people seeing what is usually her preserve. She felt strongly that I should participate because I had so many hang-ups when I was a teenager. She thought this would be helpful for me, but also for other men.

I was always skinny, always short. Puberty hit me later than most of my friends. I was conscious that at 18 and 19 I wasn't like my friends, who were hairy and well built. I was just the skinny guy. Even in my 20s I looked in the mirror and saw the body of a 14-year-old. I equated that with how men would see me, that I wouldn't quite be part of the 'boys' club.'

My wife and I met when we were 19, in the first week of university. We were good friends before we had a relationship. My body size and shape were never an issue for her and she has never said anything that made me feel inadequate in any way.

I was brought up as a Christian. I didn't have sex until I was married. That was the norm within the small circle in I moved in. I have mixed feelings about no sex before marriage. I had a conversation with a young person recently who wanted to know about what they were allowed to do. I said that sexual relationships need to be in a context where you trust each other, and there should be mutual respect. I would say sex with a girlfriend or boyfriend is related to the depth of intimacy and level of commitment, rather than rules about what you can do.

Among the people I know who waited to have sex, there was a mixture of awkwardness, disappointment and embarrassment. It wasn't too bad with my wife and I because we talked openly, so we could have a bit of a laugh about it. But I remember about a year into marriage feeling incredibly ashamed of myself because I didn't think I was giving a good enough performance, sexually. There was a brief period of issues with impotence. I wish I could have had more honest conversations with my peers about what worked sexually and also how we felt emotionally.

The issue with desire is at the root of what it means to be human. There are major issues with how we understand desire within religion. I studied Buddhism. The one sticking point I had with it was a flight from desire, a denial of desire. That was probably my own mis-reading. But, if anything, Christianity is worse because it doesn't flee from desire, it demonises desire. One thing which distinguishes us as human is desire and, if that constitutes being human, we need to pay more attention to desire.

There will always be things wrong with the Church, because it is made up of human beings. So much of what is wrong goes back to gender, power, the language we use. I realise I am angry about it all the time. I survive because I look at my female colleagues and they are able to challenge and push and remain within the institution. I owe it to them to do the same, especially as the cost to me is far less.

The Church of England is a good institution to rebel in! Sometimes when I preach or do service I use feminine liturgy. I've used 'she' for God. It's caused a few raised eyebrows and smiles. I've used images of childbirth and breastfeeding in relation to God.

On a Sunday morning we clergy dress up. We cloak ourselves in long robes, which completely eradicate our body shape. The idea is that they take away our personality to the point where we are just a priest, not an individual. In one sense, when I stand before the congregation I am veiled. There is such a contrast between that and a priest being completely vulnerable and exposed.

My bishop doesn't know I am doing this. On the spectrum of bishops, he would be less bothered than most I think. My approach to this was, if he found out, could I justify it? I came to the conclusion I could. My congregation? *(laughs)* Some would think it is good, some would be utterly flabbergasted.

Thirty-nine years old

"I've spent my life feeling my penis is too small"

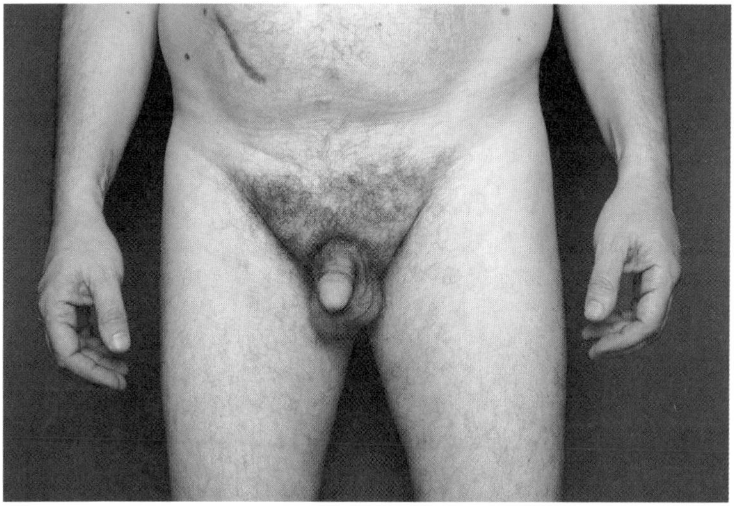

I've spent my life feeling my penis is too small. For as long as I can remember I have felt shame about it. I believe how I feel about my penis shaped my life, particularly up to my mid-20s. I'm doing this to help other men.

My teenage years were difficult for me – I'd look at other guys in the showers at school and think they were bigger than me. I felt ashamed and 'less than'. I was worried about it being too small to function. I went to an all-male school and then an all-male college. I was worried about being 'revealed' somehow.

As I felt my penis was very small, I didn't have sex till I was 21. I wanted to have sex before that, but every time I got close I went, 'Ah, she's going to discover my penis is so small.' In the end when I finally had sex it was with someone I felt very close to and trusted, and I was relaxed about it. It stopped me having more sex earlier, with women I didn't feel so close to. I'm not saying whether that was a good or bad thing.

At times I've gone to public toilets and been too tense to pee. That still happens sometimes. If you are lined up with lots of people sometimes you worry people are checking you out.

If I'd had a larger penis I think I would have moved in the world of men with more confidence. You see men stroll through the showers and gym all confident and 'Look at me,' and I don't, I'm in the corner with a towel. That seems minor, because I'm not in changing-rooms that much, but I think it would have given me more confidence.

I'm successful in my life, so I don't think a small penis has held me back. I'm a business leader, a leader of groups, I perform on stage. It feels like it's more of an inner wound, and it has served me by giving me humility. Instead of walking through life with a swagger I've always been a bit tentative. I've also thought more about who I can trust and who I can't.

I looked at penile enlargement in magazines and thought it was a complete waste of time. I knew that the journey for me was accepting how my body is. I also don't like my nose. The way forward is to make friends with the body I have. I never thought about body surgery seriously.

Size has never been a factor with partners. In fact, it's been the other way round. A couple of partners have said they like my size because it doesn't hurt and they can take me orally more easily. Close female friends have told me that large penises have been intimidating or painful. I remember overhearing one female friend say to my partner that she could never go out with a man who didn't have a large penis because she wouldn't feel like he was a real man. I thought, 'Wow, that would rule me out then.' I wondered how many other women think that. It's never been an issue with my partners though.

I made my closest friends at college, but much about the environment was horrendous. The attitudes to women were Neanderthal, terrible. Behaving with women like that now would be unimaginable. They were seen as sexual objects to be preyed on, seduced, grabbed, grappled with, fucked, and that's it. There were about five men to one woman overall at university and it was hard to get a girlfriend. All the guys were seriously frustrated.

I know men who got raped by other men at university, although it would have been seen as 'high jinks'. A guy I know was pinned down while a few other men performed oral sex on him. He acted like he saw it as some sort of initiation and thought it was a laugh. Whether he really saw it like that I don't know. I would call it rape.

There was a regular night of absolute debauchery at college, with everyone getting drunk, hardcore pornography around, and throwing things out of windows. It's a whole other story about public school and that kind of life. People might get stripped naked. I remember one time people grabbed me and ripped off my clothes, and I was super worried they would rip off my pants and start laughing at me, but they didn't. I think they must have sensed my terror and stopped. That fear was with me all the time.

I was abused twice on trains when I was 11. The first time I was travelling home from school. It was a 45-minute journey. I would normally travel in the small compartments. I was sitting in one corner and this guy got into the same compartment. At one point he looked over at me and said, 'Oh you look just the right age to be advertising yourself.' I was wearing shorts and I'd accidentally left my flies open. He came to grab me. I pushed him away. He carried on talking to me and asked me to go home with him. I was so innocent. I said I couldn't go with him because I had a piano lesson. He said he had a piano at his house. Fortunately, although I didn't say anything when I got home, my mother was sensitive enough to notice that something was up. In the end I told her what had happened. My older brother travelled with me on the train for the next couple of weeks to see if we could see him again, but we didn't. For a long time I was worried I was being followed by guys.

Maybe about nine months later I was travelling home from school, in a single compartment, putting out football cards. A guy sat opposite me and said, 'Oh, you want to be a footballer?' I said I did. 'Why don't you come over here and I'll see if you have the body to be a footballer.' He started feeling my thighs and legs and said I had the right body. Then he said, 'I'm going to give you something really hard to see if you have the strength to be a footballer.' So I was standing in front of him, facing away, and I put my hands behind my back and squeezed this thing. I didn't know what I was touching at the time, I didn't know what an erect penis felt like. It was only about five years later I realised what had happened.

I've done a lot of work around it, a lot of work on anger. I still occasionally feel really angry about it.

Fifty-eight years old

“I use my body as a shield”

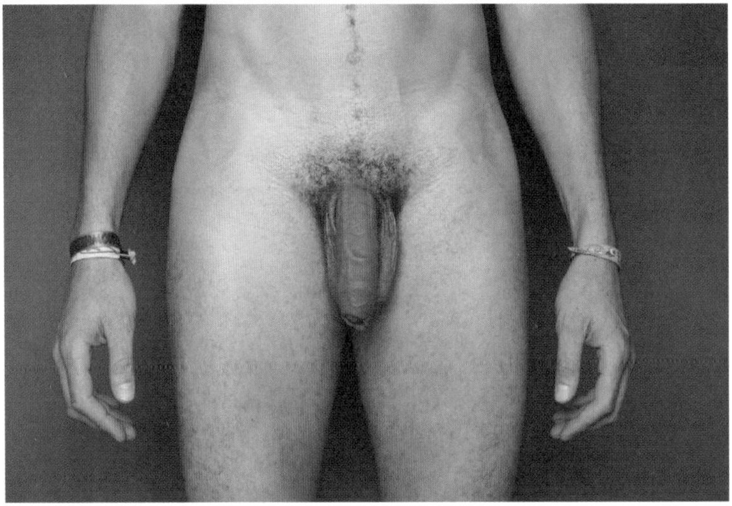

I have a big penis and that gives me quite a few advantages if I choose to take them. I have mixed feelings about having a big penis. It’s seen as a bonus. I suppose life has been easy in some ways because of that. But I’m quite conflicted because I fundamentally disagree with the idea that a large penis is better than a small one. I don’t like the effect of this perspective on penis size in people and in the world around me. Men’s personalities can be defined by believing they are too small. So in a way I like having a big penis and in another I dislike the way society perceives big penises.

I find on a personal level it's quite easy to use that attribute as a bit of a screen. If I get naked I tend to get quite a lot of admiration and it's been easy to hide my insecurity about how my personality will be perceived. 'I can be naked. You'll like me, fantastic.' I have to try not to use my body as a shield to hide behind.

I've had self-image and self-confidence issues from childhood. I've worked on it and come a hell of a long way. But part of that journey was to realise that in the past I've hidden my personality, which I'm not sure people will like, behind a body that I'm pretty confident they will like.

I've chosen scenarios in which I would meet someone through Grindr and we'd meet and get naked straight away, rather than going for a coffee and getting to know them and then deciding whether we wanted to go back and sleep with each other. That was very much because I was nervous of how my personality would be perceived and, I suppose, scared of rejection. It was far easier to be naked because I was pretty sure that I wouldn't be rejected because my body shape, my penis, is something that society values as attractive.

Gay men tend to be a lot freer about nudity. There's less of a stigma about a guy asking a guy for naked pictures, than a guy asking a female for naked pictures. Typically I will send photographs, I don't see it as an issue.

There are unsaid rules in men's toilets: you choose the urinal furthest away from another man and you only stand next to another man if there are no other urinals available. You look dead ahead, you don't look left or right. The unsaid rule of the changing-room is that you change as quickly as possible, you face the locker, you don't linger. Speaking to many of my heterosexual friends, that means they've only seen a handful of penises in the flesh apart from theirs, and they don't always know what's normal or not.

I've seen my pictures being used by other people twice. I had their accounts closed. They'd taken photographs from my profile, basically pretending to be me. My face and body. I've had instances of finding photographs of my penis being uploaded onto Tumblr too. I made the mistake when I was quite a few years younger of sending a picture that had my penis and my face in it. It was a foolish thing to do because that is out on the internet somewhere. I can Google it and I can find it on public places. So now I only ever send the two separately, so you can't actually match penis to face.

I feel annoyed that my photograph was put out there without asking, that the confidence and trust were broken. That really angers me. I have a very laissez-faire attitude to nudity, I'm not prudish, but it felt like a bit of a violation. I'm grateful that I don't have a job which will be impacted if that picture surfaces.

I am white British and black Caribbean, my dad is from Trinidad. In London I feel safe as a gay man, I think we have a very diverse and tolerant society here. I don't feel the same when I'm back in Trinidad. The few times I've been there I've been quite careful to not look overtly gay. I act more masculine. I'd reveal my love of cars, for example, rather than clothes. I've quietly pushed aside some of my interests. I wouldn't wear what I'm wearing now in Trinidad.

Thirty-three years old

"Prison is a warrior society"

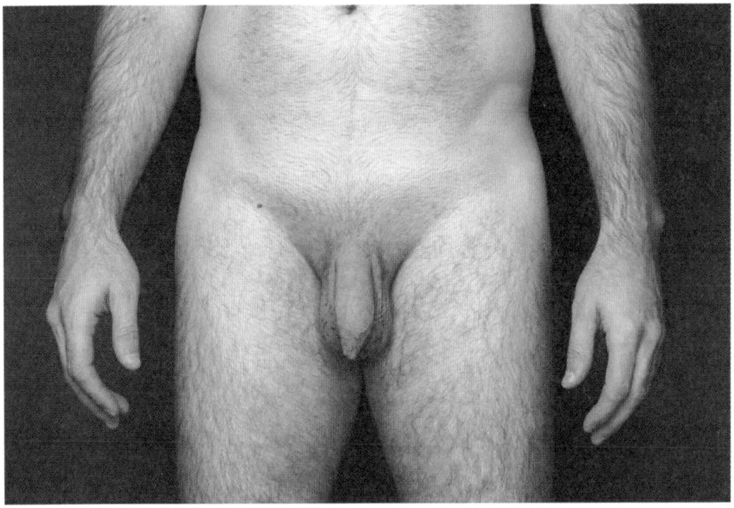

I've been married multiple times. My penis has got me into a lot of situations in the past. Fun situations! As I get older I calm down a bit.

I have an addictive personality. I went from relationship to relationship from the age of 14. I think sex was a driving factor; I couldn't be without a woman. Looking back I might have been a sex addict. It was exacerbated by drugs as well.

My wife tried to slash my penis off with a knife once. She thought I'd been cheating on her. I hadn't. One night, when I got home, she demanded that she smell my penis to check for secretions from other women. She ended up chasing me around the house. When I wouldn't let her and went to have a shower she tried to cut my penis off.

I was wild and I attracted wild women who reinforced my behaviour. I would say my little brain used to run the show back then. My normal brain tries to screen these crazy, wild people out now.

My counsellor said that the key to managing addictions is to channel them into positive addictions. I know I have an addictive personality type, but I don't consider myself a drug addict anymore. I do sports, tai chi, kick-boxing and meditation now.

Drugs got me into prison. I started hooking my friends up with drugs. I saw the business potential and built a drug business. It caught the attention of law enforcement in the US, where I lived.

I was terrified when I got to prison. My heart went all night long against the mattress for the first few nights. You have to get used to the sounds of people being smashed against walls and toilets. You hear those sounds every day. I saw an old man get attacked and blood sprayed out of the back of his head. I adapted by making friends with the right people. I had family support. I got into fitness and working out as well.

The prisons are completely gang-controlled. If you disobey the gang rules you are beaten up or killed. So you have to follow gang and prison rules. There was constant pressure on me from the gangs. They knew about my drug connections and they wanted me to smuggle drugs in.

The white gang is neo-Nazi. If you are white you come under the control of the white gang. Segregation in the US has kind of ended in the public domain, but it's kept going in prison. It's enforced by the inmates. It's really about controlling the drugs in prison.

Prison is an excess of masculinity. The testosterone in the air is palpable. It changes people. You don't feel like a human anymore, you feel like an animal. Your sense of danger is very alert. A guard who has good intentions to help prisoners will change over six months. Their face will harden and they will end up doing bad things.

Prison is a warrior society. Men in prison go back to what feels like a prehistoric masculinity. Prison doesn't help people stay out of crime; people convert into a product of the environment. Most young people in prison in the US have been arrested for marijuana. You go into prison and end up shooting heroin with the gang, making your criminal connections and getting your neo-Nazi tattoos, and that's it: your life's over. It's tragic.

Prisons were designed to house people who hurt other people. In recent decades the definitions of what puts you in prison have been warped, and now people who are low-level drug users and people with mental health problems are in prison. The media keep people frightened by constantly focussing on rapists, murderers and paedophiles, and don't let the public know about all the other people who are in prison. There are so many people making money out of the private prison system in the US. It's going that way in the UK too. It's a huge racket.

UK prisons aren't as bad as the US prisons, but they are getting worse. Murder and suicide are at an all-time high in UK prisons. The UK prison is being deliberately destroyed. 'Oh it's broken, how do we fix it? I know, let's privatise it.'

I've never seen so many penises as I did in prison, because sometimes you are all strip searched in a room together. You have to spread your buttocks so they can check there are no drugs up there. My foreskin was searched for drugs. The first time I was asked to pull my foreskin back, I thought, 'Are you serious?' You get hardened to it over time. It has certainly made me less self-conscious about being naked.

People are constantly hitting on you. You have to go to a rape class to be taught how not to be raped. You are told to report rape, but if you are a snitch you get killed by the gang. If someone has raped a woman outside of prison, they have to be separated from the general prison population when they arrive, or they will be stabbed or killed. But a gang member could beat that person down and rape them, and that would be acceptable. A man I know who was raped in prison by a gang said he felt it was about power and violence and control, not sexual drive. I was constantly worried but I was protected by some friends.

Masculinity can be defined by looking at the difference between men and women and what they tend towards. Men tend towards violence. Women rarely used to go to prison. Women raping and robbing banks is extremely rare. Once drug laws were introduced, women became the fastest-growing prison population. There are half a million women in prison right now. That tells you there is something different between men and women.

I do kick-boxing, otherwise I hardly see any male friends. I live with a male friend, but I would classify him as metrosexual. Actually, I would classify me as metrosexual too. We stay in our separate rooms like cave men. When I am around people I prefer to be around women now.

I brought prison on myself. It forced me to examine my past behaviour. I've learned to not get involved in negative addictions. I am now on a positive path in life.

Forty-eight years old

"I use dance to challenge the idea of the 'perfect' body"

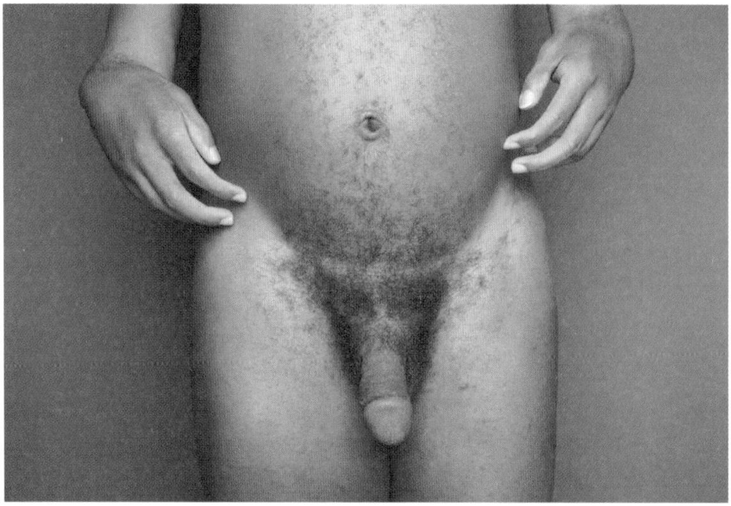

I was curious to take part in this. I thought *Bare Reality* was interesting – the women's bodies were exposed in a way that was comfortable. It made me feel safe to look at the variety of different bodies and breasts. I wanted to contribute to the conversation about manhood and men's bodies.

I think my penis has a nice shape, a nice form, but when I see it in pictures I think it is a hindrance and looks like it shouldn't be there, in aesthetic terms. I don't think penises are ugly in general. I don't think mine is ugly either, but I don't like how it looks in photographs because I don't have control over it, it just dangles.

I consider myself as a performance maker, or as a performance artist, a dancer and a writer. At the moment I am studying creative practice. I explore the relationship between the identity of the individuality and the physicality of the body. I use male dancers and male bodies and I explore masculinity in my work and challenge the idea of the 'perfect' body.

The roots of the work are me. I use my experiences as a male and my disability. I was born with short arms. There's a very complicated medical term for it. I am missing a forearm. On top of that I was born with dislocated hips.

I had a lot of operations and physio as a kid and spent a lot of time in hospital. I have been rebuilt, in a way, so I can live a normal life. Despite that I was a happy child. I look at pictures and I remember I was happy and chirpy. I also had to have an operation because I didn't have balls, they didn't drop down. One is down now, and one didn't come down. You cannot necessarily notice easily.

I was circumcised because I had a tight foreskin. I was old enough to remember it. It hurt a lot. I remember wondering when I was younger if the penis would function properly, after the operation and only having one ball. I thought it wouldn't work well. Of course it does work, but I don't think it's the best one when I compare with other men. It's stupid to compare, really, when experience tells me it works and it's fine.

I am more affected by my body now I am a dancer. You have to be in shape and be strong to be a dancer. Dancers carry an image of beauty, perfect femininity or perfect masculinity. Technically I expose my limitations; there are things I can't do. That is all I can see. I have to be reminded by others that what I do is beautiful and precise and that I am OK. I can't dance conventionally, but I can dance. If there was no disability maybe I would have a different frustration about my dance.

My disability also affects how people see me. There is an assumption that I am not sexual, that maybe I don't have 'the goods'. If I have short arms, maybe I have short everything. I've been seen as the disabled guy who can't perform, can't fuck.

First of all, men see my arms. They have to see beyond that. Until they see me naked I don't know if they see me as a man. Then they realise I have a penis and I am somebody who is interested in sex.

My relationship with my penis has changed over the past ten years. As a performer who has been photographed, I worried about it artistically and aesthetically. I'm in a bit of a grey area now. Maybe my relationship with my penis will be more positive and peaceful when I am more comfortable with my body as a dancer.

Forty years old

"I am in chastity until I see her tonight"

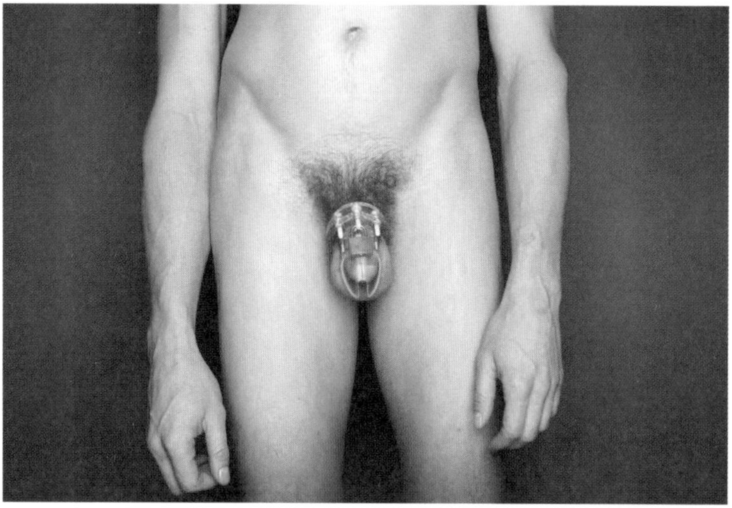

I'm wearing a chastity device. I'm part of a subculture that you might call kink, or S&M. What I like about the culture is that it gives you an ability to talk very openly and honestly about yourself in ways that you can't in normal society. In each of us there are sexual desires that we keep close to our chests.

For me, the best things are rope bondage, or perhaps something quite degrading like worshipping someone's high heels, or cleaning for them naked, or even something more extreme like taking pain, or taking something inserted into me. From when I put this device on until

I see my girlfriend tonight, I am in chastity. She is bringing the key and will unlock it later.

Something that has long turned me on is the idea that somebody else controls parts of me and controls my orgasms. I think, in part, it's because I had a very liberated childhood and a large part of me seeks discipline. There are a lot of men who really just want to serve in this way.

I have had vanilla relationships. A really good-quality vanilla is amazing, but it's just slightly more limiting. The kink aspect opens up a hundred different flavours that you can't access if you are a vanilla-style person. Kink is not essential, but it's enriching and I wouldn't want to do without it. In the same way I don't want to do without cheese or chocolate. They are naughty but nice, but you don't need them.

I remember watching Batman and Catwoman: she would capture him and tie him up. From a very early age I was like, 'Wow, there's something really hot about that.' I remember wanting girls to tie me up. Of course the classic social pressures mean that it can feel very shameful for a boy to want to submit to a girl, or be perceived as weak. So you would never reveal such a thing. I think that repression just increases it even more.

My cock has its own story, because I'm circumcised. When I was nine or ten my foreskin was tight and my pee was spraying and making a mess. My mum took me to the doctor and the doctor said, 'Oh yes, it's probably easiest to just chop it off.' I think a lot more options could have been explored.

Otherwise I love my penis. It's a grower not a shower. Then when I have sex it's got a lovely curve coming upwards, like a slight banana, and very useful for hitting G-spots. So I find that it's a good tool for her pleasure, which is great and I love it.

I have the opposite problem to a lot of men. Some men have a pent-up energy that leads to premature ejaculation, whereas I have difficulties ejaculating. I feel that pornography at an early age, in my teenage years, overstimulated me. So there's often a need in my mind to go to a place of visual or imaginative stimulus. So I've been trying to be more in the moment and less in my mind. But to be honest, actually I think there's a degree of acceptance needed, and I am being honest with my partner about it.

I do like – and it's a strange term – ball busting. I've no idea why, but just the threat of being kicked in the balls is arousing. Who understands why we're sexually aroused by certain things? It makes no sense. But for some reason being kicked in the balls by an attractive woman is a turn-on.

Thirty-three years old

"I was pleased to have finally lost my virginity"

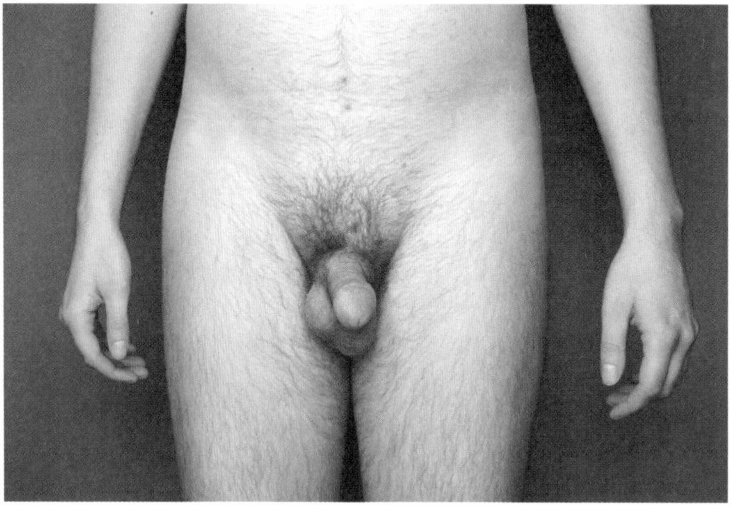

What being a man means is becoming quite blurred. Talk about masculinity is gaining a bit of momentum. This project could help the movement, and hopefully share the issues men have. I think it will shock some people, because the penis is the most taboo part of the body. It's normally mocked.

Growing up being circumcised was the biggest factor influencing how I felt about my penis. When I was about 11 I became aware that I was different to most of my peers. I believe I am circumcised because of medical grounds but I'm not 100 per cent sure. You get to an age where you don't really want to speak to your mum or dad about that sort of topic, so I've never asked why I was circumcised. Part of me would like to know, but not enough to want to broach it with my parents! I guess fear of embarrassment stops people from talking. Maybe I'll go to the doctors and see if I can find the records.

I started to become a bit more self-conscious about undressing after a couple of lads in the changing-room commented that I looked different from the rest of them. When I was at high school I'd always try to get out of any sport that resulted in needing to shower. My mum used to write a note to say I couldn't do sport because of asthma.

Most young guys wanted to do sport and that's what they did to socialise. It probably wasn't until I was about 16 or 17 that I found people who just wanted to play a board game or do non-traditional blokey things. At break time I'd be inside messing around on computers, hence the IT career now, I guess. I felt like I was waiting for high school to finish, rather than enjoying it.

I think the anxieties I had about my penis being small, and being circumcised, would have been reduced if sex education went beyond the basic biology. The use of cartoon imagery only during sex education does not do a lot to help you understand what things should really look like. I only found out recently that penises don't grow by some fixed ratio when going from flaccid to erect! I would have loved to have known this as a teenager. I only learnt it in my mid-20s when I overheard two female friends talking about whether some guy was a 'shower or a grower.' It seems obvious now, but I hadn't worked it out for myself.

My family went on a couple of naturist holidays. Then when I was at university I thought I'd give it another go. Since then it's been a good part of my life. I've met people through it, including my ex-girlfriend. It helped my body image. I'm fairly happy with my body now. It's not perfect, but I am content. I used to worry about being circumcised, having a small penis, being skinny.

I think being naked makes you feel maybe a bit more vulnerable, and because of that it makes people a bit kinder, a bit nicer. You don't judge other people when they can judge you. There's nothing to hide behind.

I'm not currently in a relationship. I had my only serious girlfriend when I was 25, three and a half years ago. It was the first serious relationship for both of us. It was nice to have someone to share spare time with. She went abroad for a year and she didn't want to have a long-distance relationship, so that was the end of it. I'd have given it a go, but I think she was probably right.

I was pleased to have finally lost my virginity. It would have been nice to have lost it earlier, but I'm quite shy and not the sort of guy who goes out and looks for a one-night stand.

Our first time was quite awkward; neither of us knew what we were doing, and it didn't last that long. It was more important emotionally, rather than physically. It's nice to have shared that moment with her. I think she could have had a one-night stand before that point if she had wanted to, but the fact that I was her first... It was nice to know that someone found it comfortable with me, I guess.

We had a couple of failed attempts before that. By failed attempts I mean we either couldn't get my penis in, or I couldn't stay erect due to the fumbling about. In a lot of ways this brought us closer, and made the times when everything worked more meaningful. I think we both blamed ourselves. I blamed myself for not staying erect or not knowing how to get things in the right place, and she had some idea that maybe we weren't physically compatible, like trying to put two incorrect jigsaw pieces together. We both hoped after we finally had sex successfully that we had found the key to success, but we still had failed attempts maybe 30 per cent of the time. I guess we tended to focus more on foreplay than sex because of this.

Since then I have tried online dating. It's quite hard work to filter through the masses of people who might be a match. I have had a couple of dates out of it. I think it works for some people, but it's quite a lot of effort. I tend to go to a lot of music events and book readings, political events, so hopefully I will meet someone through those, but I'm shy.

The peer pressure from other men to be laddish about your sex life and to brag about what you have got up to can be awkward to deal with. When I was at university this resulted in a lot of times where I felt I had to come up with an excuse to get away from the conversation. I don't really like this boastful culture anyway. The conversation was never about love, emotion or even the physical pleasure, but just talking about sex as some kind of conquest.

Twenty-nine years old

"The penis has the capacity to heal"

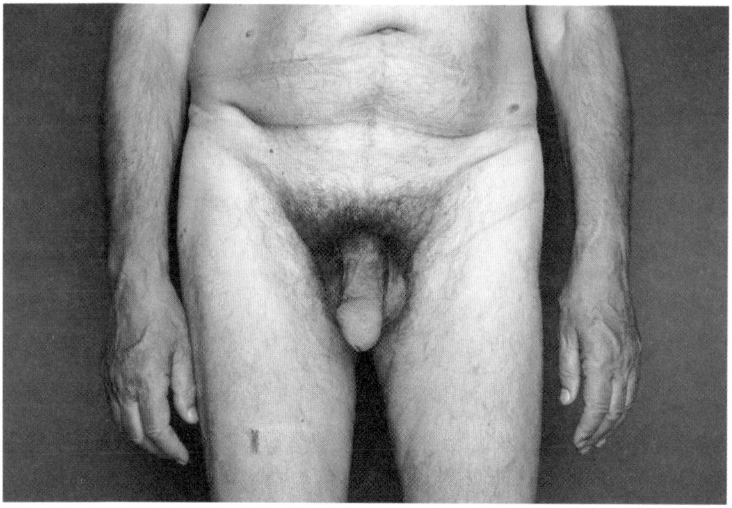

I have experienced an awakening as a result of an increased interest in the divine feminine. I just spent time wandering around Jerusalem. Three great religions hold Jerusalem sacred and they are all so masculine-dominated. The sacred feminine got lost along the way, but more people are becoming interested in different ways. I think it will change our attitude towards Mother Earth and the feminine principle of nurturing, as opposed to a dominance and exploitation of the earth. That is my hope and expectation.

I woke up to these ideas through Tantra. It opened my ideas to a different spiritual tradition: Hinduism, particularly tantric Hinduism, which is about equally honouring the divine masculine and the divine feminine. It resonated with me very strongly. It starts with seeing the divine masculine and feminine in everybody.

I've been involved with Tantra for nine years. The divine feminine found me through Tantra, but I didn't set out to look for it. After the ending of my marriage I was a pretty lost soul and didn't know what I was going to do. I'd been involved with personal development before, but it was based around talk and the mind. When I discovered the Tantra scene by accident I liked it because it was about the body and senses. I experienced a radical rebirth.

My friendships have changed too. Tantra marked a completely new, dramatic stage of my life. I'm a new man. It's hard for me to imagine myself as the man I used to be. I feel very blessed that I have discovered all this, even late in life.

I really like my penis. I have a good relationship with him. I like how he looks, how he operates, the pleasure he gives me and the pleasure he gives my partner. Sometimes he feels like a separate entity – he goes his own way. I can't control when he decides to have an erection. But he's very much a part of me.

My relationship with my penis has changed through Tantra. It has been hugely enhanced. The value I place on sexuality and the healing capacity of sexuality has expanded. There is a concept in Tantra that when a man is really present and conscious in lovemaking, there is a white light that comes from the head of the penis, and it has the capacity to heal. I have experienced it.

My partner and I were both very focussed on this healing recently in our lovemaking. She described to me how she suddenly felt a dramatically enhanced sense of feeling in her vagina, like a waking up. And this is not unique to me, this is talked about a lot.

There is a way of thinking that if a man enters a woman he is either going to make things worse or he is going to heal her. And that is his choice. There is no half way. It feels like an amazing responsibility and an amazing gift. I want to tell more men about it. I think it is more important for a woman to intuitively feel the man is fully present. I've not seen it scientifically verified, but I think evolution has instilled into a woman that she must be able to fully trust her man. As men we need to acknowledge and honour it. I think it's important for men too, but not so fundamental.

I like to take time and tune into her energy. I want her to feel that I am tuned in to her, with no sense of me trying to override her or persuade her, or seduce her.

Most women in my experience have had plenty of occasions where they haven't said 'yes' fully consciously, and there can be a traumatic effect. That's a strong word, but that's what it's about. So where is the healing going to come from? It can come from a man, although I'm not saying the only way a woman can be healed is through having a penis in her vagina!

The contributory elements include trust. There has to be a deep level of trust in the woman for the man. A man is generally larger and stronger and he will enter her body. The other element is slowing it right down so that both the man and the woman can focus their consciousness entirely and completely on what is happening in the moment in the head of the penis and the walls of the vagina. The other element is for both to intend to heal and to be open to the experience. The intention is very important in my view, to set the scene.

Slowing down is very counter to our culture. How do men learn to be with women? Often it's through their peers at school and through porn. And those messages are completely counter-productive, in my view, to a healing relationship. A complete relearning is needed. A slowing down is needed. When a woman has had unconscious experiences the walls of her vagina can be affected. The healing happens with a complete slowing down.

This extends to all touch. How do you touch a woman? It's about full presence; she should know you are fully with her. I've asked women about the early stages of attraction and intimacy, what works and what matters. Presence is the number one factor. It is also about slowing down. It's also about touch without an agenda. That is difficult for a man who is turned on. But when you slow down and touch without an agenda, the woman can expand into the experience. The way I have talked about the penis is an extension of this.

I might think it's the perfect time to penetrate a woman, but my penis might have other ideas. Fine. Do something else. Also you can go in soft and come out hard. More often than not, what happens is that the erection comes from being inside the woman, if there is presence.

Hard and fast porn-style sex numbs men and women; it's the wrong direction to go in. If you aren't healing a woman, you will leave her worse off. The most pernicious effect of porn sex is how men learn how to be with a woman. I feel for young men who have porn as their starting point. There is much for them to unlearn, and luckily I didn't have that.

Seventy-four years old

"If I had sex every day it would be like having pizza every day"

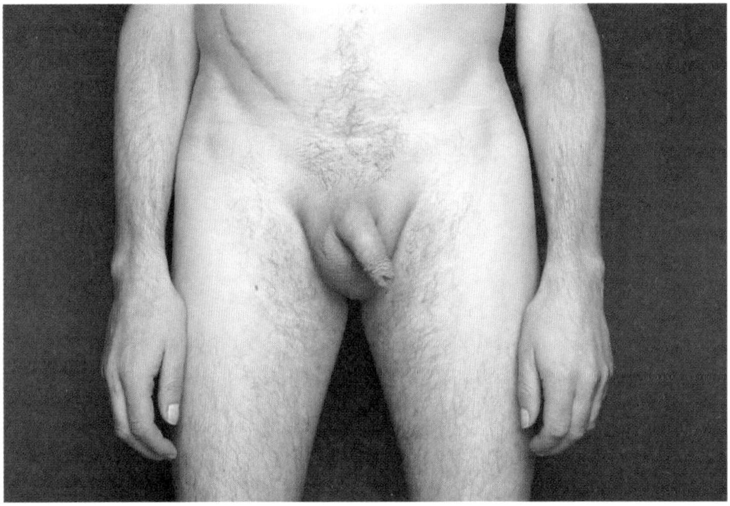

I don't think about my penis much. I only think about it really in sexual terms. That is when it's useful and important. The rest of the time it is tucked away. It's important symbolically. You could say having a penis determines your place in the most important hierarchy. It decides your privilege and power in life.

I lost my virginity when I was 18 to my first serious girlfriend. We were penfriends first, so that was back in the day. We'd been writing to each other for six months before we met. Then we dated for several months before we had sex. We did it about five times that day after the whole build-up. There was a lot of enthusiasm and inexperience involved. In terms of doing it there was a lot of hit and miss. Symbolically I felt it was important to have sex.

People never used to have sex as quickly as they do now. I used to enjoy foreplay a lot, mostly turning on the woman actually. I became good at that. I didn't have so much sexual intercourse casually. I feel I became good at sex because of that. Not having so much full sex helps you enjoy other things.

My sex drive died down a bit in my 30s. I didn't want it so much. I feel sex is like a certain type of meal, something you might have about once a week. You only want a nice burger or a pizza about once a week. If I had sex every day it would be like having pizza every day. I wouldn't want it. I could have Margherita on Monday, Meat Feast on Tuesday and Hawaiian on Wednesday, but I still wouldn't want pizza every day.

I see sex as less important now, but it is an important way to reaffirm that you fancy each other. There are many aspects to a long-term relationship, like going out for a drink together, doing household jobs, talking about work and having sex. If one person never put the bin out, something would be lacking too. I think I have quite a pragmatic approach to relationships.

I have felt flirtation and chemistry with trans women. I can find them attractive as women. At the back of my mind I think they are biologically men, or like men, although they wouldn't like to hear that. But socially I would treat them as women. We're in a kind of social contract where they are presenting to me as women and so that's how I will treat them; there is a niceness and generosity and social giving. No one wants to be unkind to someone who is vulnerable.

Some trans women have gone a bit over the top, putting on a very high-pitched voice and a stereotypical representation of femininity. It's an off-putting parody, a bit like doing 'blackface'. But if they are doing it in good faith and acting natural I am happy to flirt a bit. I don't think I could go to bed with a trans woman though.

It becomes quite politically problematic for me here. Like when trans women say they are lesbians and that other lesbians should fancy them and have sex with them. I understand where they are coming from, but that crosses a line for me. I wouldn't want to be unkind, so I would never say it to anyone, but I think it's my right, and anyone's right, to fancy who they want and sleep with who they want.

I am biologically a man, and that is that. Nothing can change me being male. We have a right to choose how we present ourselves. There are different types of masculinity. Wearing make-up isn't considered traditionally masculine in our culture, but it has been traditionally masculine in other cultures and other times. I'm not bothered if someone says I'm not masculine. I wear make-up a lot. I'm wearing foundation and powder today. Can you tell? Well, it's supposed to look natural. I wear jewellery and nail varnish and I colour my hair. I've worn women's tops if I like them. I wouldn't even call them women's clothes. I'd wear any type of clothes that suit me if I like them.

I'm slightly on the unusual side in my gender presentation, I'm more on the feminine side in make-up and hair. I think it would be better if people could be more flexible if they want. And it's nothing to do with being transgender. I am cautious about different presentations of gender being labelled as non-binary. Nothing is going to change my biological maleness, that is just a fact. Someone could look at my make-up and say I'm non-binary, but that's not true, I'm a man. I think this non-binary thing is a regrettable trend. I don't think it helps feminism either.

It feels like a failure as a man if you can't get an erection. That's when the penis is very important, in a sexual context, and if it fails sexually then it feels very bad. It's happened when I've taken certain medication, or if I'm not aroused by the person I'm with. It's the one time when you feel like your whole self is centred around the penis. You both want something, but you can't go ahead without it. Girl wants cock sometimes. The whole point of you has failed.

A lot of importance is placed on something the size of a finger. At least a finger can move! I can do a lot with a finger. A penis can't move, it's just a floppy thing. You can't send the blood there, it's involuntary. But when you want to have sex it is incredibly important.

Forty-eight years old

"From impotent virgin to womaniser within two weeks"

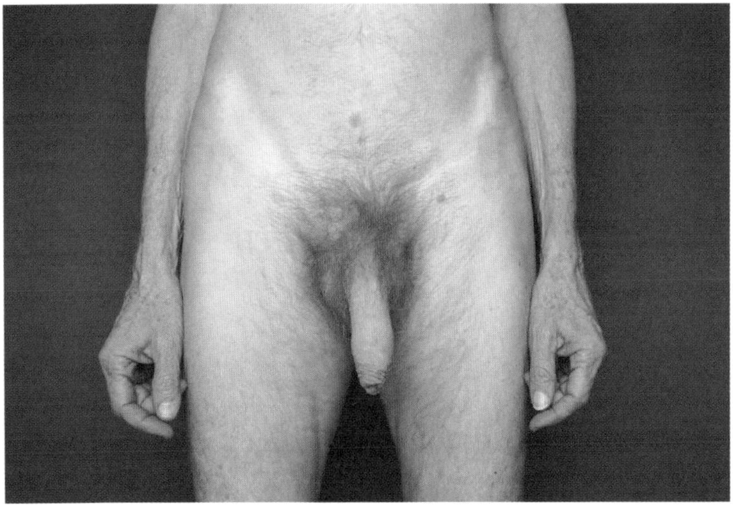

I've been friends with my penis since I was a young child. I'm the single child of divorced parents. I lived with my mother and she needed to work so I spent a lot of time on my own and, in spending a lot of time on my own, I explored my body. I can remember masturbating from when I was three.

I had a couple of critical years where I was a bit nervous of being impotent. That was because I felt that I was being disloyal to my mother. When I was connecting with girls there was always a sense that I was betraying my mum, so I just couldn't get an erection. My mum was actually sleeping within 12 inches of me at the time, because my bed was on one side of a wall and her bed was on the other side. So when I brought girls home I knew that she could probably hear what was going on and it kind of made me nervous.

I lost my virginity when I was 16 and away from my home and my mum, doing a Duke of Edinburgh's Award Scheme. Thank you Duke of Edinburgh! We were both 16 and it was wonderful. We woke up in the morning and she was convinced she was pregnant and we had to get married. You know, she'd never had sex before and nor had I, we had no idea what was going on. Obviously it turned out she wasn't. But I'd lost my virginity and I felt terrific.

While I was away I also met a girl who was older than me, 18, and she was really experienced. She was married to a sailor who was out at sea and I got into a sexual relationship with her too. And at one point the girl's father came up to me, he kicked me right up the arse and I fell on the floor and he said to me – I'll never forget these words – 'Stay away from my daughter, you womaniser!' And I'm on the floor with a bruise on my bum and I'm thinking, 'I'm a womaniser?!' This was a transformational point for me, the road to Damascus – from impotent virgin to womaniser within two weeks. It felt like the biggest compliment anyone could pay me.

When I lived in New York I was married to a Californian woman for ten years and she actually ventured into the pornography field a little bit and did some acting. She would come home and do the acting with me, which was kind of jokey and fun. She was a very sensuous woman and she was really, really into sex. I was working in the rock and roll industry at that time doing hospitality for rock and roll bands, so I was very connected with that side of life, which also included a lot of sex with groupies and all that kind of stuff. The frustrating thing was that I wanted to work in porn as well and the director took a look at me – I was only about 39 – and she said, 'Well, sorry, we don't actually need anyone with the ageing rock star look.' *(laughs)*

I'm infertile. My wife was a very fertile person and had a few abortions before we got into a relationship. We sort of just noticed that we had had sex during the ovulation period and nothing had ever come of it for months and months. She said, 'Do you know what? I'm not sure I should really be worrying about you. You don't seem to be able to...' So I had my first test then, about 30 years ago.

Somehow, I already knew I was infertile. I know my body very, very well. I had a test and it turned out that I was 93 per cent infertile because I don't have tails on my sperm. And I've had about three tests since then and it's always been the same. I took quite a lot of LSD in the hippy period, as well as other drugs, and I wonder whether that had an effect. Because LSD was supposed to destroy chromosomes and all kinds of stuff.

But really, I think it's just not my time. I'm not supposed to have children in this life. I have had an incredible life and I'm so glad that I didn't have children. I've travelled all around the world. The relationship I've been in for the last three years is with a woman who has a child. I love her, I love them both, and having a child is such hard work. I cannot imagine... my heart goes out to mothers, or parents, but particularly single parents. Don't even think about unconditional love until you're a parent, because that's where unconditional love really is, that's how you learn about it.

Sixty-four years old

"I am all about the woman's satisfaction"

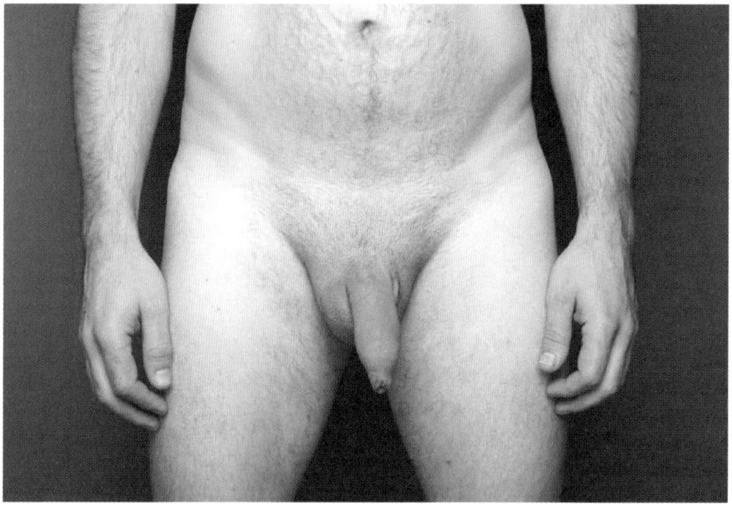

It's funny, I'd never really thought much about my knob till I heard about this project. When you're a teenager and in your early 20s, it's on your mind an awful lot: your knob, the size of it, sex. I used to be very self-conscious, I was shy as hell. 'God, is it big enough? What will girls think?' I'm a lot of more comfortable with myself and my knob these days.

There's talk of knobs in mannish circles, but you don't 'lob 'em out, and say, 'Yeah, right, nice.' People say they have a big knob, but you don't know. Unless a rather unkind girl says something. A girl was unkind about my size when I was only bloody 14, and not even in an aroused state! You know some guys have colossal knobs, and it becomes a joke among your friends. A friend of mine is about 6ft 4in and his wife said something once, since then we say he's hung like a bear! *(laughs)* Jokes about how a girl is walking afterwards, brash stuff like that.

I remove my pubes. I think it looks nicer, to be honest. I think it aids sex as well. It's nicer for your partner to do certain things if pubes aren't in the way: blow jobs, sucking your balls, that sort of thing. I know a few guys who tidy up – 'manscaping' – but it's not widely talked about.

I'm going to sound like a right slut, but the more women you sleep with, they've all got wildly different experiences. Some will not say anything. One called it a 'monster.' Bloody hell, you need to get out a bit more! I guess it's what you're used to, and there's a lot of scope out there. I haven't had any bad press.

I am all about – it's going to sound like a right line – the woman's satisfaction. That really turns me on. If they are enjoying how big you are, then great. But there are other ways and means of giving satisfaction. Bit of a stereotype, but there are two types of women: those who get off on penetration and those who need clitoral stimulation. Size is less important for women who aren't as into penetration.

The size of women varies massively too. Massive differences. The outside of women looks very different, obviously, but the tightness varies too. There have been some I've really struggled with in terms of gaining penetration. I'm going to sound like a right tart again, but there are some you don't feel like you're touching the sides, as it were. Yeah... Massively different. It's the luck of the draw. Childbirth has a bearing too, I think. One girl had had two kids but she had been cut and sewn up afterwards. I struggled because she was too tight. She was loving it though.

I used to work in IT sales, I just fell into it after uni. It was OK, it paid pretty well. I was looking at other jobs and my shoulders were slumping more and more. My marriage also came to an end. I decided to do something completely different, and I'm setting up an escort business. For a start, I love having sex. Without sounding too big-headed, I've always managed to attract women. I love spending time with women. Hey, if I can get paid for it as well...

There will be things I won't do; the whole bondage side of things doesn't appeal at all. I'll always speak to the client first to find out what they want to do, whether it's going out for dinner or just staying in. I want to make sure the experience is as good as it can be and not set unrealistic expectations. No being tied up and smacked with a pole!

Being an escort will be about repeat business. I want the experience to be great so they won't bother going anywhere else. Obviously, the ideal client would be absolutely stunning and engage in fascinating conversation, and not some horrible old ratbag, but there will be a mix I'm sure. You can't pick and choose, you have to just get on with it. We'll see if there are any performance issues, but I've never had any before. I rise to the occasion. I feel confident about it. Can I make a living at it? We'll see. I'm going to give it a bloody good go.

My soon to be ex-wife doesn't know about this. I don't see it as any of her business, but I guess it will be out there in the public domain, so she might find out. Apart from interacting with her because of my daughter I'm planning on having nothing to do with her!

I've told a couple of friends who are very supportive of what I'm doing. Some are open-minded, like me, others, er... wouldn't react in a good way. My marriage has been in the toilet for years. I happened to mention to one of my friends that I'd started having sex with other women. Oh my God, I hadn't realised he was so old-fashioned. He reacted in an extreme way, he couldn't believe it. He said 'What about *(my wife)*?' and said I had to end my marriage before I started anything else. It's interesting to see what people's reactions are.

I would have found this project really interesting when I was younger, it's why I agreed to take part. There is this shroud of mystery, a taboo, about penis and penis size. Why should there be a taboo? There is no reason for it.

Forty-four years old

"My dick needs friendly, open, non-judgemental company"

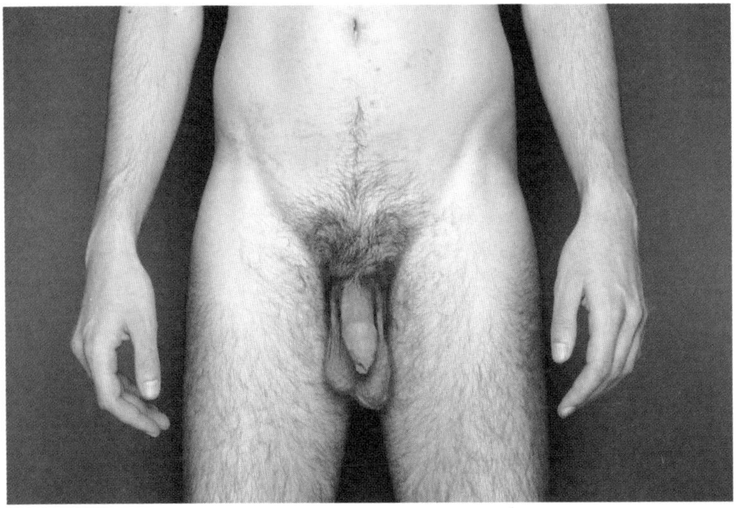

I wondered what I'd be able to contribute to this. I might be too mundane. I was talking to a girl at a party and said I don't really think about my penis. She said, 'That means you don't have a nice cock. Guys who have a nice cock know they have a nice cock and like talking about it.' That threw me.

I was 18 when I lost my virginity, during the first week of university. I wanted to get it out of the way and move on, not make it a big deal. I almost preferred it to happen with someone I didn't have strong feelings for. I couldn't get it up at first, I'm not sure why to be honest. Nerves? I don't know.

In certain cases I can't get an erection. Is it a concern? Yeah, kind of. It only comes into play if you are naked in bed with someone, in which case life is not that bad. Failing to get an erection is just a bit of a frustration, like getting out of breath when I'm running. If I ran more, I'd get out of breath less. If I had sex with more people it would be less of a problem. When I'm in a relationship with someone, and have that emotional aspect, it happens less. I wouldn't say I have erectile dysfunction, but I would I say I can experience erectile dysfunction.

I would say it's a one-night stand situation. My dick needs friendly, open, non-judgemental company. One-night stands are pointless. If it's good, why wouldn't you want five nights instead of one? Sex gets better as you know each other better. The majority of girls I've taken home I've wanted to see again. Because why wouldn't I? It's the start of something great, whether it's a relationship or a friendship. Two interesting people hit it off, find each other attractive, see each other naked. So many boxes are ticked.

You can have those magical moments when your lives cross. Life is best when you enter someone's life, whether as a cameo or main character. It's just a slight misfortune that I can't always fully round off that experience with the actual sex part. I do worry that she might think at the end of the night that it was a waste of time. You can feel like you're falling short, even though you've done so well till then. There's always going to be that part of me that goes, 'This girl put so much time and effort into talking to me, and got me back to hers, and now I can't properly have sex with her and now she's thinking it's a waste of her night and when is he going to leave.' Thinking about it becomes a minefield.

It was so exciting downloading porn as a kid. It's like your first cigarette, or your first beer. Doing something you're not supposed to do. Back in the day, computers were quite an effort. After hours of download you got the reward and excitement. Now with porn sites, everything is on tap, at the press of a button. It's depressing how immediate the gratification is.

I'm pretty sure the first thing I searched for when I was about 11 was 'naked women.' It wasn't boobs, I've never been a boobs person, I'm in the 10 per cent of men who are into legs.

The first search term that was really rewarding was 'blow job.' They made sense, they looked fun. Porn is really great, it's a self-discovery. What is fascinating about it is that it's so universal and diverse. It's like going in to an art gallery, and going 'Ooh, I like that, but I don't like that. Now why I do like that, but not that?' You see yourself reflected back.

As you grow up, you think, if I had children, what would I think of them using porn? Did it damage me? Has it hurt me in any way? Obviously, the landscape has changed a lot now. A lot of porn is so fake now it's unreal. I miss that it's not as appealing as it used to be.

I always have an erection watching porn, drugs and alcohol aside. I think it says that I feel more comfortable being naked around myself than other people. Actually, no, it's not about being naked, it's more about performance. The sex part is more intimate. If I'm with someone I am comfortable with and we've had sex before then I know I'll be fine, so it's also about comfort. I think the main problem with porn is that it's overly visually stimulating. It's fascinating that by looking at something you can feel so much. It's like being plugged in.

I think my sex life would improve if porn wasn't a thing, I think it's distracting. But I feel that implicit in that conversation is that porn is bad, that it ruins your sex life, but that's not the argument. I think I am at an age where I am outgrowing porn. It doesn't have any additional benefits, it's becoming mundane and routine.

Twenty-three years old

“It got stiff in church”

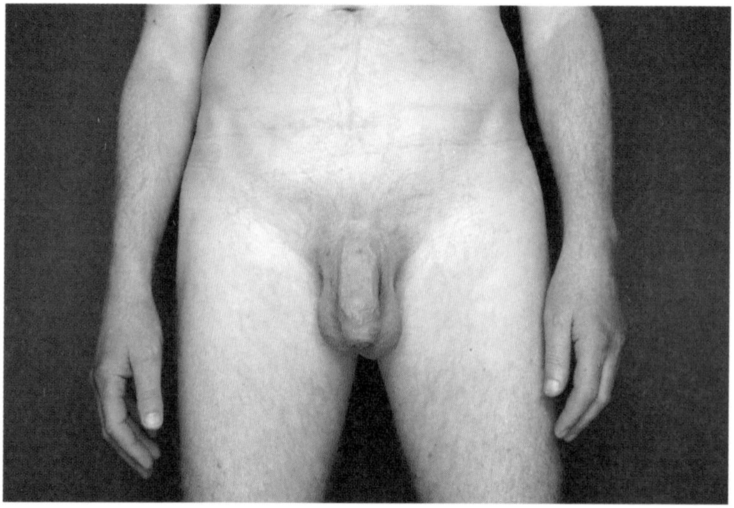

I’m quite happy with my penis. I don’t really think anything about it. It’s not very deep. *(laughs)*

I remember measuring it and thinking that it was about average. I last measured it when I was a teenager, but other people have measured it since! If it’s cold it can be tiny. Tiny! It’s quite amazing, where does it all go?

There’s a little old Chinese guy who can suck his nuts up. He’s a well-known martial artist and it’s a form of self-defence, because obviously you don’t want anything exposed because you can get kicked there, so he can suck his nuts up. You need to train to do it. Can I do any tricks? I’ve put glasses on it, that looked funny. Penises do have a fun side. I think it's a very comedic organ.

I've been teased about ginger pubes, the same old, same old. Gingers are the only ones who it's still lawful to take the piss out of, aren't they? I learned to deal with the ginger thing when I was quite young, so it's never really had a negative effect. Men take the mickey out of each other.

My penis felt difficult to control sometimes when I was growing up, so it was a bit embarrassing from that point of view. I can remember being very young, maybe four, and standing in church, because we used to have to go to church every Sunday, in the row behind a girl who was in my class. I remember it getting all stiff in church. It was a nice feeling and so I let it carry on, but I knew I couldn't be seen to be fiddling with myself. Even at four I knew it was a kind of naughty thing because of the way I was brought up. That's when I started becoming aware of my penis and that it felt nice. Well, church is pretty boring when you're four, so week after week after week... I'd look at something nice, it wouldn't have been sexual... It's quite funny that it was in church.

Dad made us go to church until we were sixteen and then it was our choice. So, I haven't been to mass since I was 16. Catholic guilt. *(laughs)* I don't agree with the Catholic Church's teachings on sex only for reproduction, and no condoms.

I lost my virginity when I was 16. It was at my Catholic school. It was at the bottom of the field so we were pretty much out of sight. She wasn't a virgin and she made it quite relaxing. I had all of those feelings of, 'Oh God, is it going to work?' We didn't go out together or anything like that. It was just a one-off.

Apparently you can tell by your thumb shape what shape your penis is. And the woman's thumb reflects the shape of the inside of her vagina. So, for instance, if our thumbs were to match shape, not size but shape, then my penis would theoretically excite all of the area within your vagina and therefore we would be sexually suited. Yeah, have a look at men's thumbs. Thumb wars are excellent! And then you look at length of fingers to compare size. So you might meet someone who has got a similar thumb shape to you, but it might be too big and so you might not be able to handle it. *(laughs)* So then you can look at fingers and so on. If your finger length isn't right, then the woman might not be able to take the man's full length and she won't be able to excite all of the zones on the willy.

I think it does stack up, actually. This mate of mine, he had a real bend on his thumb and his knuckle stuck out a lot further, and that was the shape of his willy when he was erect. Some willies have got quite a bend on them, like a banana, haven't they? And other willies are just dead straight, aren't they? So, if you're a girl with a bent thumb then you're probably looking for a guy with a bent thumb as well.

Forty-eight years old

"My relationship with my penis is crap"

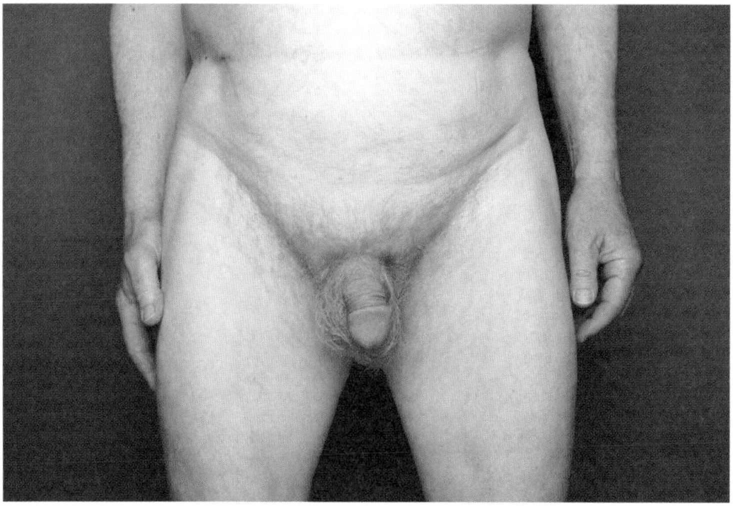

My relationship with my penis is crap really, because of my age and because I'm diabetic. What I have is an excretory organ and not a sexual organ. That's quite difficult, because desire doesn't go away even though I'm 75. And I've got an enlarged prostate. It's not cancer, but I do take a lot of medication to keep it from enlarging any more.

I go to the gym three times a week, I like to keep fit, but it's quite hard because I used to walk 20 miles a day. My body is slower than it used to be.

Throughout most of my married life I've been very happy with my dick. We had a good sex life, but then there was the menopause, then I was kind of less vigorous, and now it's all gone, really.

I don't think we manage this well in our relationship. It's an issue. I haven't had sex – penetrative sex – for about eight years or so and it's disappointing really. If you have diabetes you're likely to be impotent. I mean, I have used chemicals like Viagra and I had a pump and all the rest of it, but if your partner's not 'there' then it's quite a difficult issue, isn't it? If she doesn't want to be with you. I think she doesn't.

I'm a Buddhist and I meditate, and I try to work on the images that arise during meditation and become a bit detached from them. But it's taken quite a bit of work, really, to keep them away. In the past I didn't have any issues to do with masculinity. It makes you feel a bit inadequate really. It's what the Buddhists call suffering. *(laughs)*

Society doesn't address, either for women or for men, that desire continues for quite some time.

The prelude to sex is about comforting and warmth and feeling and all that. So now I think there is less... I'll put it this way: there's less affection than I would like. So, there we are.

As an adolescent you're always wanting to get your leg over. It's a struggle finding adequate outlets. Because you want to be a bloke, you know. But life has changed, women are stronger now, and rightly so. Don't get me wrong about that, but it's hard for somebody of my vintage to take all that on board, when basic affection, if you like, is sometimes not there in the amounts that you might want.

I wanted to be closer to my children when they were growing up. In my working life there weren't the opportunities, the expectations were different. Sometimes I didn't get anywhere near the kids. If you talked to my wife, I think she'd say that I had quite a close relationship with my kids and the grandchildren. I think she's got a grip on those relationships and you try and break in on that and you find yourself... We look after the grandchildren three days a week so she takes them off to school, because they're seven and nine, but if I offer to take them, ooh-hoo, not a hope in hell. Not a hope in hell. There's a bit of me that really is quite angry about that and I resent it, really.

So, don't get me wrong, there are rights that women have fought over and it should be equal, but I find feminism a bit tedious. There's no doubt in my mind that there should be equal pay, and considering that there has been an Act of Parliament that's supposed to give that, it surprises me that it just hasn't happened. I really don't have any difficulty about that, I mean, that's how it should be. We're equal, it's just working out what the roles should be that's difficult.

A lot of stuff falls to women by the very nature of their relationship with a child – holding and feeding, being pregnant, all that kind of stuff. When I was young I'd have been afraid of looking after the children. You know, I was glad of having a more distant role. I'm sure it's better nowadays for men and they do have different kinds of relationships. But if you feel as if you're kind of pushed out a bit then you lose the skills and therefore that desire to be closer. In broad terms we both have good relationships with the kids and grandchildren, and hopefully that will continue.

Seventy-five years old

"I wear a packing cock"

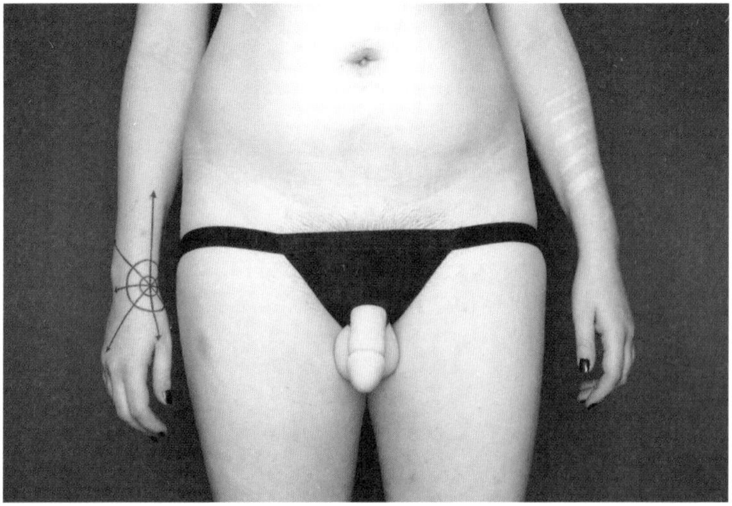

I identify as non-binary. Genderqueer is another word. Basically I've never felt like a woman. I didn't get into girlie things when I was a teenager, I didn't really like hanging out with girls, I didn't get into make-up or shoes and I didn't like the kinds of conversations that girls had. I thought if I wasn't into all that, then maybe it meant I'm a guy, maybe I'm a trans guy. So I thought about whether I should transition and live as a man and what that would mean, and that didn't quite feel right either.

I don't even know what it would mean to be a man. The more I think about it, the more I just think that society has created really fucked-up structures that don't fit people, that force people to try and uncomfortably be something that maybe they're not and I think that's very sad. In my ideal world genders wouldn't be a thing; you wouldn't separate male or female, you wouldn't have masculine characteristics or feminine characteristics, we'd all just be people.

I try and match how I look on the outside to how I feel on the inside, which is generally something in between genders. Occasionally someone will see me from behind and say 'Sir' or 'Bro' or whatever, like if it's a quick glimpse. My face is too feminine to pass as a man. There have been occasions when I'm going about my business, wearing my chest binder and my packing cock, feeling very masculine and then I've walked into a shop and the person's said, 'Alright darling?' and that's just felt like a slap in the face.

I wear a packing cock for the aesthetic and the feel of it. It doesn't have any real practical purpose. I can't piss through it. I can't have sex with it. I can get a blow job with it and that's really quite hot. I like the feeling of having my genitals on the outside sometimes and like just feeling the way that my clothes rub against it. It can be arousing. I can feel it press against my clitoris. I like being more aware of my sexual organs, it feels kind of nice to walk around the world being more aware of my sexuality. I wonder if it feels like that for men, but maybe if you have a cock every single day you're not so aware of it.

I bind my breasts more frequently these days. I first did it about a year ago and I looked in the mirror and I was like, 'That's what I look like in my head!' I used to be really skinny and I had little B cup boobs that were kind of flat so they weren't too much of an issue. And then I put on a bunch of weight, so now I'm a size 14 and I've got 36C breasts, which feels fucking big. I don't like what I see when I look in the mirror, they look really odd to me. When I put the binder on it feels like that's what I should always look like.

I feel very vulnerable going out in a skirt. It feels like my genitals are more accessible and I feel off-balance in heels. I feel very aware of who is around me. It's very, very vulnerable and quite uncomfortable.

I noticed recently that I tend to try and dress for minimal reaction from people. If I go out wearing make-up and dressing more feminine then men will comment and I don't like that. If I dress more masculine, in a suit, people look and that feels less comfortable. I like to dress more gender neutral, so I can just slip by people's radar, but that's kind of sad.

I've thought quite a lot about getting my breasts removed and that's still an ongoing thought process, but my work is a big concern. I'm a pro Domme. I really love what I do for a living, I wouldn't want to damage that. I play a more feminine role for my clients. I wear girlie underwear.

I enjoy playing with people's bodies, seeing what you can do with them. I like connecting with people and being very intimate. So in my sessions I tend to be quite sensual and get quite physically close with people. It gives me a rush hurting people, if they're enjoying it. If they're not enjoying it that's a different thing, of course.

In my personal life, I tend to have sex with people who have penises or who identify as male. I find masculine people attractive, but that could be a trans guy; it doesn't have to be someone who has got a biological penis, but someone who identifies as male. My current partner identifies as genderqueer as well, so they have the pronoun 'they.' They have a biological penis, but sometimes we have sex where they're more female and I'm more male.

There'll be plenty of times when I'll have sex with my partner and my vulva doesn't get involved at all, so I'm just wearing a cock and I'm fucking his arse and it's like I'm fucking a vulva. So the experience that we're both having could be straight sex, but the other way around, and that's our experience of it. But it could sound complicated to someone who doesn't understand.

The interesting thing is that I can orgasm very easily from penetrating someone with nothing touching my vulva, no pressing against my clitoris even. Yeah, really! I think it's because I spend a lot of time imagining that I've got a cock and then I can imagine the sensations of it. If I just put my hard cock on now and rammed it into somebody I wouldn't feel anything, but if I put it on and get someone to go down on me for a while I kind of watch them and see what their mouth is doing and imagine how that would feel if that was a real penis, then I kind of get my head in that place. Sensation is all in your head really. Someone could be rubbing your clit and you're totally not turned on and it would feel terrible. In a different headspace it could feel great.

When I'm penetrating someone with my fucking cock, I forget I even have a vulva. I've got this whole piece of anatomy that I've forgotten about. So it takes a little while to get my head back round it again. But my vulva works very well indeed, I have really great sex with it.

Because I can orgasm from fucking a guy in the arse, because it's just as intimate as penetrative sex, I don't do it in my work as a Domme. I'm not comfortable having that level of intimacy with my clients. If I'm fucking them I'm going to get selfish and want to have more orgasms. It's going to become about me rather than them. So I just don't do anything like that with clients.

Thirty years old

“Being a man means being wrong all the time!”

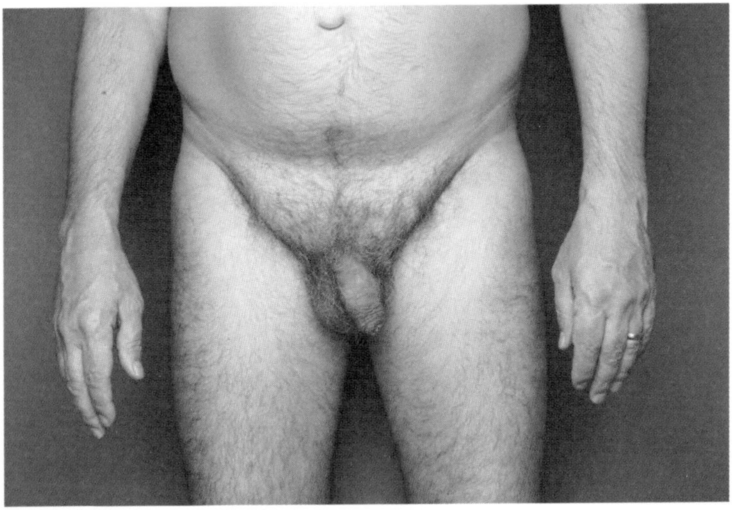

I’m pleased to be involved with something that takes a positive view of penises, because I feel positive about my penis. It is very expressive and variable, which is unusual for a body part. You wake up with the same nose you go to sleep with. Your penis can drastically change size and shape in response to cold, stress, illness and arousal. It’s a constant source of interest.

It’s also a source of pleasure. I came to that early in life. We are brought up to feel shame about the body, but I went against that. I am not self-conscious about allowing my penis to be seen. Not that I want to go around raising offence and causing upset. I'm not an exhibitionist, but in a situation like this I am not uncomfortable.

I'm against any kind of body shame directed at women, so on the rare occasions I have experienced it directed at me, I have really felt it. I once did life modelling for a further education college. I asked if there was anything they wanted me to change, meaning my pose or something like that. One of the students, an 18-year-old girl, said, 'Well, yeah, everything.' I wish I'd had the self-possession to stand up and walk out. I was there as a subject for them to draw. This is it, this is who I am. It was horrible. To be fair the rest of the class did react against it.

Ageing is hard. I don't look old for 51, but I look older than I did at 24... I enjoyed the time of life when I was most out of control. I wish I'd done more with it at the time, to be honest! I'd like to have been more of a wild beast! My penis is still a beast, but more like an old dog that has to be encouraged to go for a walk, but always enjoys it when it does. Everything is slower and turned down a few notches. I don't have problems getting an erection, but I don't get the spontaneous ones I used to.

Across the board, I want things to be more or less equal for men and women. I'm very keen on making sure that my daughters aren't disadvantaged in any way for being girls. My family and my wife's are mostly male, so having daughters has been a puzzle to learn about. How do girls grow up in the world? I haven't seen any obvious barriers put in their way. But when they were younger there was a school play in which there was a chorus of scientists. I thought it was disappointing that none of the scientists were girls. I spoke to the headteacher about it, who said there had been girls until the last day of rehearsals, but then they had said they didn't want to do it.

I got into a terrible row when I was younger and referred to myself as a feminist. A female academic said, 'You can't be. You're not qualified.' I sort of agree with her, but what does she want me to be?

Being a man means being wrong all the time! *(laughs)* You can easily get that impression. If you read and pay attention to women's issues, men don't come out looking that great. There are lots of times when I would want to say I am not like that.

Being a man also carries the residual expectation that you will be the breadwinner, the leader, the head of a household. That doesn't disappear in a generation. In our household there are jobs that I typically do, and jobs that she typically does. But we don't do them for gender reasons, it's because of what we like and don't like doing. You can agree a division of labour, but it doesn't have to be for reasons of gender. It's my job to reach high shelves though!

As a man, I enjoy the physical strength. I'm not stronger than all the women I've met, but in general I am. It's also nice to be granted a degree of privilege. On those occasions where you deal with women who like men, it's a nice stroke to have.

I like to join in with football talk. It's a nice vehicle for being in a conversation. My men friends and I don't have the sort of friendships where we talk about emotions and personal things. I've had deep and strong friendships, but a lot was left unsaid. I never really knew how to make it different. I don't think I wanted it to be different, or we'd have had to be different people, and I wouldn't wish that. I can see why being more emotionally articulate would be a good thing, but I can't visualise myself doing it.

My experience is that men don't talk like this with each other. My supposition is that women do talk frankly and emotionally. I wonder if I have been discussed by women?

When did the penis become an object of fear? Why are there taboos around the penis? Why is the erect penis more threatening than the flaccid penis? I think this is a good opportunity for people to enjoy visually and emotionally the defining characteristic of being male.

Fifty-one years old

“I thought it was normal for sex to be painful”

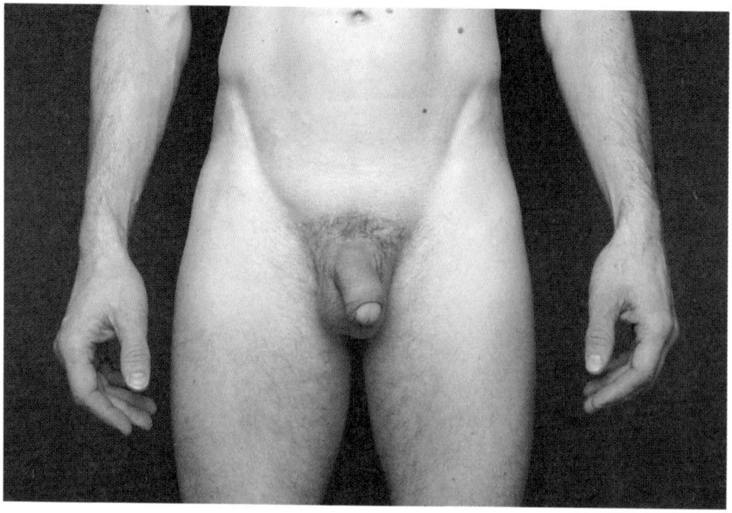

In my family we always called it a ‘sparrow.’ One of my enduring childhood memories was my grandma calling my penis a ‘sparrow’ when I was in the bath. Yes, sparrows are small, but I was only young at the time, and it sounds nice and innocent.

I know some people really worry about their size. I’ve got no angst about that. I’m probably normal, not big or small. I’ve always had a very sensitive penis though, and that has restricted pleasurable sex to a degree.

I thought it was normal for sex to be painful, until I had a long-term partner in my early 30s. So I had a circumcision quite late in life. It was difficult to go from having a proper foreskin, which I could pull all the way back even though it was painful, to suddenly not having any foreskin. There is a little bit of foreskin left and that is still very sensitive, so I have to be selective what I do. I have to be very clear that I want to do it. If someone mishandled my penis it could be very painful. It becomes abrasive and sore and red very quickly. I have no idea how normal this is.

The circumcision did help, because it was a lot more painful before. Now there's just a residual sensitivity if it's handled wrong. I have to lubricate very carefully to avoid it getting chafed. I'm lucky in one sense, because I don't have a problem with erections or orgasms. Some of my friends in their 40s are now getting the beginnings of erectile dysfunction problems. That began for a few friends in their 30s. One of my friends can't get it up at all. So I suppose I'm lucky.

One friend bought one of those tubes off the internet that you put your cock into and pump it up. It's supposed to give you an erection and make you bigger over time.

I get 'green' pills online, similar to Viagra, the ones that help get your cock erect. They are a herbal equivalent. You get an instant erection if you are stimulated, but you get red in the face too. I don't have a problem getting it up, but it's not as hard or rigid as it used to be. These pills make me harder.

I announced my circumcision in a funny way. I was going on holiday with friends, but I hate flying so I drank a bottle of Jack Daniels. I was quite sleepy, but about half way through the flight I got a surge of energy, stood up on my seat and announced to the entire plane: 'Oh, did I tell you what I've just had done...' I went through a period of being very private about the sensitivity. I didn't want any questions about the circumcision, my sex life and relationship. But then I had the Jack Daniels!

I think taking part in this project is a good thing, because you don't see penises except in porn films, and they're all the same. Porn men are in porn films because of their huge, perfect penises, they are all uniform with perfect shapes and the same colour.

I do watch porn, especially as I have a single life now. I do tend to start thinking, 'Ooh, that's the norm', but then my rational brain engages. I'm pretty sure all penises are not like that! Luckily I've got some inner confidence. Perhaps it all goes back to my grandma saying I have a nice sparrow. *(laughs)*

Kids now have the internet. Me and my mates, our only reference point for sex was going into the local newsagent and looking at this magazine called Face to Face, which had men and women in sexual poses. We used go round and round the magazine aisle, choose an innocuous magazine, then grab Face to Face and put it inside the other one so we could have a look at the pictures. It was the first time we'd seen another naked man or woman. It got us all excited. Now it's a different ball game, it's all out there.

I think there's a lost innocence now. I'd worry if I had kids coming up to puberty seeing porn. You would not want your son or daughter to see a lot of the porn out there. It's usually demeaning to women. Gay porn is more equal, there isn't the same power differential. Straight porn invariably involves men calling women particular names, which I find demeaning. I don't like to see women treated badly and called 'whore' or 'bitch.' Even the names of porn clips and films are part of the problem. It's repulsive seeing men slap women around. I saw a man holding a woman down by the throat. That's supposed to be a sex act? No, it's an act of violence. So, if kids are getting to see this... I think if people watch this at an early age it will condition them. They might think it's the norm. Girls will think they should allow boys to treat them like that, and boys might want to do it.

Despite having problems with my penis and a late circumcision, somehow it's not become an issue. I'm glad I've done this, and hopefully it will be of interest and solace to men with similar issues.

Forty-two years old

"I want to work hard and fulfil my potential"

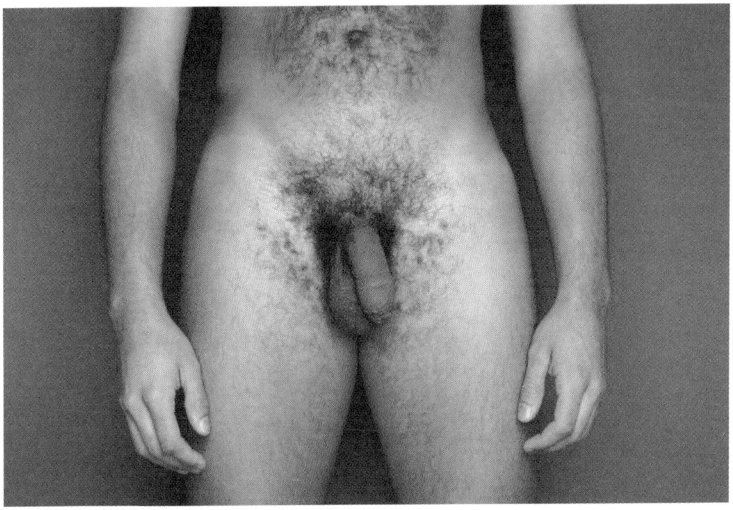

I am very happy with my penis. It's a very healthy, positive relationship.

I am in the performing arts. You see a lot of male dancers who are quite feminine. I want to say that male dancers can also be masculine. I want to portray masculinity as a dancer. I do this using the dance itself, with posture and how the movement is executed. There's an idea that male dancers are gay, but this is not true, it's not always the case.

I wouldn't say that being heterosexual means the same as being masculine. You can be gay and masculine. Masculinity is not limited by your sexual orientation. Masculinity is driven by testosterone. The balance of hormones, oestrogen versus testosterone, affects you. I think it works at a chemical level. I think one masculine trait is ego. Men have egos because they want to prove themselves to females.

I think 20 years ago people would have had more distinct ideas about what men and women should be like. It's the 21st century now, we're not as rigid about things. Jaden Smith wears women's clothes, but it doesn't make him any less of a man. Young people are more likely to wear clothes of the opposite sex now. I am wearing women's jeans today. You wouldn't know they aren't men's jeans. They have more stretch in them than men's jeans, so they're more comfortable and it's easier to dance in them.

I'm 25 and the last eight years have been very busy. I went to performing arts college, I crowdfunded to travel and train in LA, I've run community workshops where I live, I've taught, I've danced for a company, and now I've set up my own dance company.

I think my drive comes from a positive mindset. If I'm going to do something then it's going to work. My mum is a really strong role model. I see how hard she works and it inspires me to work hard and fulfil my potential. I don't want to look back on my life and wish I'd done more.

My dad passed away seven years ago. He had prostate cancer. I created a dance performance for my final year project and I invited Prostate Cancer UK to watch. It combined dance and spoken word, it was a hip-hop theatre piece. I actually shaved off my hair live as part of the performance. A lot of people in the audience were gasping, 'Oh my goodness, he's actually shaving his hair off.'

I wanted to create awareness of prostate cancer, I felt passionate about it. I have a personal experience of it because of my dad, so that helped but it was also really hard.

My dad always wanted me to push on and do more. He was the dad who was always, 'OK, you've done this well, but you could have done a bit more.' I don't try and prove a point about anything in life, but I do want to push myself to the best of my abilities now. I felt really sad about my dad, but it happened, and he wouldn't want me to feel sad forever. I celebrate his life and pursue the things I want to do in a positive way. Without forgetting what has happened, I can use the energy to move forward in my life. I think I'm fortunate in how I see life.

Twenty-five years old

“I brought up three children on my own”

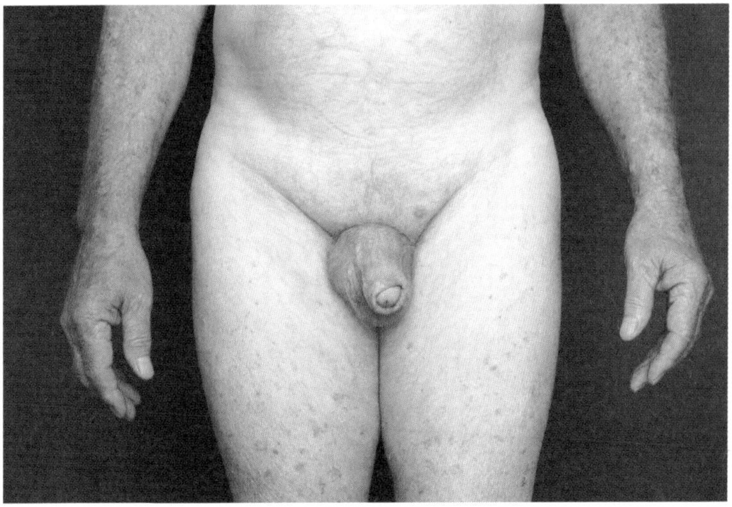

I’m really quite an independent person. I question just about everything. I think I’m a good person with good values and because of that I don’t really have any hang-ups about anything. As far as my penis is concerned, it’s a tool, it’s there for a purpose and I’m really quite laid back about it. Some things I’m not very laid back about at all, but they’re things like injustice and prejudice and stupidity and all those sorts of things. But in terms of anything else then I’m quite cool, calm and collected.

I brought up three children on my own for about seven years, while having a full-time job, and just learned to cope.

I was married for 16 years. My ex-wife came from a large family and wanted quite a few children, but didn't discuss it with me. I thought she was taking the Pill. I'm not blaming her, because I could have used protection. I didn't want lots of children.

She met a man and became pregnant by him. I'll always remember we had a discussion on the settee about trying to reconcile and she just calmly announced, 'I'm pregnant.' And I said, 'OK, well that's it. That's the end.'

I said I wouldn't have another man's child in the family home, but I wasn't prepared to kick her out because of the children. She would never talk about anything. I instigated counselling for couples who are about to separate, the impact it has on the children, all those sorts of things, but she never bothered.

Our children were five, eight, 13 and 19 on the morning her waters broke. For the previous nine months there had been no discussion about what might happen to the children or what we were going to do. I think she had been torn between the children and this man.

She calmly announced 'Right, I'll take the younger ones, you can have the older ones.' I had a deep attachment to the children because I'd spent much more time with them; she was off going out with him on a regular basis, at weekends and during the evenings and what have you. And I said, 'No, that's not happening. You're suggesting that they move away from the area where they live, change schools, change everything.' The two youngest didn't want that to happen either, they were very close to me. So what I did say – and I'm glad she turned me down – was 'Look, if push comes to shove I'll live where your boyfriend lives and you can move into the family home.' She actually tried to drag my daughter, who would have been eight at the time, away with her, but she wasn't having any of it, she didn't want to go.

So I just said to myself, 'Well, I've looked after myself before, how difficult can it be? I'm good at organisation and logistics and things like that.' Cooking for five is just a bit more than cooking for one. We had an arrangement about school runs and sharing the car. I was mindful of their best interests, I felt that I could cope and therefore I just got on and did it. Extremely unconventional but I'm not one for convention. *(laughs)*

I use the phrase 'I love children', and that's not a good thing to say these days. I'm fascinated by children, the way they learn, their expressions. I remember being up at my golf club and saying to one of my friends that I like children. He's quite a staid sort of man and he said, 'Oh, you shouldn't say that.' I think it's because of paedophilia. I understood where my friend was coming from, but it wouldn't stop me saying I like children, because it's other people's issue. I think that adults really underestimate and undervalue the abilities of children, I really, really do.

I don't think it's fair that we see women as more nurturing. Human beings have evolved through various cultures and society changes. I think that both sexes ought to be given the same opportunity to develop themselves as they see fit. But often both men and women have expectations of what marriage and having children will be like.

I wasn't experienced at all when I met my wife. I've only ever had sex with two women: my wife and my current girlfriend. I couldn't have sex with any woman that came along. I would certainly never consider sex outside a relationship. I know that I think very differently to a lot of people. There are so many pressures on men by society, by their peer groups, by the media, by films or anything which portrays men. They try and meet those expectations rather than be true to themselves. I was very fortunate because I didn't take notice of any of that. I was comfortable with me. I think the majority of men are very susceptible to external pressures about their masculinity.

The advice I would give other men is what I've always said to my children, 'Be yourself. Learn about yourself.' People should have confidence in themselves. Just tell yourself, 'I am a good person.' But I think, sadly, the human condition doesn't really lend itself to that. I think we're a whole load of sheep, to be honest.

Sixty-eight years old

"I tried penile enlargement"

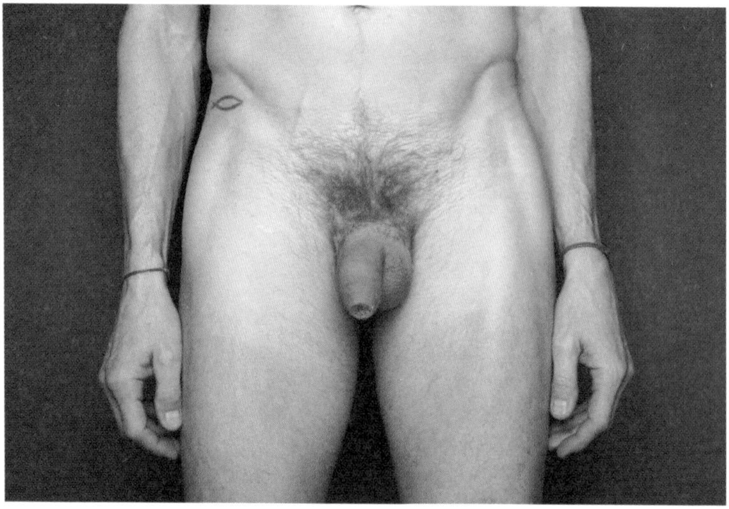

At boarding school I always felt my penis was too small. Three times a week we would play sports, get into the showers and I would be terrified. If I could, I would hide and then sort of wait until everyone was finished. Sometimes I'd go into a toilet stall and I would try and masturbate myself just a little bit to make it big enough so that I could get into the shower. It was torture, it was the worst thing in the world, the deepest, deepest shame. And I felt utterly alone with it. I spent a whole section of my childhood strategising and dreading sports in this boarding school. Then I didn't do well academically so I got taken out.

In my early thirties I was depressed and I was doing drugs and alcohol. I had one suicide attempt. I had this feeling that something had to change or I would kill myself. I read about penile enlargement in the back of a magazine. I had some money saved up. I thought I could use the money to go travelling for six months, or maybe I could try penile enlargement. There would be a miracle, the operation could work and I would be so much happier. It was supposed to make the flaccid penis bigger, not the erection.

I was incredibly ignorant, I didn't do tons of research. I just rolled the dice. My penis was wrapped in bandages and a bit swollen and I went home. Every day I would look at it, it wasn't painful at all and I'd just think, 'If it just stays like this, it's OK. If it just stays like this.' But it went back to normal. It may have been a little bit fatter afterwards, I'm not sure.

I was terrified of women as a teenager. When I was 17 I met a woman I felt comfortable with. We were friends and sexual. After a year and a half I would have liked to break up with her, but I didn't know how to say that, so I stayed with her for seven years. Then I had exactly the same thing again; I stayed with someone for three years because I didn't want to break up with her. After that I didn't have a girlfriend for 10 years because I was terrified of getting out. This was about permission, about being honest. I took everything on me, I felt responsible for causing pain.

After coming out of those relationships I'd go out and get crazy drunk. Mostly I was more interested in getting crazy drunk than I was in being sexual, but occasionally I would end up in bed with someone. I think I would usually fall asleep after five or ten minutes and just wake up and sort of disappear or something.

I've never been able to sustain sexual interest in a partner for very long. I sometimes think it's because I spent so long masturbating and in fantasy. I'm a bit curious about that, so I'm exploring intimacy through workshops. Intimacy doesn't necessarily have to do with having an erect penis and fucking, it could be just touching or massage. I wonder if I hadn't had so much time in fantasy I'd be able to stay a bit more present with reality. I've never orgasmed without fantasy.

I would like to be able to sustain an erotic intimacy. It's not crucial, but if I could actually stay present and orgasm with my partner and not use fantasy, that might be the ultimate symbol.

Fifty years old

"It's nice to get a gasp of surprise when you get it out"

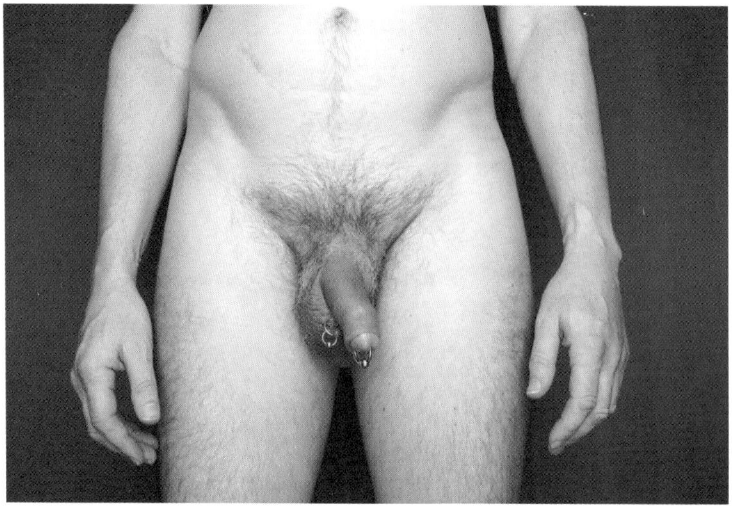

Like most people I'd much rather that it was bigger and more showy. I'd be more confident. I went into life modelling to get some kind of gentle validation and boost my confidence. I realised that I was willing to take my clothes off. I thought, 'Well, how can I use this super power I have?' *(laughs)*

Life modelling is a nice opportunity to think. I think about building work. I have designed roofs and things, decided on plans for diving surveys in the year ahead; just noodling away in my own mind while people draw me.

After quite a few years of doing life modelling, I saw an advert for an agency for hen party life modelling. The money was better, it was £40 an hour, and it sounded like a laugh. And the women were funny and giggly. Willies are funny and they would point and you could jiggle a bit. But most girls seem to prefer bums and my bum is very popular; I'm very lucky, bum-wise.

I modelled with a tutor who really had no aptitude for teaching hen parties at all. And I thought, 'Actually, I'd quite like to do this.' So most of the ones I do now, I do solo. I tutor and I model. So it's almost like a couple of hours of stand-up; you do a couple of hours of naked stand-up chatting to people. They laugh because there's a funny naked man in front of them. Then within 20 minutes they're actually talking to you normally. They'll ask you how you are, and you can talk to them, you can talk about modelling and they'll very matter-of-factly say, 'How do you draw a willy then?' And you say, 'Oh no, it's an easy bit. It's like a sausage that's swallowed a strawberry.' It's very light-hearted, they're very relaxed about it. It's charming and you almost get Stockholm Syndrome; it's almost like you're held hostage because you're there for a couple of hours and you don't quite fall in love with these people, but you feel like very good friends, because you've given up a lot of yourself. Then you leave before anybody is bored with you. And that's really good for your self-esteem. It's a lovely, bubbly group of friendly hens who, without exception, have been just lovely to be around. I've been doing it for five years now and it's the best job I've done.

I think the dynamic with a stag party and a female model would be quite different. I'm not a bloke who thinks, 'Oh no, I'm only here to model. Please don't joke about my penis or even look at me.' *(laughs)* I've been very flattered that these very lovely ladies are interested at all. People have grabbed my bottom and maybe patted it and that's just sweet and it comes with the territory and I don't feel violated. People have asked if they can look at the rings and hold the rings *(laughs)*, but they're ever so careful about it.

My mother is very worried that all this will end my political career, which hasn't started. My father is sure that every party is a complete orgy. They're both quite wrong. It's drawing, not a strip show. It's a hen party, they want it to be hen-themed by having some nakedness, but they want it on their terms and for it to be defensible, almost arms' length. And that's quite sweet.

At the end of the '90s, everybody was having metal through everything. My girlfriend had her navel done and I thought, 'That actually looks cool.' She got hers done in a rather tedious little hippy shop in town and I said, 'I'm going to go to a proper piercing shop.' As you're a bloke, the obvious thing is to have metalwork through your bits. Obvious, yes. *(coughs)* Why wouldn't you want metal through your bits? So I sort of started off with a navel thing and then I got some in my knob and scrotum. I think it's one of those things, like tattooing, there's an endorphin rush and it's brilliant. After the fear of having someone stick a needle through your scrotum and then the endorphin high afterwards. You think, 'Ooh, what shall I have next? I've been so brave, I can be brave again. I can be a successful grown-up.'

My genitals had begun to seem boring and I thought it brightened the area up. It was a bit like Christmas decorations, a definite pejazzle. A bit of shine. Scrotums are dangly and they're a low stress place to have a piercing. I thought it brightened up an otherwise rather uninteresting area, because the balls are not the big deal, really, they're just sort of along for the ride. Again, you learn this in life drawing for hen parties – nobody cares about the balls, nobody. As a man I wish I had huge, magnificent balls.

The Prince Albert looks the most dramatic. It goes through the urethra and out underneath. It was a nerve-wracking one. Lots of people faint and fall over. I think it helps with the legendary G-spot.

I think men are sexually very simple. Every time I go to a hen party I hope people will find me super-attractive and this will be good for my self-esteem. Every time I go, I worry about my knob being big enough, the balls being the right shape, not too big, not too small. It would be marvellous to be some kind of animalistic totem that was just admired for the fantasticness of my genitals. I could probably retire without ever doing anything else. So, as a simple bloke, that would be the very thing. It's lovely to meet people and be friends with them; it's lovely to have warm fuzzy feelings and people to treat you normally even though you're naked. But at the heart of every man is someone who would love to be a tribal leader simply because of the magnificence of their widget. I do not believe I fall into that category, but it's always nice to get a gasp of surprise when you get it out.

Forty-nine years old

"My partner and I haven't had sex for three and a half years"

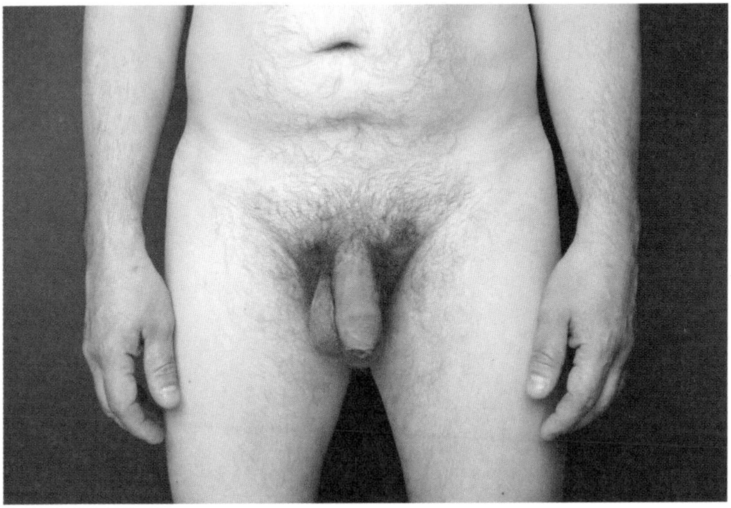

I have an obsessive compulsive disorder. One of the early problems I had was spitting. That was very embarrassing. I had a compulsion to spit after someone coughed, because I was worried about germs. When I was in my early 20s an old school friend of mine died of meningitis. It was a defining moment in my life. He was an old friend from primary school. I realised that germs and disease can spread, and it's not just old people who die.

When my partner got pregnant, the spitting thing subsided, but was replaced by worrying about her getting ill and losing the baby, and fear about childbirth. I had to coach myself and look at statistics. The web checking I do when either of my children get ill is endless. It's to reassure myself they are not fatally ill. My own self-preservation has disappeared and it's all about the kids. I am completely obsessed with them using antibacterial hand lotion. Changing my behaviour is a challenge. If my children turn out to be hypochondriacs or obsessive I will blame myself, because I think it's learnt behaviour.

I haven't analysed it for a while. I've been feeling quite low and I think I need to get on top of it. I think fear of death is the underlying theme.

I found this year difficult. I had high levels of anxiety about my kids. I can't talk to any of my male friends about anything meaningful emotionally or psychologically. Most of the men I know are quite blokey. It's a constant puzzle and frustration to me. I've always wanted to talk to male friends about anxiety, which I've had for the last 10 or 15 years. It's as though when you even get close to broaching the subject, there is a machismo effect. People close down. I think there is still a stigma about admitting weakness.

It's probably a vicious circle. Since my partner and I have had two children I've become more distant from my male friends because I am so absorbed in domestic life, and obsessed with anxiety. And when I do see them it almost always revolves around alcohol. Alcohol drives the conversation towards jokiness and blokiness. If anyone turned up at a night out, had a few pints, and then started talking about their recent depression, they'd probably be ostracised. Maybe ostracised is the wrong word, but they'd be the subject of banter. The 'bloke effect.' There would be comments like, 'Don't be such a big girl's blouse.' It is counter-productive for many men who want to improve their mental health and their ability to cope.

Since my son has arrived I can see first-hand that it is damaging to teach boys not to cry, not to moan about the knee they have just scraped, but I still find myself saying, 'Come on, you're alright, you're a big boy, big boys don't cry.' I hear myself say it, and it's utterly ridiculous. I would never say that to my daughter.

My partner would probably say I am quite a big crier. I would cry more, but I stop myself. It's therapeutic. If any of my local male friends saw me cry I would be mortified. It's like you have to do it in secret, which is not healthy.

I want my son to see me as confident, strong, powerful and in control. I want him to feel safe with me. But can I succeed in presenting that image to him, when some of it isn't necessarily true? I do get anxious and sometimes I'm not in control and can be a ditherer. The thought of him seeing me dither is quite upsetting. I wouldn't want him to be like that when he's older. I'm convinced that my dad didn't want me to be anxious like him, so he played a part, which he was good at.

The defining moments for my penis were in my early to late teens. I'm renowned for a particular story where I grew up. I was being lined up with a girl at the girl's grammar school disco. I was hoping to get a snog or something. I was 13 and hadn't remotely hit puberty. I was so concerned. Naïvely I thought I might even get a fumble, so I thought I should pretend I was in puberty. I got some black wool from my mother's knitting – it's absolutely absurd, I can't remember if it was loose or sellotaped – and I put it down my pants. I made the mistake of telling my best mate at the time. Everyone found out.

I didn't lose my virginity till I was 18. I was paranoid that the girl would laugh. Once I was in my first serious relationship insecurities about my willy became a non-issue. I stopped thinking about it completely, although I was concerned when I started trying for children that it wouldn't work.

My partner and I haven't had sex for a long time, not since we conceived our youngest child over three and a half years ago. I wouldn't have sex with her when we were pregnant in case my knob damaged the baby. *(laughs)* At least I can see the funny side. We found it hard having children at this age, there's my anxiety, and I guess we're tired. My partner has made a bit more effort than I have to sort it out. We can't quite understand how it's got to this point. It's an issue which bubbles away in the background, but to be honest we're both preoccupied with getting through the week. We're not sure how to deal with it. Over time it's become a barrier. I do want to have sex with my partner again.

We don't know how to address it. We argue so much that a lot of the time we don't want to be near each other, let alone fancy each other. We argue more when we're tired and we're fed up with the drudgery. We're both the sort of people who would probably be better off on our own. I joke we'd be better off buying two houses next door to each other and live as a family over two houses.

We haven't done anything on our own for years, not even gone out for dinner. We're anxious about our children sleeping without us. Maybe we should go out, have some good talks, have some champagne and get back in the saddle.

Forty-five years old

“Today I am wearing a long, black dress”

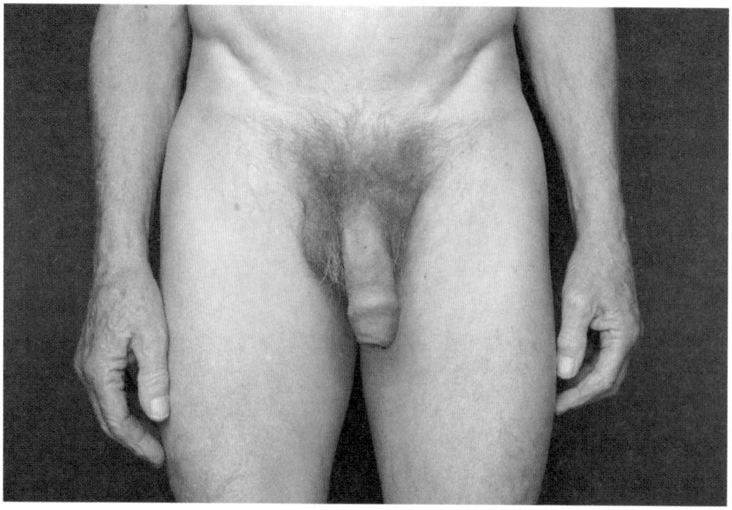

Something has started, but I don’t know where it’s going yet. It all started in a charity shop. I had been thinking for some time that men’s clothes are so boring and grey, all the same. The designs and colours are predictable. I was by the dull men’s rack and was looking over at the fantastically interesting colours and designs in the women’s section, all colour-coded. It looked fun, interesting, exciting, stylish. I decided to buy a few women’s outfits.

Today I am wearing a long, black dress, with a split up the sides. I am wearing it with a man’s shirt and a belt. It looks a bit priestly. I’ve tried to make it look in between masculine and feminine. I first decided to wear a dress to a political demonstration, a big flowery dress. I thought it was ideal for a refugees' march.

I am fascinated by the responses of people when boundaries appear to have been broken. Why is it that a dress is only for one sex? Women can wear anything. They get a lot of telling off and abuse if they don't wear the right thing, but in principle they can wear anything. Men can't wear anything; dresses are forbidden, dresses are women's territory. Men don't wear dresses or skirts, because they call them something else: kilts, cassocks, sarongs, nightshirts, dressing gowns. There are an awful lot of garments that could be called dresses and skirts, but they aren't.

Most people have accepted it on the street and they have treated me in a very friendly way. I feel more caring, friendly and outgoing when I wear a dress. I don't feel like it's a new me, I think it must have been in me all along. How can one garment make that difference? But of course, clothes do make a difference. Military outfits make people feel military. In this particular outfit I feel more priestly, because it has that look about it.

I have five dresses. I don't wear them every day, although I do wear them as much as possible. I look for opportunities to wear them. I didn't leave the house wearing this; I changed at the train station. I have yet to relate all of this to my wife. She knows I've worn these outfits to marches. But this is now something I want to do much more of.

I don't think I am a cross-dresser or transvestite. I'm not dressing as a woman, I'm not in drag. I don't want to be a woman, I'm not gay, I'm not trans – I'm just me. This is not a sexual fantasy. It isn't like that and I don't want it to be like that. I want to be able to choose a garment regardless of my male form. I'm not interested in high heels, or stilettos, or make-up or doing my hair. I am taking more care of my appearance though, and I do want to have a new haircut.

I've explained it to some people at my art group. They are all steady, stiff people. I turned up one night in a dress and I rippled the waters quite a bit. They were very taken aback. I explained the idea of being 'gender free' and they didn't understand. In the pub afterwards, one guy said to me, 'I don't understand, you're not homosexual, are you?'

Men are about competition, not cooperation. There is an idea that men are not emotional. This is not true. Men are emotional, they learn to cover it up. At the art group the women embrace and kiss in greeting, as women do. One week I saw something incredible: a couple of the men danced towards each other and did a pretend embrace. Why did they do that?

There's nothing unusual about what the women were doing, that's what women do. Why did the men put on this performance? I think it was to distance themselves from it, to show that what women do is silly, and men don't do that. They want to have a laugh about it, but it goes deeper – they have learnt that men do not display that emotion and affection. If they behaved like the women did, people would wonder what was wrong with them. It is lovely that young men, my son's age, do embrace in greeting, like women do.

A good friend has advised me I should tell my wife soon, because if I don't it will look like deception. I'm worried about what she will think it means. I think a man wearing a dress is a bigger taboo than a man being naked. One woman told me she would feel threatened if her husband wore dresses. She thought it might mean he was going gay. What will my wife think... yeah. I have to find the time to explain it to her properly, that it has been a precious discovery.

Sixty-seven years old

"I'd like to switch sometimes"

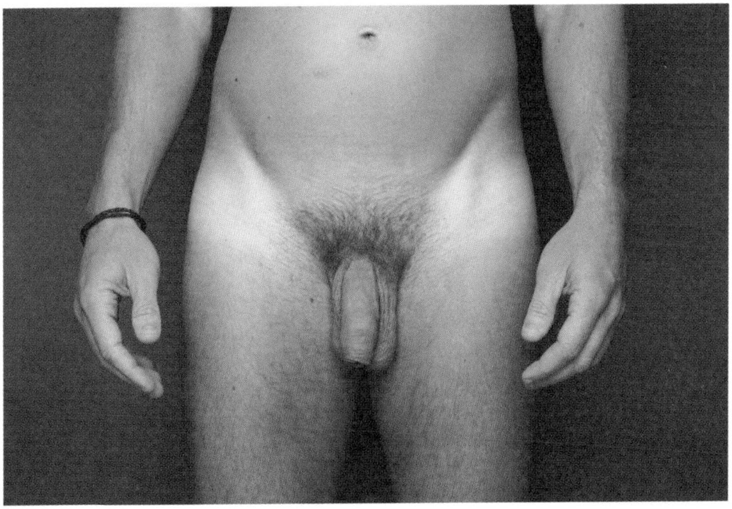

I'd rather have the smaller penis in a relationship, so I'm with someone who is bigger. Mine is big enough. Is size important? It does depend, but if you're confronted with one that is very, very small, you do wonder what you're going to do with it.

The penis is pretty nondescript and boring until it comes to sex. I'm a gay man, and I don't think all penises are equally attractive. Most guys look better in a pair of trunks, leaving something to the imagination. Just seeing everything all flapping around, soft and flaccid, isn't that attractive. I have a good relationship with my cock. No great love or admiration, but

I'm not unhappy.

I had a long-term relationship with one boyfriend for nine years, but in the last year I've been on a journey of discovery, playing the field and being with different men. I was acting straight before that. When I stopped pretending to myself I wasn't gay, it was a game-changer.

After I got together with my boyfriend, I told friends first, then my brother, and then my mum quite a long way down the line. She passed on the information to my father. Then me and my dad spoke. My mum was worried it would make my life harder and that I wouldn't be able to have children. It hasn't made my life harder though, it's made it better, more enjoyable, more open, more happy. I can have children if I want to, but I don't have any desire at the moment. Apart from that she said if I was happy then she was. My dad was a bit more emotional, but he also wanted me to be happy.

I know more what my male partner would like. With a woman it was more like, 'Is that too much, not enough, too soft, too hard?' You have the same questions with anyone, because everyone is different, but I know more about how to handle a penis because I have one of my own. I know where to start. I'm more confident with a man than I ever was with a woman, but I'm also older. My relationship with my penis and sexuality has changed as I age.

I only have limited experience of fucking men. I'm the receiver, not the giver. My ex-boyfriend was a complete top, so he would never contemplate anyone near his bottom. So that was me done in, I only had one option. I think that's how I came to enjoy being a bottom. And he had a really nice penis, which helps.

When I have tried being the giver, it's made me very anxious, because I feel like I need to perform. I found it very tight, much tighter than with a woman, for obvious reasons: it's a different part of the anatomy. It really turned me on and I'd like to switch sometimes, give it more of a go, but I think I'd need to be in a loving relationship because it makes me nervous.

There are orgasms and there are orgasms, aren't there? You can have a wank for a quick release, it can be over in five minutes, and it's pleasant, but nothing to write home about. I had a recent experience on holiday, which was amazing. It was extremely intense and exciting. I had sex with a gay married couple. They both had really nice penises. One was just the right shape and size for me, straight, a nice uplift towards the end and a full engorged head. And it was very stiff. Big and bold. His husband had a huge penis, the biggest I have ever seen. He had a problem getting it completely upright, because it was so big. The excitement level was high. The sexual encounter was an hour of this, that and the other, and it ended with the guy with the really big penis fucking me, and the orgasm was pretty intense. To have an orgasm while being penetrated is the icing on the cake.

We're taught that men must work hard, provide, be the breadwinner, be strong emotionally and physically, and that's it really. I feel like that myself. All my friends from university are married and they nearly all have children. So, that's the male and female role working together. That's the end point, the classic ideal. Sometimes it's hard being single and gay, although I don't want to be married and straight. Maybe I want to be gay and married.

I'm sure in the 1950s, male roles were far more strictly defined. You couldn't go into certain professions as a man then, like nursing. Being gay had huge implications beyond the law. We have more freedom now.

I was walking home one night from a club with a new friend, hand in hand. A drunk woman was vicious in her language to us: 'You fucking queer bastards! Disgusting! You should all rot in hell.' That was the first time someone had said something like that to my face. We were just holding hands. Maybe she was angry with the world. I was surprised. Shocked. Afterwards it made me quite angry.

Forty years old

“Porn gets the blame”

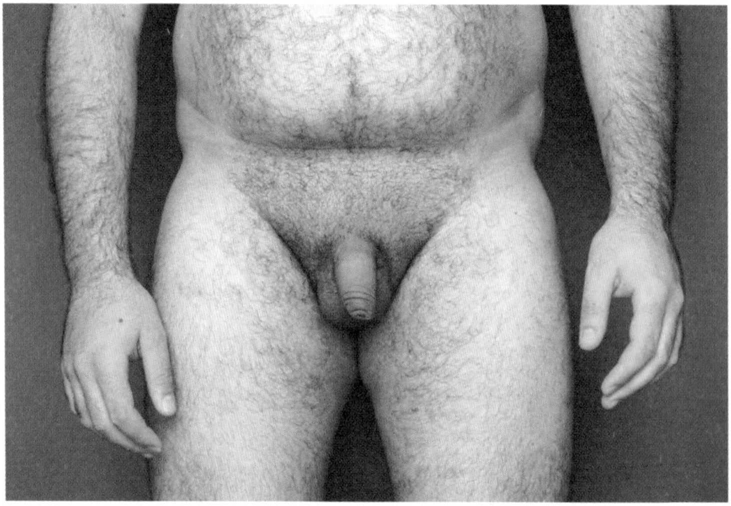

I like my erect penis. It’s had compliments. It might be a mistranslation, but a Finnish girl described it as pretty, which is a bit effeminate. I’ll take the compliment though. I don’t think about my flaccid penis at all. Apart from here, or at the doctor’s, it never makes an appearance.

I made a video called ‘Freedom to Fuck.’ I think there’s a moral panic surrounding sex. It’s good to see women asserting their ability to determine what sexual experiences they want. But I get the sense that men are seen as inherently dangerous and that what they want is bad. Pornography is seen as for the male gaze, for male pleasure, as though that's a bad thing.

Sex is a completely normal thing, and yet there's a real worry about the way young people are having sex, as though older people don't approve of it. Porn gets the blame. Older people say they didn't have anal sex when they were younger and blame it on porn. That's fine, I don't have a problem with that. It's when it goes from an observation to saying anal sex is a problem and asking what can be done about it.

Pornography alerts people to things they may not have been aware of, but it doesn't make them enjoy them. I don't think people directly copy porn. I've only come on a woman's face once or twice. I've never particularly felt moved to do it, and I grew up in the age of internet porn. I've had anal sex once or twice, just to try it. Now I don't actually tend to watch porn with it in. There's so much porn out there to suit your taste.

Before fast internet speeds we used to have to download it overnight. We used to watch more extreme stuff then, because we didn't have a reference for real sex. I'm not really that interested now if it's very different from my own experience or what I know to be relatively normal.

I think I was 11 when I first downloaded porn. It was exciting because it opened up a world of adult experiences and it was so different to sex education. You would imagine from sex education that a penis is put into a vagina and that's it. We used to watch it together in a group so there was no whipping our dicks out. It was like watching horror films or video nasties together.

I was 17 when I lost my virginity. It was intuitive. I didn't think about pornography at all. In fact, I wasn't even thinking. It just made sense. The whole process just happened, it's a mystery to me. Even though I've had a lot more experience since then, I do feel like there's a build-up to a point when it becomes inevitable. I don't know what the secret is, I wish I did. I don't even have to have kissed them, I just know if we'll have sex. There have only been a few times when I've been pleasantly surprised to find I'm having sex with someone, when I didn't know it was going to happen.

I'm naturally quite cautious. I don't want to be openly rejected and feel like I've made a fool of myself. I wouldn't want a definite 'no'. If I was more than a bit unsure I wouldn't want to make any moves at all.

I've always felt this way, even before more recent talks about 'consent' came to the fore. There are movements in universities, but people also want to introduce it into schools as well, that you have to give verbal consent for each individual sex act. It gets more bureaucratic each time it's talked about. There was one popular feminist website that said you should ask for consent every few minutes during sex. I'd be shocked if people really do ask permission to kiss, to touch each other. You should be relying on non-verbal cues. You know if someone's not interested and it would be stupid to ignore them.

The suggestion is that if you don't ask for consent – and I don't, and no one has ever asked me – then potentially it could be a rape situation. What are we saying about sex? What are we saying about the capacity of women to say what they want? It belies a distrust in sex and in human beings. Sex is one of the most fundamental aspects of our lives. Every adult wants to do it. OK, apart from a few asexual people. It's misanthropic to clamp down on it and make up more rules about it. Maybe we're trying to find a balance; it's a swing too far in one direction and it will swing back.

When I was at university we went on football tour. One year we were in Spain and it was carnage, more than usual. Someone's penis was always out, in clubs, in the hotel. We knew it would wind people up. It was only among fellow students, we weren't terrorising the locals. We got in the hotel's hot tub naked and the hotel manager threatened to call the police. We laughed it off. They persuaded us to leave the hot tub. There was a lot of alcohol involved.

Taboos are for the stupid and superstitious. Penises provoke people a lot and you can be arrested for getting them out. If people do fear penises, I don't see why that fear should be indulged. I think it's equally crazy that women can't be topless in public. I, for one, would like to see more topless women. People find nudity difficult.

I didn't tell my parents I'm doing this. I don't think they'd mind, but I don't know what they'd say. They'd find it strange. It's easier not to tell them. There's loads of stuff I don't tell them anyway! I'll definitely tell my friends though – it's quite an exciting and funny thing to be involved with.

Twenty-four years old

"My dad was an über strict Jehovah's Witness"

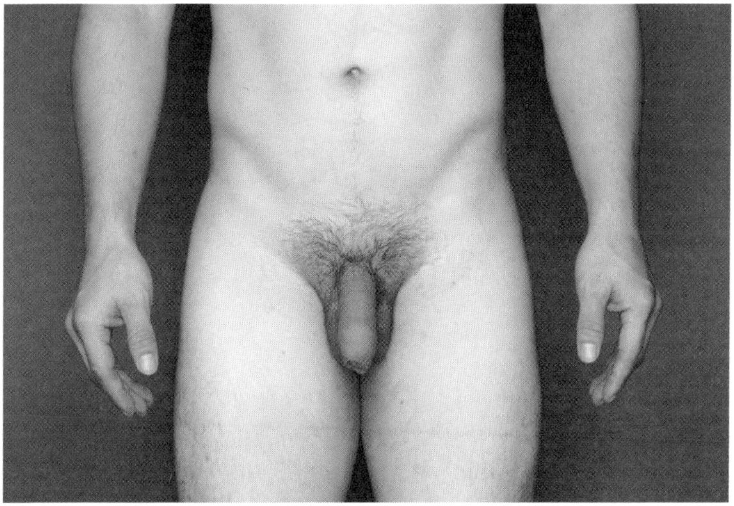

I really like my penis. I love having sex. Penises are quite funny things, but they make the world go round.

I was quite fixated on it as a teenager. I was horny all the time, and everything was about sex. I've had two children now, which changes your view. I've had a little girl and it's made me realise how I've dealt with women in the past. You know when you ruminate on your life and look back? I had intense relationships with a couple of girls. I can see what a knob I was now. Boys and girls are different, I guess. I used to think you can treat women the same, but you can't talk as roughly with women as you do with men, you need more sensitivity. Listening and knowing there is a difference is important. I've had to learn to step back and let my daughter get more emotional. We're both stubborn and we'd lock horns otherwise. She needs a wig out and a tantrum sometimes. I'm more at ease now. You see yourself reflected in your children.

Getting down to my children's level to talk to them has changed me. I don't have to be 'the man.' I want to be relaxed. Being a man means being protective of your family and being there for them. It doesn't have to mean being strong. Showing your weakness is important too.

I was selfish. I used to cheat. I had low self-esteem so I had to keep topping it up, by cheating, have someone new look at me and make me feel attractive. I didn't see anything wrong with it, I thought everyone did it. I objectified women to a degree. I had some success with women and it gave me a power trip. Maybe it's part of growing up. Having a daughter made me realise I'd treated women like objects. I am her 'first man', the first point of call, she'll learn about men through me. I need to be calm.

My girlfriend and I started going out when we were 16, on and off. There were all these things about her I wanted to change; you know, that immature thing where you want to change someone. But as soon as we had children, some of her traits, like being organised, made sense. I saw her from outside my own little bubble. I try and apologise to my partner. It's one of the hardest things, but one of the best things you can do, it frees up a lot of energy.

I'm Chinese-Scottish. When I was growing up in London, being mixed race didn't make any difference to me at all. There were black, Indian, Pakistani, Chinese, white in my class. People used to take the mickey out of each other, obviously, but people didn't dislike each other because of their race.

I had a good, but fractious relationship with my dad. He clearly loved us, but he was a bit crazy. He's a Jehovah's Witness. He's quite smart, but totally deluded. He wasn't just a Jehovah's Witness, he had to the best one, über strict. He'd do 90 hours a month. The religion felt like a tool to beat us around the head with. It felt like a justification for being strict. You end up feeling like you did everything wrong. We were good kids – there was no need for all that guilt. There was impending doom hanging over everything, what books you're reading, what music you listen to, who you talk to. The fun police.

My dad called someone a liar in the fellowship and wouldn't back down and got kicked out. He couldn't apologise. It was his pride. He fucked his whole life. I saw how they all treated each other, and they are supposed to be Christian. Jesus is about love, when it comes down to it. You shouldn't be judging each other on minutiae.

My older sister is still a Witness and she has cut off me and my family. She feels bad about it. You don't have to not see your family, it's down to your interpretation. But maybe they want to be the best Witnesses. *(mimes self-flagellation)* I've been depressed about it for the last month. I think she's batshit mental, but I'm sort of at peace with it now. I don't mind if they want to believe it, but they shouldn't impose their religion on us.

There are positives to Jehovah's Witnesses. People are polite, respectful, well-mannered. We knocked on doors, so you learn to deal with rejections and develop a thick skin. It's helped me with selling and being personable in my own business. There was community spirit and respect for elders and strong family units.

I grew up in a massively patriarchal society, where the men are always right. If there was a meeting, a young man would take the study, the meeting, rather than an older woman. Only men could do things in the hall. Women were just there to prop up the men. Growing up I had to untangle myself from that sexist upbringing.

Thirty-one years old

“Being made redundant at this stage of life was really hard”

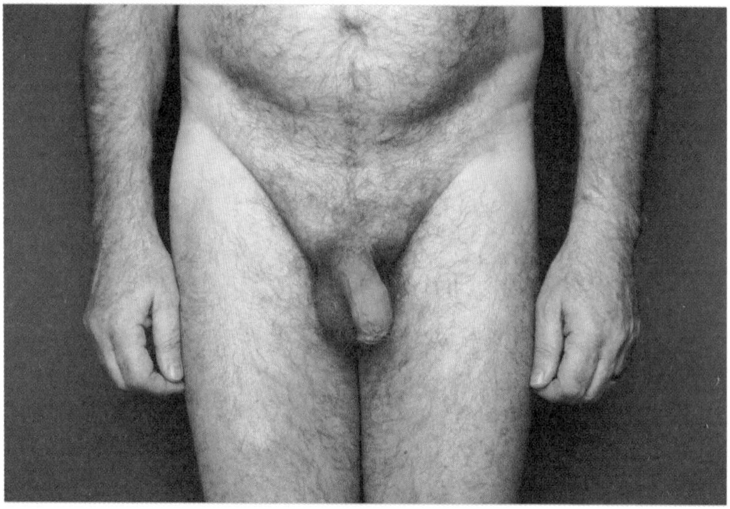

I like my penis like the rest of my body – it's part of me, just like my face, neck, leg, foot, any other part of the body. I'm not immensely proud of it, I'm not ashamed of it. I've always had a pragmatic approach to the body. I've always played team sports and used communal showers.

Bodies are just bodies. It's the person who matters. I think it helps in life to realise that. My mother always said that when she died, as far as she was concerned, you could put her body in a bin bag and take it down the dump, because she didn't need it anymore. The body is just a carrier for the person, the brain, the emotions, the attitude to life. My mum taught me that from an early age.

I used to play football and cricket. These days I only play rugby. Sport is a way to keep fit. I'm not mega aggressive. I play to the rules and the spirit of the game. We have a huge mini section, for the little ones and under-16s, in our rugby club. Our ethos is about the team sport, respect for you, your team, your ref and the other team, and it's about friends for life.

When I was younger I used to play opposite the Borstal team. Of course, these kids all had big, big problems. They were allowed to play rugby as a treat, and in order to do that they had to play properly and have respect. Rugby as a whole still has this ethos. You can have a 5ft 6in referee telling off a 6ft 8in guy. You do not get players crowding around a referee demanding and shouting like you do in football. There are laws, rules, in rugby – you can't be disrespectful to the referee. Football doesn't have sanctions for foul language.

I wouldn't tell the men on my team that I'm doing this. I can't explain it. I think maybe I'd be embarrassed. I think some people wouldn't understand why I'm doing it, even though they wouldn't be surprised!

I love women's rugby. I'm very lucky, my club has one of the top women's teams in country, and much higher nationally than our men's team. I love watching women's rugby. There is a difference: they aren't as physical and as big as the men. Well, some of them are close! *(laughs)* They can't generally kick the ball as far as the men. As a result the game is more skills-based and their technique is better. In the men's game, some men simply use their physical presence. I love watching our ladies play.

There are social pressures for men and for women. The social pressure on men is to be the breadwinner. That comes with a certain degree of pressure, particularly when you have lost your job and you are trying to build up your own business, like I am at the moment. There are feelings of inadequacy if it doesn't go as quickly and as well as you'd like. The other pressure is being 'mother's little soldier'. Men are not expected to cry, or be emotional. We are supposed to be the rock of the house, and we don't always feel that way. As a small child, no matter what happened, you were told, 'Big boys don't cry.' Not to complain, not to get emotional, becomes routine. I think this is why men sometimes have a higher incidence of some of the serious illnesses, because we don't like to complain about being ill. I think it's also why men commit suicide.

I've lost a couple of friends to suicide. It's very unpleasant. One had depression and nobody knew, outside of his family. People don't talk about mental illness.

I lost my job earlier this year. The firm reorganised my department out of the business, they decided they didn't need an in-house sales department. Some finance genius worked out they could reduce their fixed costs. It's the accountants' way of looking at things.

I set up my own business about six months ago. It's growing slowly. Being made redundant at this stage of life was really hard. It can be hard to think positive if you have a week of essentially knocking on doors, and none of them opening. The rewards are potentially greater and I try and have a positive outlook. Hopefully I will be able to earn more. The risks are higher too though; if I don't get a sale I don't make any money. Business is slow at the moment and so I am a bit down. On a weekly basis I think I should get another job. At the end of the day the mortgage has to be paid and sometimes just doing that is really, really hard.

What does being a man mean? It means that as you get older, the hair that used to grow out the top of your head grows out of your nose and ears. Your prostate gets bigger and you don't get a full night's sleep ever! Your stomach gets bigger and you can't get rid of it. As you get older, bits of you stop working.

It's not necessarily to do with being a man, but you don't realise you are older. I still think I am 17 in my head. I go out and play rugby with 17 and 18-year-olds and I think I can do it, but my body says otherwise. You don't have the stamina or the strength.

I'm not a particularly macho testosterone-fuelled man. In fact I hate testosterone-fuelled men, they are normally the racists and the sexists. I don't mean all boys together having a laugh, I mean men with harsh opinions about what Muslims are, or what women are, or what gay people are, that's the kind of macho I can't stand. I think they're insecure, it's as though they can't admit someone is as good as them.

Fifty-seven years old

"I drank too much"

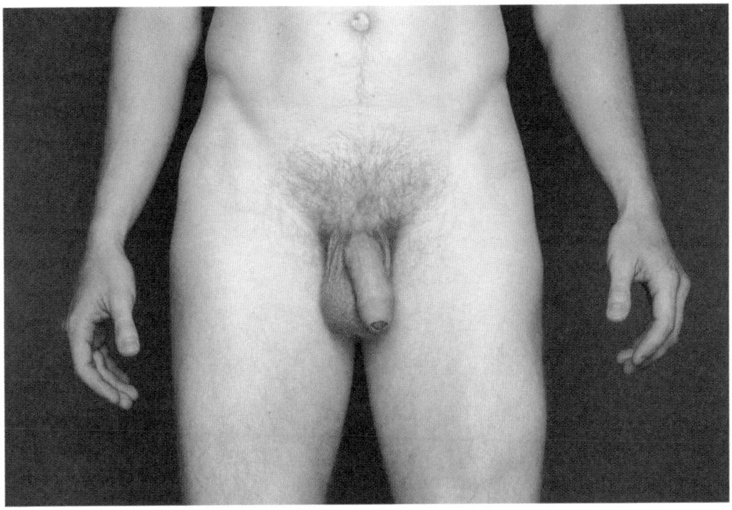

I like my penis, it's alright. I've had people comment on it and say it's a nice-looking penis. I have a very decent sized penis, it's a grower not a shower.

A lot of my friends growing up were women. Most of them preferred oral sex and said penetrative sex is not the be all and end all. Size doesn't need to define you, if you know what you're doing in bed – talk to your partner, and often they might prefer oral sex, then you're alright regardless of size. You can be lazier I guess if the woman prefers penetrative sex. *(laughs)* But there's something really nice about doing something that doesn't give you sexual gratification. I wouldn't say it's a sacrifice, but it certainly shows you're willing to put effort in. Whatever you do is fine if you both leave that time feeling connected and you've enjoyed it.

My first sexual experience was awful. I was so drunk at a house party, this girl was on top of me and I just remember really needing the loo. *(laughs)* After a while – oh it was awful – I just pushed her off. Because I didn't have the confidence to say, 'I'm not going to be able to really enjoy this because I could do with urinating right now.' Awful.

I've had about 30 sexual partners. Women vary a great deal in size. I've had partners for whom certain positions are just a straight up no; it would be too deep and uncomfortable. And other partners where any position is fine, there's no position that is too deep and uncomfortable. I had one partner who was very tight and it took a few weeks of other things before penetrative sex could happen. Then on the other hand... I don't know how much I want to say. I've had partners who I can have penetrative sex with and insert a dildo in the vagina at the same time as my penis.

I was in the Territorial Army for a bit and that had a really big drinking culture. Even when you'd done really vigorous activity during the day and your body needed to recover and you needed sleep, it was seen as a given that you should go to the bar and have a few beers before you went to bed. Socialising, being part of the group, camaraderie and stuff.

At university it was similar. Dirty pints were a thing, a little bit of everyone's drink around the table mixed into one pint cup. Wine, vodka, coke, beer, cider, they all just get mixed together and downed. It tastes pretty grim. You sing a song as someone downs it: 'We like to drink with [name of the person] because [name of person] is our mate. And when we drink with [name of person] they down it all in eight, seven, six, five, four, three, two, one.' And you've got to down it before the song finishes. It's a peer pressure thing. I certainly used to do it at 18 and 19, but by 21 I was like, 'I don't care. I'm not going to drink that because I know I'm going to be hammered as soon as I've finished it.'

I drank too much and ruined my pancreas. I had acute pancreatitis. The doctors said if I kept on drinking the same way I was likely to be diabetic before I was 30.

It was one big heavy night that did it. I must have had maybe eight pints and about half a bottle of whisky. It left me feeling rotten. And then a few days later I drank again, although I only had four pints that time, but the damage was done. My pancreas went into some sort of shock and there was a searing pain. It was a horrible experience. I went to hospital in an ambulance. It's supposedly quite common, especially among young men who are drinking heavily.

I started drinking a little bit again, having one or two pints, but it was a waste of time. I can have as much fun teetotal. Not having hangovers is great; I love getting up the next day and just getting on with stuff. I do find it strange how much productivity is lost when people are hungover.

Not drinking has helped with my athletics and rock climbing. Recovery times are just so much shorter; you can train day after day after day. Alcohol certainly does not help muscle recovery.

Sport is about competition. I always loved winning stuff. I don't know whether I was naturally very gifted, but I was always fast in school, good at sports, competed in all the sports – tennis, basketball, cross-country, athletics, football – to a pretty decent level.

It's expected in our culture for men to like sport. If a guy isn't in to sport, it's like, 'What? Why don't you want to play? Why don't you get involved?' I would do sport rather than sitting down all the time. I'm very active.

Being sporty is seen as an attractive trait in society, I think for both men and women, but some men prefer it if women aren't sporty or muscly or whatever. I find it very attractive if a woman does sport.

As a child I really cared about winning. I'd be so angry if I lost. I've grown out of that mentality and now I do sport for the fun of it. I'm less competitive, but I like beating my own time when I sprint. For climbing, it's you versus the wall, it's climbing harder routes than you've climbed before. It's not climbing a harder route than your friend.

Being a man means being loving, caring, kind, compassionate, being there for your friends and loved ones. Being resilient when times are tough, a bit of a rock for other people if they need you to be stable, consistent.

For a woman it's also about being loving, kind, caring, compassionate... it's similar. I like it when a woman has independent strength, and an ability to deal with her own problems, but isn't afraid to ask for help when she needs it.

If I'm watching a film with my girlfriend and it's a sad bit I can bawl my eyes out and cuddle up to her and she's fine about it. If something is sad then it's sad, I want to cry. A large number of people hold on to traditional views, but I think the world is changing.

Twenty-six years old

“My cock is the essence of me”

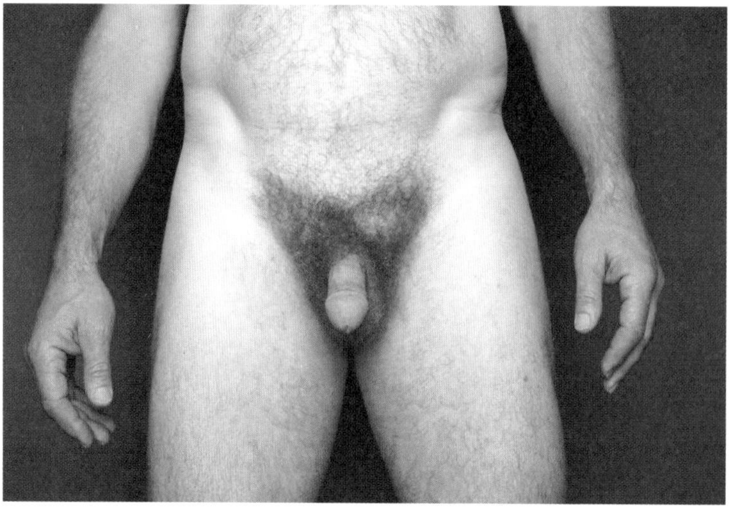

I know I am not alone to think it feels nice to touch your testicles in the bath. I was fondling them and I noticed that one was not right. My wife thought I shouldn’t leave it to chance, so after half a dozen baths I went to the GP. The day after an ultrasound, I was on the slab having my testicle removed. The biopsy is the removal of the testicle. If they took a bit out there would be a risk of spreading cancerous material.

The whole process from start to finish and right up to now, is terribly matter of fact. It was uncomfortable for a couple of weeks but it was fine. I had absolute faith in the medical profession. I just thank my lucky stars I didn't ignore the early signs. I was offered a prosthetic testicle, but I wasn't bothered. I have had my children, and I was happy with the aesthetics.

Remarkably it had no effect on any aspect of being a man. It didn't affect my libido. The difference between having one and not having any at all is enormous. It's miraculous how well just one works. My sense is that two are more than most people need. Maybe because it's such an important organ we are doubled up and have two.

I don't spend hours awake worrying about it at night, but there is a 1 per cent chance I could get it in the other testicle. I'm not terribly comfortable with that.

I've got all sorts of issues about my genitalia! *(laughs)* As a man who is entering the middle chunk of his life, I am getting over a whole load of them now.

I had a lot of shame attached to size in my adolescence. A lad could be gangly, spotty, anything, but if he's got a big dick then he has a major box ticked. Being circumcised and having one fewer testicle than most men I feel slightly... what's the word... mutilated. I'm not all that I came into the world with. Hacked at.

I was circumcised because my father had a strong colonial past within his family, and in those countries it was considered to be healthier. It was the done thing. In fact, in boarding school the uncircumcised boys were in the minority and they tended to have grown up in England then moved away. I don't feel too strongly about it, but I do wonder what it would be like to have a foreskin. As I become older and my glans becomes less sensitive I can see the advantage of having a foreskin.

I went to boarding school when I was nine. An event when I was 11 affected me. In the dormitory one night after lights out, a group of older boys came in, pulled my duvet back, shone a torch on me and tried to teach me how to masturbate. I was in a bit of state for a week or two. With my adult head on, it was definitely abusive. I felt terribly dominated and out of control and what have you.

At my boarding school I got on particularly well with the girls in the sixth form. I think that some of the boys, having seen me in the shower with hardly the biggest packet, married that with my relationship with the girls and didn't like it. One time, a group of them presented me with a clay sculpture of a big fat knob with 'Penis Royale' written on it. It was a gift to rub it in that I had a small dick and they didn't like me getting on with girls.

I count myself very lucky that I wasn't sexually abused at boarding school. My father was. At my school we had a housemaster who I think abused some boys. It was a behind-the-times Empire boarding school. We'd be told to strip and line up, there could be 100 boys at a time standing there and we'd go into the shower six at a time. You had a hot shower, but you had to go through a cold shower at the end. It's a boarding school thing. There was absolutely no privacy whatsoever. You couldn't shut the door if you wanted a crap, you'd have the stuffing taken out of you. Boys would wipe their arse, opposite one another chatting, doors open. You were stripped right down in every way.

I think men who went to boarding school fit into two different categories. Some float, bright-eyed and bushy-tailed, happy to be away from their parents. They take it all in their stride. Others, like me, sink. They feel abandoned and isolated. I've done a lot of thinking and working through this as an adult.

One of my sons was really into dollies right up till he was five. To this day he has a very strong connection with younger children. One day he was sitting on the carpet, a beautiful dappled light was coming through the window. He was on the floor of his bedroom hugging a little dolly, and it was just so sweet. It was a gem of a moment. I'm really chuffed that despite the weak parenting at times, I'm proud that I didn't apportion any discomfort to playing with dollies. I wanted to support him with what was right at the time.

I would like to talk around size and shame. Although it's got much better as the wisdom of my years helps me, I still don't feel comfortable in my nakedness. Speaking as a heterosexual man, it's one of the most attractive traits in a woman when she is at ease with her own nakedness, but I find it difficult myself. There is such a strong visual impact of a big penis and dangling testicles, rather than what I have which is small and looks pre-adolescent. I feel shame and incompleteness. Although when I am with my wife I am completely at ease, and I am perfectly at ease with my erect penis.

There are two things I love with my wife, that really turn me on. One is when we are deeply connected and kissing. The other is when I give her cunnilingus. I absolutely swell to the top. The penis is a wonderful barometer. When I am genuinely turned on I get stiff. If I'm not turned on it goes in reverse. What really turns me on with my wife only happens when we are really intimate.

I'd like to talk about porn. You can go straight to bits you want to find, but the things that turn me on are few and far between. I look in the women's eyes and I pick up that they are making sounds and doing things because they've been told to and being paid to do it. I had an encounter with a porn actress; she described a trail of misery and abuse. I'm just not interested anymore. My own perception of that and what the ex-porn actress told me have put me off. I won't for a moment deny that I've watched and enjoyed porn, but I found it a very double-edged sword. Some would really hit the button, but in some I could sense the horror, or fear, in the woman's eyes. But when I did look at pornography, the thing that turned me on the most was seeing a woman almost in love with her man's penis. Joy and adulation about touching, stroking and kissing it.

It's a relief to talk to about these things, especially those things that are the most unsaid and, strangely, the closest to my heart. I feel that my cock is the essence of me and to not express myself with complete freedom in this domain is a curious sentence. I have not yet found the confidence to talk about anything and everything with my lover. The price has been too high for one reason or another, but the time has come! It's good to explore this side of me, this inescapable core part of who I am.

Fifty-one years old

“I had a vasectomy to sever the lineage of my father”

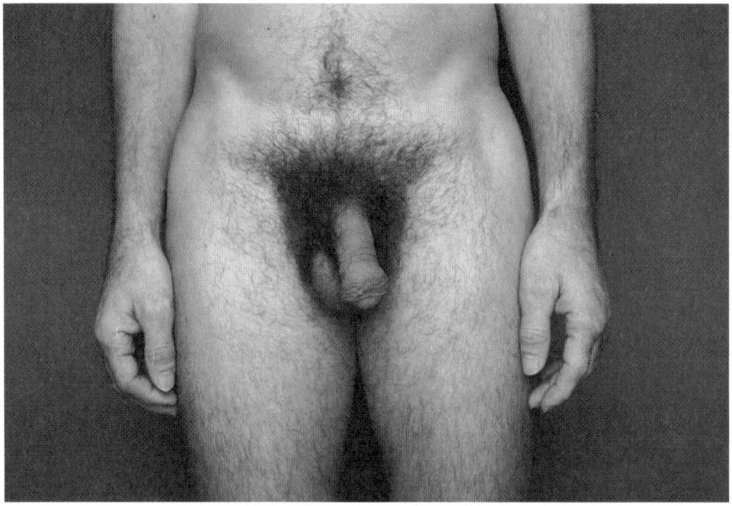

I was 21 when I lost my virginity, about the same age as my mum was when she lost her virginity and conceived me. The girl was a bit older than me and had a child. For some reason I used to be attracted to women with children. I think that while I was in the process of finding my genetic mother I was attracted to women who were mothers. It was a representation of expanding to connect with my mother.

The day I met my mother was one of the most amazing days of my whole life. There was a period of getting to know each other, and a lot of sitting, and just being in the same space with each other, conversations, and a tactileness. There was a great deal of warmth and intimacy, that did have a sensual and sexual element to it.

In the first couple of weeks of spending time together there was almost an overriding need to have that intimacy, like a baby being held by its mother. I was 21 and she was 42, so we didn't act that out, but there were days and moments when there was a tangible sexuality to the reconnection. I've never spoken to my mum about it, but talking to other people who have been adopted or separated from siblings, it would seem to be quite common.

My mother gave me up because she was quite young and at university. My father was from another country. It would have been impossible at that time for them to be together. Society was not ready for mixed-race children, so my mum felt the only course open to her was giving me up for adoption.

I tried looking for my dad when I was 32, but never actually met him. I couldn't find an address or contact. I could have tried harder, turned over lots of stones, and reclaimed who I was, but it would have upset people's lives.

For all of us in the world, our mothers were there when we were born but, for a lot of us, our fathers weren't there, and have never seen us. I question the relevance of a man who played a small part in the beginning of my life having any relevance to my life now, when he has never seen me.

I had a vasectomy when I was 45. That was deliberately to sever the lineage of my father. I have consciously not wanted to have children. I've always struggled with the male aspect of reproduction. I have never been drawn to be a father. Meeting my mother was a very important day and severing the link to my father was a very important day. Now I am just me.

I have a very good relationship with my adopted family. I am lucky I was given the opportunity to have a very nice upbringing and a good family life. My adopted family is the best family you could ever have.

When I was young I had a funny relationship with my penis. I used to have to see a nurse every now and then because I was born with a condition called hypospadias. My earliest recollections of my penis come from the times when the nurse looked at me. It's a malformation of the penis, where the hole doesn't go all the way to the end. I had an operation when I was under a year old to put another hole in. I don't have a hole right at the end, I have two holes slightly below where one would normally be. As a child and teenager I wasn't sure it would work properly in a sexual nature. That uncertainty was probably quite useful, because it kept me away from girls that bit longer. When I am in relationships I've sometimes showed the girl, but there's never been a problem with it not working.

Within my lifetime I have spent a lot of my working life with women more than men. I have the aspect of being very adaptable, very giving and flexible – a lot of the feminine qualities. I never had a major urge to do 'male bonding.' But from the age of about 30 I got involved in Native American Sundance ceremonies, where the men and women have different roles, but are equally important. Exhibiting the masculine pulls it out of you. I felt that was an empowering cycle to be involved with.

Men are confused about what men are supposed to be. I was talking to my mother a few years ago about how I feel I can stand up and be counted, and linking that to my strong male lineage. And she said, 'He didn't do that with me when I was pregnant.' He didn't stand up and support her. It obviously still hurt my mother.

I generally try to be very reassuring and sensitive, but strong. I'm not always the best at the strongest masculine aspects of taking control and giving direction, I'm not an 'alpha male', but I'm never one to shy away from an issue. I'm not one to force my view on anybody. In this day and age we have a lot of problems and issues in figuring out who we should be and how we should do things, we don't have a lot of the framework. A lot of men confuse masculinity with physical control.

Ultimately the man has to provide a safe structure for rearing children. As someone who doesn't have children and doesn't want them, I've struggled with the 'role' of the man. To be the most masculine version of myself is almost a contradiction with that. I think matrilineal societies have more solid foundations, where the family look after the child, and the house passes though the female line. The structure there is from the family.

The *Bare Reality* book showed you a whole world of women. I think it helps men to look at these things in a real way, as opposed to the modern world's way, which is all about image, and being plastic. We're really lucky that we all have bodies and that we're all unique. If women are going to stand there and expose themselves in that open way, then to be one of the men who is willing to do that is a really positive thing. If we have conversations that help us to understand ourselves, it helps us to understand each other. It gives a human side to people's vulnerabilities and strengths. It takes away the purely sexual nature of our bodies and brings it back to a much deeper sense.

Forty-seven years old

“I wanted something a bit more gentle and romantic”

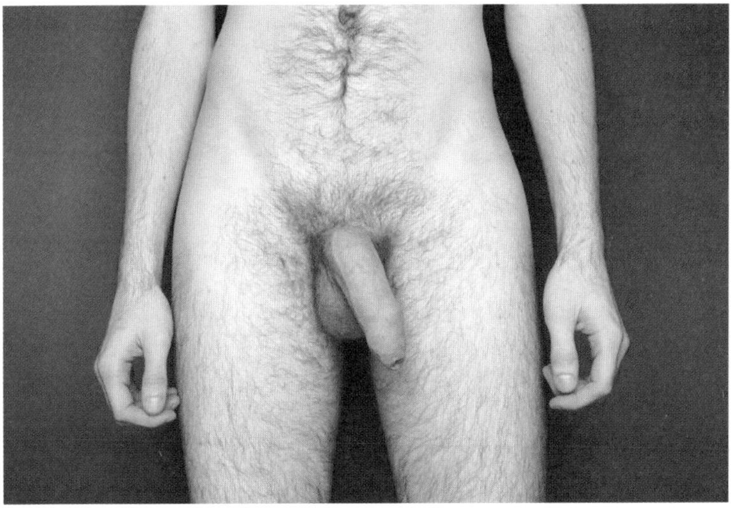

I guess I’m quite proud of the size of my penis, but it leans quite far to the left, which I’ve never been happy about.

I never say to people, ‘Oh, I’ve got a big penis,’ or whatever, apart from to my wife. *(laughs)* It’s a pride that I keep to myself. You don’t want people looking at your penis and talking about it, which is really funny, because I’m doing a photo shoot about it.

I’ve had compliments from women about my penis, that it’s nice and that it’s big. When my wife and I first made love, she told me afterwards that she was angry at me because I didn’t have to try very hard to satisfy her.

I've had four sexual partners and it's only my wife who has been sensitive and delicate. I had two one-night stands. I had a girlfriend for a couple of years and that was fine, but what we had was closer to porn sex. I guess we were both quite young so we would shag like rabbits. There wasn't much foreplay. We'd come home from a night out and take our clothes off and just do it. If there was any foreplay it would be for five minutes maybe, just a quick rub. I think she quite liked rough sex. I wanted something a bit more gentle and romantic.

Because my penis leans to the left it has contact with my testicles and that means I can get thrush quite a lot. So I never wanted to go near girls at all when I was a teenager, because I was like, 'I don't want to show this.' Yeah, it was quite a hang up for me. I have to use cream on it sometimes and I don't like wearing certain trousers.

I had a lump once. Well, I still have it. It's underneath my testicles. I went to the doctor about it a few times. The first time they just said to come back if it changes. I never believed them when they said not to worry. I went two or three more times over three years. Eventually they were like, 'It's probably only sore because you touch it all the time. Stop touching it and leave it alone and it will get smaller.' And that's what happened. It's still there, but it doesn't hurt and it got smaller, so it's just a gland.

If you have conversations with men about health, or sex, or relationships, it's one step removed. It almost feels like you're not talking about it, does that make sense? Like reading the page of a book. I've got a friend who likes to tell me about his sex life and he goes into a fair bit of detail, but it almost doesn't sound like what he's describing is real, it's almost like a story because there is an emotional detachment. Maybe we want to keep up a sort of barrier. So you can talk about that stuff, but you're not really feeling what you're saying. I think maybe it's innate to men, and then culture makes it a stronger tendency.

I can't remember ever talking about sex with my parents. My mum once found a porn mag that I had. She had a chat with me about it. She told me it was degrading to women, that I shouldn't do it and she threw the mag away.

I'd like to try and be a nice dad and make my kids better people than me. I think I would try and make sure they're confident and that they feel assured in what they do. I can be insecure in some situations. I don't want my kids to be like that.

Twenty-eight years old

"We accessed a divine realm when we made love"

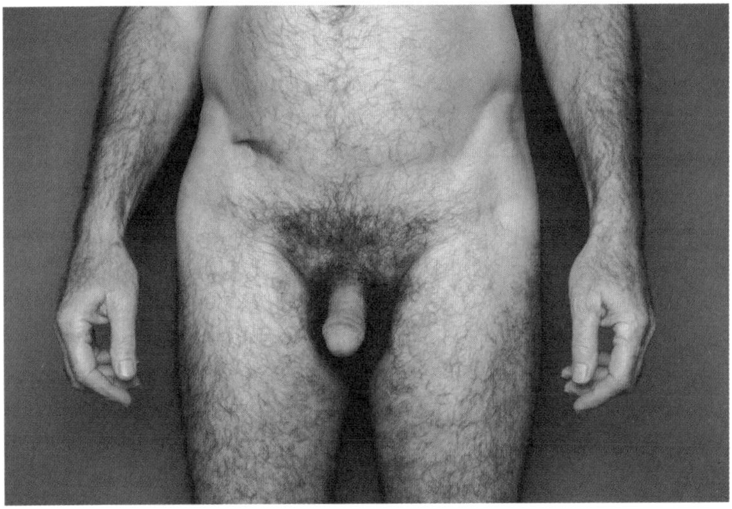

I think one of the huge problems with our society is that sexual issues are repressed. In society generally, there's no way to express one's sexuality and to heal one's sexual wounds.

I'm a full believer in transparency, to the extent that a year and half ago I published a memoir about a love affair. It was vaguely erotic, and quite out there in terms of my lover and I being honest and exposing ourselves. It was brave of us, but we thought it was important to bring these topics to the surface.

I had mixed feedback, but I was satisfied it was the right thing to do. One or two people were outraged, most people who read it were really grateful and, in some cases, quite inspired by the openness of it and the transparency, which encouraged them to be more open themselves. Society is so repressive that it needs to be loosened up so that people can be themselves and be healed and be free.

My wife and I were hippies in the 60s and 70s. We built our house and lived in a hippy community. We had beautiful home births. The kids grew up close to nature, we had rainforest all around and we grew our own food. It was the whole hippy dream. We were not strictly monogamous; when we got married we made an agreement that should one of us feel attracted to another person it might be OK to act on that, provided we were transparent about it. In fact, that agreement got tested very early in our marriage, about a year in. My wife was away at a meditation course and she called me one night and said she was attracted to someone on the course, and would it be OK if she slept with him? And because that was our agreement and I felt confident in our relationship and I trusted her, I said yes. It was a good confirmation of the agreement, that it could work.

There was a lot of nudity at home. It was the sub-tropics so I think we went for about nine months of the year hardly wearing clothes at all in the house and garden. We used to keep a sarong hanging on the fence in case a stranger wandered in, so we were all very relaxed with nudity.

For the first six or seven years of our marriage we had a great sex life because we were very much in love. And yet, in retrospect, with what I know now, I don't think I did it very well. I don't think we did it very well as a couple. We weren't very exploratory. We were in love, so in a sense whatever we did was fulfilling, but in terms of exploration neither of us pushed boundaries with the other very much.

It wasn't until I turned 50 and got divorced that I actually started playing around. I started dating much more seriously. I went out clubbing two or three nights a week, having a great time, meeting lots of women and having lots of sexual experiences. I got the chance to explore my fantasies, which was great. To carry around fantasies in your head and not live them out is very frustrating.

Then, at the age of 63, I had the best relationship of my life in terms of sexual compatibility and sexual attraction. That was the relationship that I published the book about. It took my sexual experience to a whole new level – at the basic physical level it was wonderful, but we took it to a more spiritual level that I had never experienced before. It felt like we accessed some kind of divine realm when we made love.

She taught me a lot, she was a great teacher. The most important thing was to slow down and to be less goal-oriented. Prior to that, all my life, I'd been quite fixated on climax and whether that was mine or my partner's. But she insisted that we just slow down, just be in the moment, be in the present. We would make love for hours and in the process we would each orgasm several times, she multiple times in a way that I'd never experienced with any partner, just through being slow about it and being present with a lot of eye-gazing and our heart connection.

There was a lot of beauty to our relationship, but there was a lot of challenge as well. It lasted seven months. Basically, she wanted to be polyamorous and I didn't. I'd done my polyamorous thing in the past. Here was a woman I was prepared to settle down with. I would have married her on the spot, but she was quite a bit younger than me and she certainly didn't want to marry me. We spent half of the relationship in a kind of honeymoon period, which was just unbelievable, and then the last half was a slow break-up. She explored with other guys and I got frustrated and hurt and crazy-making. It never had long-term prospects really.

I would advise young people to talk about sex and process their sexual issues. I would encourage them to be very cautious about devaluing sex. They should try as much as they can, with their partner or partners, but remembering the sacredness of it.

Sixty-five years old

"I like that it's unpredictable"

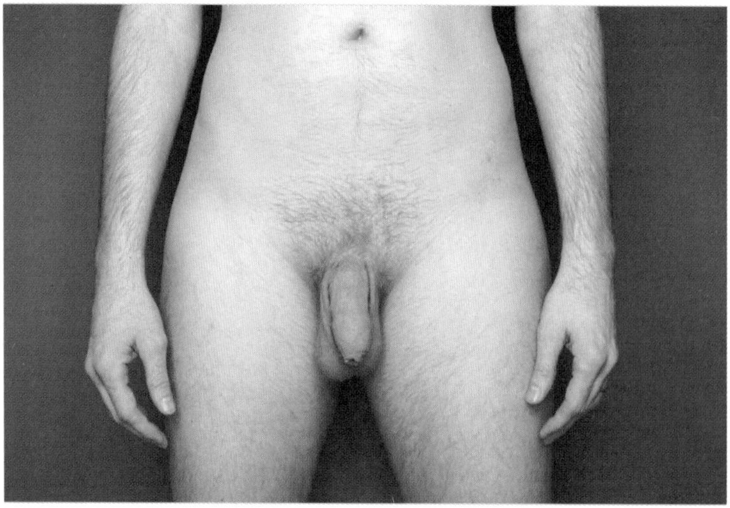

I call it my 'widge.' It's a northern word. If you talk to someone in the north-west they'll know what a widge is. 'Stop holding your widge!'

I really like my widge. It's always been there. It's one of my most favourite features. I grew up with hippy, kind of naked parents. My mum would go topless on any old beach, and my brother and me ran around with nothing on till we got too old.

Do you know what 'cotch' is? It's when you sit with your hands in your lap and cup your penis. It's really warm and comforting and safe. I have to stop myself doing it in front of other people. I'm not doing anything,

I'm just holding it. Apparently it's a very young, boyish thing to do. But I think real men cotch!

My widge has been there through the good times and the bad. It's there when I'm happy and there when I'm sad. I know most men don't like theirs, but I do. I think it has a life of its own. It's like a barometer. I can tell a week before that I'm going to get poorly, because my balls will ache. And if you're happy and excited, then you're happy and excited!

It is what it is and I've got no hang-ups. It's one of the few bits of your body you can't change, so just as well.

It probably has a life of its own. I'm quite excitable. I get all erections all the time. 'Dog with a bone' is how my friends describe it. I have to keep covering myself with a towel on holiday. I hope that never changes. I like that it's unpredictable.

Ideas about the ideal penis vary. Most men worry about the size. I think mine is fine. If anything I wish it was a bit smaller. This is embarrassing... When it's hard it's quite thick, and I think that can be quite challenging and uncomfortable for some people. When I was younger and dating it used to put people off.

I wish I was more handsome, but I guess everyone does. Some of my friends have very classic male good looks: broad shoulders, narrow hips, chiselled features. If I could change one thing I would have narrower hips. But it is what it is. I'm not that confident about the way I look, but I'm very comfortable with my widge. I wish I felt that about my face, to be honest!

I have a fear. I worry about getting an erection if I get naked. I could have had an erection today and had to completely question my sexuality! *(laughs)* I sometimes have a massage. You know when you are naked under the towel? A massage can be quite sensual, it's intimate, the lights are dim. I quite often find myself not relaxing because I'm thinking, 'Don't get an erection, don't get an erection, don't get an erection.'

A few years ago I was persuaded to have a boyzilian wax: your balls, your crack and the base of your cock are waxed. Basically for vanity. It's the most bizarre thing. At this stage it goes from being a 'widge' to a 'cock', because this is grown-up, serious business. It absolutely killed. It wrecked more than anything I have ever experienced in my life. Once they start it's a full commitment because it would look ridiculous. Once the wax is lathered on you can't back out. I nearly kicked the guy. It was awful. It's degrading to kneel on all fours and have someone play with your bits for vanity.

Having absolutely no hair on my balls or around my cock was weird, because I am an adult. Being hairy is part of being grown, and being a man, part of your masculinity. I just didn't like it. And as it grew back it was itchy. I would never do it again.

I came out when I was about 15 or 16. I had a girlfriend, had a boyfriend... Classic teenage stolen kisses and things. I played around a bit, and realised over time. When I was 17 I realised I was definitely gay. I thought coming out would be a massive thing, a difficult thing to do, but in hindsight no one cared except some guys at school who bullied me a bit.

I was singled out for being gay and being a podgy boy. At the time I was bullied quite badly, in my mind. At the time that felt terrible, but worse things happen. I think it made me stronger.

When I was bullied for being gay I didn't deny it. I could have shut it down, but why deny it? I was bullied for being fat, and I probably am more body conscious now. But you move on. I'm sure they've matured and grown up to be great people.

I've never had any STDs because I'm a nice boy. I've been in a relationship for 15 years. I think it's really important that you have respect for your body and for other people's bodies. I'd never intentionally do anything to jeopardise my health or my partner's. Even in a long-term committed relationship I go for checks every six months, I think of it as being like going to the dentist. As a part of the screenings you get health checks too, it's like an MOT. I did this before my partner, and in the early days of a relationship you don't know whether it will last or not, but it's stayed my routine. I'm not sure if my partner does, we haven't talked about it.

We've never talked about our previous relationships anyway. Not interested. We're not married, you couldn't get married when we met, but we wear rings anyway. By the time civil partnerships came along we were very comfortable in our relationship and had bought a house, so we just didn't do it.

We have a really strong relationship, but we enjoy our own lives and our own friends. We have active social lives and a good home life and lots of trust. We were raised with similar family morals. I think how you are raised as a kid stays with you into adult life.

Thirty-five years old

"I wouldn't mourn the loss of my penis"

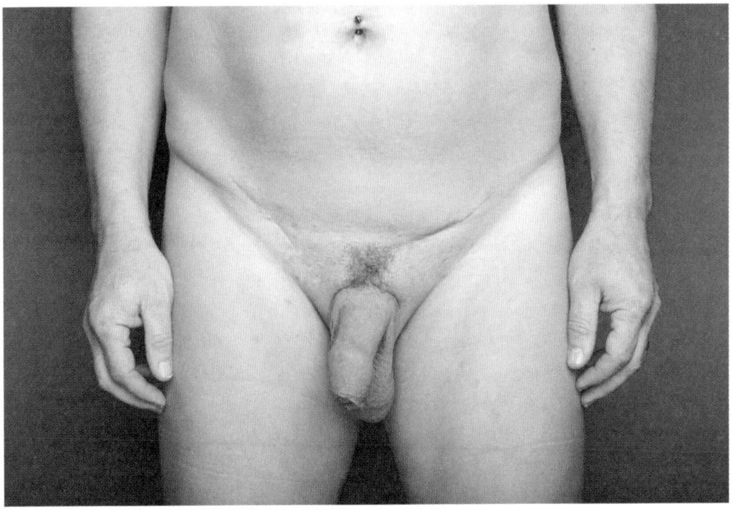

All my life I've known in some way that my gender doesn't match my birth gender. But I have suppressed it and repressed it. I went strongly into denial and chose very macho jobs, without knowing why. I went to a traditional all-boys school, where if you didn't act like a 'proper' boy you would be beaten up. I've learnt to live how people expect me to be. I joined the forces, then the fire brigade.

I'm under a gender identity clinic. I generally present as androgynous, but sometimes in a female role. I don't like the word 'role', but people know what I mean by it. It implies there is only one way to be a woman, and actually there are as many ways as there are women. It also implies acting, which I'm not.

I could really manage without a penis. In an ideal world I wouldn't have it, and I probably won't in the future. But I still need it because they'll use it to make the bits and pieces that I want. It's almost a necessary evil. Would I mourn the loss of my penis? Oh God, no.

There have been times when I've loathed it and sat in the bath and seriously had thoughts of taking a knife to it, and getting rid of my penis, testicles, the whole thing. You don't act on it, you know it would be fatal. It wouldn't have been a resolution.

I used to have a kind of hypochondria about my penis and testicles. I've found things wrong and needed to go to the doctor, like lumps on my testicles, and imagined them to be more significant than they are. I used to turn up at the doctor quite regularly. I'd have been so grateful if a problem had required the removal of my testicles. It would have made the decision for me and almost solved the problem for me.

They probably labelled me as someone who liked being examined, maybe they even thought that I was a man who liked getting his dick out in front of women doctors! When I did have a problem, I thought, 'Finally!' You know, 'real' men do not want something wrong with their dick or penis. I had a hydrocele, like a varicose vein in the testicle. I now have a platinum coil in my testicle.

I'm married and I love my wife. We still don't know how it will pan out for our relationship if I have my penis removed. Do I carry on living in this in-between space, where I'm neither properly male nor female, but wanting to be female, or do I go through with it and run the risk of losing the person I love most in the world?

Her reactions to this have evolved over time. She used to say if I fully transitioned she would be my friend, but not my life partner. She says she would be living as a lesbian, and she's not a lesbian. It's so complicated. She didn't fall in love with my gender, but would she have fallen in love with me if she hadn't perceived me as a man?

My penis still comes into my sex life with my wife. Sometimes it works naturally, but it takes some time. But our sex is not all about penetrative sex, it's a lot about touching and holding each other beforehand. Some men just think about sex and they get an erection, but that doesn't happen to me. Sometimes to be sure of an erection I take Viagra. My other half doesn't know. I'll be aware of where my body is and how it's likely to react and I'll take one without her knowing. Rationally she would know it's an effect of the hormones, but she might worry that she thinks it's because I don't find her attractive. I prefer not to shove it down her throat. *(laughs)* Sorry.

With all the hormones I take, I don't wake up with a morning erection anymore. I hate the occasions when it happens, it's a reminder of real masculinity. 'No! Go away!' I cope better than I used to – now it's annoying, but once I would have wanted to take a knife to it.

I prefer lesbian porn to straight porn. I don't mean lesbian porn for straight men, I mean porn for women who fancy women. I've watched straight, 'nice' porn with my wife; not violent, not where anyone is being degraded. Most porn you can stumble upon on the internet is not 'nice'. I don't identify with straight porn, it's like watching a horse race: I'm interested in watching the jockey, but it's not something I can do myself. It leaves me feeling as though I'm missing the point. It's not particularly erotic. It's about atmosphere. If I watch porn on my own, it doesn't massively turn me on. If I watch it with my wife and she's aroused, if I can sense that, then that has an effect on me.

I sometimes say to women that men are quite horrible. Men behave differently when women are around. A woman who's always been a woman has never seen that. Men adjust their behaviour when women are around. Sometimes it's horrible and scary. I think it's getting a bit better now, maybe because men are becoming more aware, but also the workplace is better policed than it used to be. When men are on their own watching TV, it can be all 'I'd fucking do her', 'She fucking wants it', 'Look at the tits on her.' It's almost like a parody, but it's not, and it can be done in a nasty way. Some of the sexually suggestive phrases are quite aggressive. 'I'd fucking smash her back doors in' is an extreme example. Generally, men would not behave like that if women were in the room. A trans man I spoke to said the most shocking thing for him was the difference in how men behaved when they perceived him as a man, not a woman.

Dicks are a huge part of how normal men feel about masculinity and being a man. When my mother started working, my father, who was a very traditional man, said it made him feel emasculated, like he'd been castrated. It's interesting. I don't think a woman in the same position would say she felt like her vagina or vulva had been removed if something happened to make her feel less feminine. A euphemism for a penis is 'manhood.' I don't think anyone calls a vagina a 'womanhood.'

Fifty-five years old

"This older woman took a shine to me"

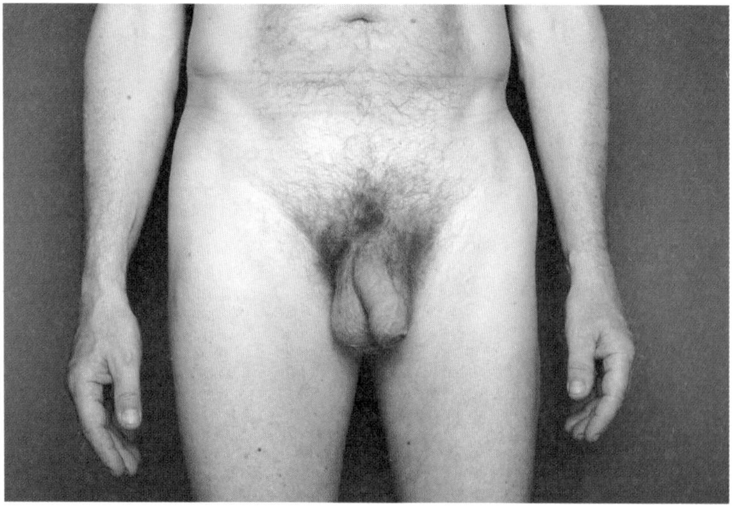

At school I felt inferior in terms of penis size. I am self-conscious about having a small penis. Your relationship with your body is a strange, complicated thing.

I always had this idea that I have a small penis. I wouldn't shower after sports, not just at school, but in general. Around the age of 40 I decided it was ridiculous and that I had to accept we are all different. I don't remember many endorsements from either parent, and my father was quite critical. My mother doesn't say she loves you, and she's a cold fish if you go to hug her. I think having a small penis contributed to my inferiority complex.

My current partner is a psychiatrist and I can speak freely to her. She has assured me through scientific methods that I am actually average. *(laughs)* I just needed a tape measure and accurate figures for the normal range. I'd like to give a message to young men, not to compare themselves to other men. There is more to men than the size of their cock. I hope that this project will make men feel better about being physically different, or developing late, and stop them worrying about size.

My relationship with my penis is better now. Today it's good! I've become a bit of an exhibitionist of late. My partner is a wild thing. We go to festivals and get our kit off. We've been to fetish clubs. We don't fully engage, but we show off a bit. She looks great whatever she's wearing or not wearing. I join in a bit. We're playful rather than risky, we take considered risks in the things we do.

She makes me feel good about my body, whereas historically I have felt bad about my body. I didn't get compliments in the past, so I thought maybe it wasn't that good.

My first sexual experience was not great. *(groans)* I was about 14, in a youth club playing pinball. This older woman took a shine to me. She wasn't very attractive. She lured me back to her place. I didn't know exactly what was on offer, but I was up for anything really. We had sexual intercourse. I ejaculated quickly. I was going to go and she went all coy and did this weird 'Hello Daddy,' psycho routine. It was freaky, she was scary. I was traumatised and ran home. I think she was quite a mad person.

My second sexual experience was a year later. I was knocking around with these Millwall thugs who were older than me. I met a woman at a party and we were having sex behind a car, when a load of these football hooligans joined in. It turned into a gang bang, basically. They were abusive to me and to her. They ended up urinating on her. It was terrible. She went along with it, I don't know why, but she didn't like being pissed on.

I felt really bad for her. Even though they were abusive, I was quite brave, because I said I would take her home. They taunted me about that. So I took her home, I apologised. I didn't see her again.

It looked consensual at the time. But looking back... it was not great. How do you even say no in a situation like that?

The separation from my wife was traumatic. She found a photograph on my phone of my current partner. She got violent. She punched me in the face and threatened me with a knife. I was very angry with her for doing this in earshot of the children. I called the police. I thought the police handled it really badly. She was taken to the police station. It all got totally out of hand. I basically lost seeing my kids, because they didn't want me there anymore. I left home, and lost contact with all our friends. I've never been able to put my point of view and version of events across. I'm pretty sure she will have painted the whole thing as though she is completely innocent. She won't divorce me either, which is frustrating. I am in contact with my children again at least.

I really enjoyed fatherhood. Once we got over the shock of being parents to newborns I really enjoyed it. I was an active and hands-on father. It was great until my wife and I had differences of opinion about how we wanted our children brought up. It annoyed me that I had to concede on nearly everything. She wouldn't consider my rational, logical arguments. We agreed we wanted them to be happy, healthy and self-confident, and with my knowledge of psychology I would have ideas about how to do that, but we didn't agree. I'd like to think I'm a good dad.

Working in psychiatry I see a lot of female leaders: nurses, psychiatrists, commissioners. I am very easy with the idea of total equality. In fact, I think women should have a go at running the world, because the wars we have are due to male aggression. It might sound stereotypical, but men have pretty much messed the planet up.

An aspect of masculinity I am conscious of is anger. I feel that I have a lot of anger and I have to channel it and suppress it. It worries me how violent I could be. I have felt that blood lust thing inside me. I've been in fights before. I know I give off a lot of calm, which makes it more scary that the anger is inside me. I could do a lot of damage to people. I used to be a boxer. I took up Aikido to neuter that aggression.

Fifty-four years old

"Cold bums touching each other when you go to sleep"

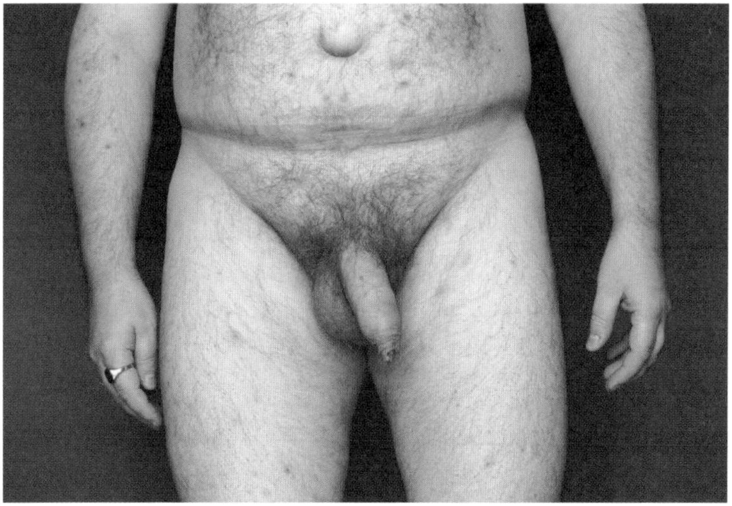

I used to feel dirty, naughty, different from everyone else. I used to worry that I masturbated too much or even whether I should do it at all. When we were kids we used to say if you wanked too much you'd go blind.

I'm quite happy with my penis now. I've got a fairly good relationship with it. It's become healthier over the last few years through being in a brilliant men's group called the Mankind Project. There was an initiation weekend. I can't tell you about it because it's confidential. Things happened that made me able to talk about sexuality, my penis and masturbation more easily. It's helped to know that other men feel the same. I realised I'm not that different and I relaxed a bit more.

I don't get to use my penis as much as I would like to because of back pain. I have a spine disease called ankylosing spondylitis. I started getting backaches when I was 17. I was sent for tests and found out it was highly likely I had the disease. It's caused me problems with my sex life even though my genitals are OK. It's affected sex because it restricts my movement and because of the pain. It's a hereditary, degenerative disease; the vertebrae crumble and try to join up. It's painful, it inflames and gets stiff.

My dad mind-coached me a lot. He used to be a sergeant in the Paras. He played it down a lot. He was absolutely doing his best for me, and it got me through a long way. I still had to go through the emotional side, but in a way you can't understand the pain to come at that age. My dad didn't want me to worry too much when I didn't need to.

It's a horrendous disease and there are young people who have committed suicide when they've found out they have it. With improvements in medication the outlook is less bleak. At the moment it is fairly good because of my self-care. I take medication, do exercise and pace myself. If I do too much I can end up in bed, but I have to do some exercise or the vertebrae fuse up.

I can't work full time. Since my last full-time job in the 90s I've only been able to do voluntary work. Employers have said I don't work fast enough. That's down to being tired. I'm unreliable, and there can be days when I can't go in because of pain.

I was classed as disabled once, but I'm not now. I used to get Disability Living Allowance, but I no longer get that because my health has improved. Disability is a subjective thing according to politics. Over the last ten years they've raised the bar. People who were once judged to be disabled are now judged to be fit and healthy.

I have felt emasculated by not working. I was brought up with the model that the man works and is the provider. I realise now I was worried about what other people thought, rather than what I thought. Actually I'm 90 per cent OK with not working now.

I wanted my last partner to go on top because of my back pain, but she had some issues with that. We had to work out a system, using two mattresses. She would lie on a thin mattress and I would pull it and pull her on top of me. You can get leaflets about how to manage your sex life for people with back problems and arthritis. They are designed for older people who want to carry on having sex. The main thing is you have to talk about it. People don't talk about sex problems, and before you know it, it's cold bums touching each other when you go to sleep.

Before that partner, my marriage was definitely affected too. My wife and I enjoyed sex and enjoyed each other. We could be in the middle of sex and I'd suddenly be in pain and have to stop. That can be extremely frustrating. If that happens twice a week, just when you get to a good part, the exciting part, why would my wife bother? We tried spooning like the leaflets say, and that was good, but we weren't looking into each other's eyes. It wasn't romantic and it became monotonous. It's sad.

Fatigue also played a part. I needed extra sleep and couldn't get up in the mornings sometimes. She never called me lazy, but I believe that's what she thought I was.

We tried to have a child at one point. When it didn't happen it did go through my mind that maybe it wasn't a bad thing, so a child didn't inherit this. I wondered if because I didn't want to have a child, I unconsciously affected the sex and that's why it failed.

If I had a choice of existing or not, would I prefer my parents not to have had me? There've been times, when I've been in pain, so much that I'm crying and can't move... In fact, it's in the in-between times that I've wondered about it. When I'm in that much pain I can't think about anything.

Fifty-two years old

“If my dad hadn’t been an alcoholic I’d be completely different”

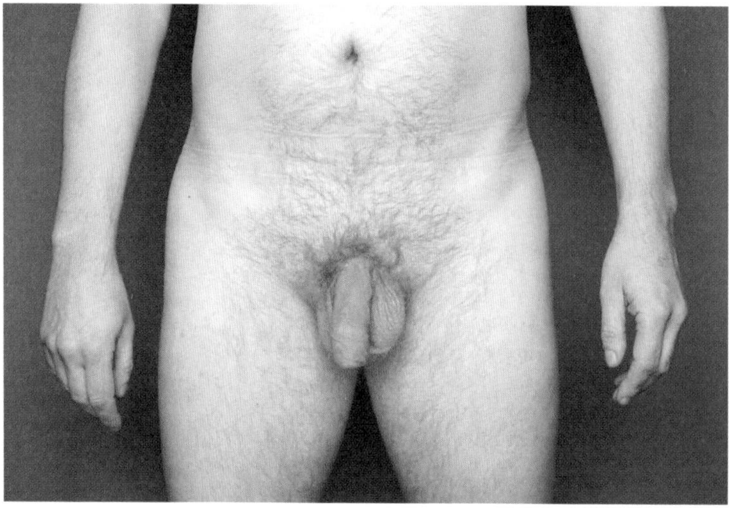

I was a massively insecure and terrified child. It wasn’t till my 30s when I started to let go of the insecurities and bullshit complexes of my childhood. Because I was an insecure person my relationship with my genitals was part of that.

In the school holidays I used to go and stay with my sister and brother-in-law because I had no friends at home. One day at their house, I found a photograph of my brother-in-law with a bunch of his friends and one of them had taken his penis out as a joke. You know, standing around, drunk. I think it was the first human penis I had seen. I was 13. Had I seen my dad's? Christ, no. We were northern working class. If someone kissed on TV everyone would get very uncomfortable and walk out of the room. I grew up with that feeling that sex is dirty.

So, this photograph. I was fascinated by it. It was quite a small penis. I tore out the penis and put it in my pocket. My mum found it and I came downstairs and there it was on the table. This tiny little torn-out penis on the kitchen table. I threw it away and none of us ever mentioned it.

I was a very insecure kid. I had these spots around my penis. I saw a documentary about genital warts, and it said if a man had genital warts and had sex with a lady she could get cervical cancer. And I thought, 'That's it. I can't have sex, I'll kill the first person I have sex with.'

For years I thought about suicide. We lived in a block of flats and I thought about throwing myself off. I wasn't really going to, I just felt really sad. In the end I went to the doctor and said I thought I had genital warts, and he asked what I'd been up to. 'Nothing!' *(laughs)* He looked and said they were sebaceous hair follicles, normal spots. So for a few years I was convinced I had a disease I didn't have.

So, the internet opening up pornography has been wonderful for helping people appreciate the magnificent array of bodies. Probably 75–80 per cent is the standard crappy mainstream porn formula, but there's all sorts of amateur stuff too. When I was growing up sex and bodies were all hidden. At least it's out there with porn. Just being able to see people naked is amazing. I would have been fascinated by *Manhood*, absolutely. I would have wanted to look at it and read it. I'm in favour of openness.

I didn't lose my virginity till I was 20. It was a long-term loving relationship. We fell in love before we had sex. The first time we tried we got really drunk and we couldn't really manage it. We never had great sex. I never went down on her, I didn't know about that. In my mid-20s I read Charles Bukowski and he talked about 'eating' a woman, and I thought, 'Oh, is that a thing?'

Our sex was nothing like the sex in porn. I've always been a snob about art and films. I don't like shit films, and most porn is shit. And some dreadful formulas have crept in in recent years, like coming on women's faces, and anal, and weird stuff. Kids growing up with it will think that's what sex is and that's terrifying. There's no love in most pornography. In my own experience, most sex has been loving. And that's what pisses me off about porn.

I've carried a lot of fear through my life. The frightened little boy is still very much there, but I've made so much progress.

My dad would binge drink and then there would be sulky, silent weeks. He wasn't often violent, but my first memory is of him holding scissors to my mother's neck, my sister and I creeping down the stairs and then him getting carted off to jail. He got put in the cells a few times. My mum and my sister tied him up a few times to stop him being violent. He was a lovely man, but he was totally ruined by his alcoholism and his fear. If my dad hadn't been an alcoholic I'd be a completely different person. I'm not going to put it all on my dad, my mum was from a similar background.

It wasn't till I got to college that I realised that people say they love each other or hug. I thought that was just an American sitcom thing. There was no touching at all in our house. I confronted my mum about it before I left to go to London. Looking back, I wish I hadn't been so challenging about it. She said she did hug us, but when I was about four I pushed her away and didn't want it anymore. But if your kid pushes you away, you don't say 'Right, I'll never touch you again.' She had no affection when she was growing up.

I'm pleased with the progress I've made, getting over all this shit. It'll sound arrogant, but I've been able to help my family. I've inflicted this progress on them too. I lived with my mum for a while after my stepdad died, and when I left I said, 'Look, I know we've never said this and it's embarrassing and everything, but I love you.' And she said it too. And then we hugged. I left, got into the lift and I burst into tears.

I'm not in a relationship at the moment and I'm starting to think, 'Shit, that's it.' I went on Guardian Soulmates for a couple of months and these days the market of people who would be interested in me is reduced because I'm old. The only women who would even consider going out with a 47-year-old are in their 40s themselves. I'm not anti-old, but I do have a bit of a reputation for going out with younger women. *(laughs)* I want everyone to be interested in me! That's going to make me sound like a cunt, isn't it? I have a very specific type of women I fancy and, by the way, young isn't part of that type. I don't want to be one of those men.

I'd love to have kids. I have so much love to give. I love my life and I'm excited about the future, but it does upset me that I'm not in a relationship and I don't have kids. I'm good with kids. I'd want to be everything my father wasn't. Loving.

Forty-seven years old

“I’m looking for someone I would have kids with”

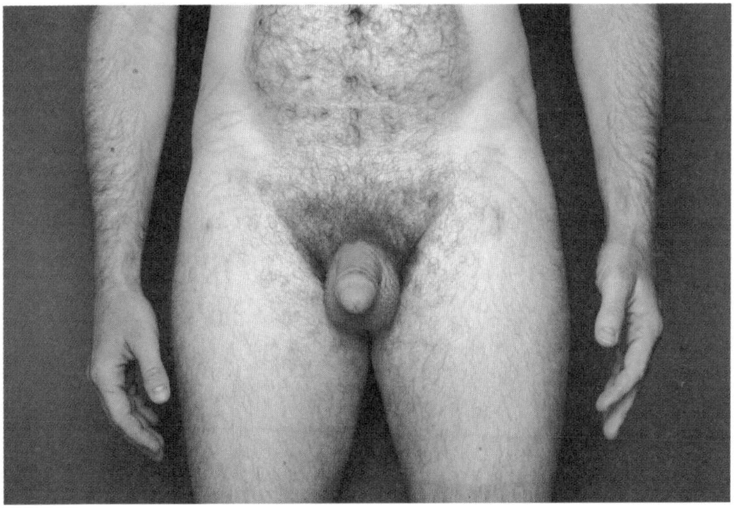

From childhood to adulthood, men use fun and games and banter with each other. Base level male banter is all about taking the mickey out of a small willy. ‘You’re really ugly, you’re crap in bed, you’ve got a really small willy!’ Even now with my friends, if we make a joke about that it’s guaranteed to get a laugh. Just with good friends, it’s not office banter. It goes back to PE sessions, football and rugby.

At the heart of it, all this joking is about sexual prowess, and being worried about no girl wanting you. Deep down, it’s about wanting to love and be loved. When you’re younger you think that being loved is about being sexually appealing to the opposite sex. What makes you attractive? Good looks, being good at sex, good body, decent willy size. Of course, when you're older you know it's more about being a good person, having a similar outlook on life and being kind to each other, and sexual prowess is increasingly less important in the mix.

Men's sexual peak in terms of performance is late teens and early 20s. I think women enjoy sex more as they get older. Talking to all my friends, we have less sex as we get older. When you're younger you're like a wild animal. You want it from everybody, and your standards are lower. It's all about frequency. It's about 'Where can I put this?' As you get older it's more about intimacy and quality, not quantity. When you're older it's about creating love and relationship with sex.

I've had sex with about ten women, more of them when I was younger. When you're younger it's fun working out who you like, what you like, experimenting.

Being circumcised sounds bigger and more important for those who haven't had it done. It's not something I think about as I was only eight days old when I had it done. I like the idea of it because it is a tradition through the ages. Circumcision feels special in a way. It doesn't negatively affect my life. It's cleaner to be circumcised for health and hygiene reasons, and it's supposed to reduce transmission of sexual disease. Aesthetically I think it looks nicer, although I don't see a lot of penises to cross-reference – women can be the judge of that! I found it distressing watching my young family members being circumcised. But I would find it distressing to watch them having an injection. It's not like FGM, which is supposed to stop women enjoying sex and exert power over them.

I don't think about my penis that much. It's a functional relationship most of the time. Sometimes it is an amazing way to give someone you care about pleasure, and have pleasure given back to you. Other than your lips and fingertips, it's the main way we do that.

Our penises are hidden away so we don't have to worry about how they look very often. I think guys worry more about how they work. Impotence is a terrifying idea for men. But then, I would be terrified about my kidneys not working too!

I last had sex about a month ago – I had a ten-day thing with a girl I met. We didn't sleep together on the first night. I did ask and she gallantly declined. But we did sleep together on the second date. I don't know... how much do I enjoy sex these days? Hook-ups aren't my thing

I guess. The first few times you have sex you're wondering, 'Are these just hook-ups or is it going to be something more?' I don't often find the first few occasions I have sex with someone that enjoyable, because I'm not that relaxed. I'm not a wild conquistador sexual being I guess! I think it brings up memories of happier sexual acts. In a way I don't look forward to it, but knowing it might not be that great the first few times, you hope it's going to get a lot better. She didn't want to continue it. I was unsure as well. She wasn't feeling it, and that's fair enough.

If I'm honest it was a big plus that she had a coil, so I didn't have to wear a condom. The first time was back at my place. We got naked in my lounge, drinking gin and tonics, and progressed to the bedroom. It was the first time in my new flat. It sounds terrible, but there was an element of christening my new flat and furniture – not just the bed!

I was quite surprised that she wanted to see our bits when we had sex. She wanted to see my willy going in and out. It turned me on actually. It was quite cool. Most girls I've been with haven't been that fussed, they've been more interested in us looking into each other's eyes.

I like it when a woman is more sexually experienced than me. I think it means she will know what she likes and what she is doing. It might sound strange, but I prefer experience.

I'm looking for someone I would have kids with, someone I could have a shared approach to life with. She doesn't have to be Jewish, but it might be useful. I'm 40 now. Kids might be out of the equation in a few years' time. It makes my heart break a little when I say that. If I haven't had children by the time I get to 45 I suppose I'll be more flexible about women, it will just be about the connection.

I think many of us have a lucky quirk of biology that when reflecting on the arc of our life experiences, we over-dwell on the happy times and gloss over the difficult ones. Therefore, when real love comes, it tends to erase the moments when we've felt alone and unloveable. Whether you call that faith in the healing power of life resilience, or optimism, or whatever, I think it allows us to persevere when life sometimes seems too much and too difficult. For me, I think I'll be happy if I do find love again later in life if it is powerful enough to fully colour the perception of my own life, even if statistically the periods of being without it are greater than those with it.

Thirty-nine years old

"I developed a sexual fetish for balloons"

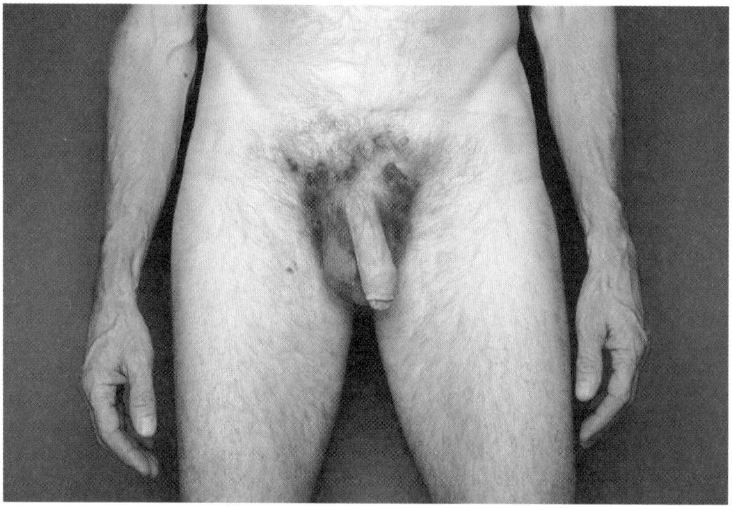

If I had to sum up what my feelings about my penis have been for most of my life in one word, it would be 'shame'. But it's not so much about how it looks or its size – though bigger would have been great – or even my penis itself. It's really about how I have generally felt about my sexuality and masculinity (or lack of it). My penis is obviously a focal point and symbol for who I am as a man.

Many of these debilitating feelings are due to a typical combination of parenting, religion, and the nature of society generally around me when I was a child. However, a huge part of the problem was also that I developed a sexual fetish in my early adolescence as the result of an event that happened to me when I was very young.

The most obvious effect of the fetish was that it intruded on my thoughts about and interactions with women. I was constantly longing to experience this with a woman, but too fearful and ashamed to even talk about it. In my younger adult years, I was able to keep it from intruding so much, but my ability to keep a lid on it diminished over time.

The other aspect of the event that gave rise to the fetish was that it involved a paralysing fear, and resulted in PTSD-type hypervigilance and other symptoms.

So what was this event that has had such a catastrophic effect on my life? Beatings? Rape? No, something much 'smaller' than this, and something which I still feel the need to justify, as I fear others will judge it as laughable that such a small thing has had such a devastating effect on my life.

My dad was in many ways a loving dad. Like all of us, he wasn't perfect, but he did many things for and with me, including playing and showing affection. However, for reasons I can only guess at (he died a few years ago), when I was around three years old he started to blow up a balloon and kept going steadily until it burst. From what I recall, even though I had no knowledge or experience of what would happen, I instinctively sensed that something wasn't right and felt concerned as he was blowing it up.

When it burst, I was stunned. I don't think I cried. For one thing, I had gone into shock, but I guess I also knew instinctively that he must have known the effect it would have, so what would be the point in revealing my upset? My mum was in the next room and came in to see what had happened. She asked him why on earth he had done it. I don't know whether she noticed the state I was in or not, but she didn't offer any comfort to me.

My dad then proceeded to blow up a second balloon just the same, while I didn't know to do anything other than sit there and endure it.

Over the years, I have come to understand the things I took on board from this. However much my dad showed love towards me, I couldn't trust that he wouldn't deliberately do things he knew deeply hurt me. Showing my fear only brought on more of what I was afraid of (presumably to make me face it). If my dad, who showed great love in other ways, would treat me like this, then what would other men do? 'Normal' boys like loud noises like balloons, so I was deficient and this deficiency was not acceptable.

I'm sure these weren't the intended messages, but they are what I unconsciously concluded about the world around me for many years.

The effect of all this was that I became ashamed of both my fear of balloons and my 'weakness', and did my best to hide them both at all costs. Of course, I could not hide from myself the fact that this 'weakness' was in me, so I felt massively insecure. I was also fundamentally wary of men.

So how did it become a fetish? I saw girls and balloons and birthday parties and I knew that girls liked balloons. When I started to become interested in girls, I was faced with a dilemma. How would I handle a situation with a girl and balloons, which would inevitably happen at some point?

When I saw or thought of girls I liked, my mind would bring up some image to do with balloons as well. The feelings of desire and fear would be present simultaneously. Ultimately, the desire was stronger than the fear and the only way my mind could find to resolve the clash of feelings was to start to link the two. It wasn't long before an association formed between balloons, girls and excitement.

Even talking about balloons now, there is a sense of energy in the genitals. Not arousal as such, but there is a feeling.

In the last ten or so years, I have made a lot of progress in understanding and healing this psychological wound. It has been a quest to seek freedom from shame and fear. Along the way, I have had the joy of sharing this aspect of my life with a partner who was accepting of it and engaged with it happily.

I am at the point where I am starting to see the gifts that I have gained that I do not believe I would have had without this experience. I am also beginning to embrace all of who I am, including my sexuality and what remains of the fetish, my fears, shame and self-judgements. That I can share this publicly is a great testimony to how far I have come, to those who have supported me, and to what is possible. I am looking forward to finding out what lies ahead.

Fifty-five years old

"More awareness of prostate cancer will create more action"

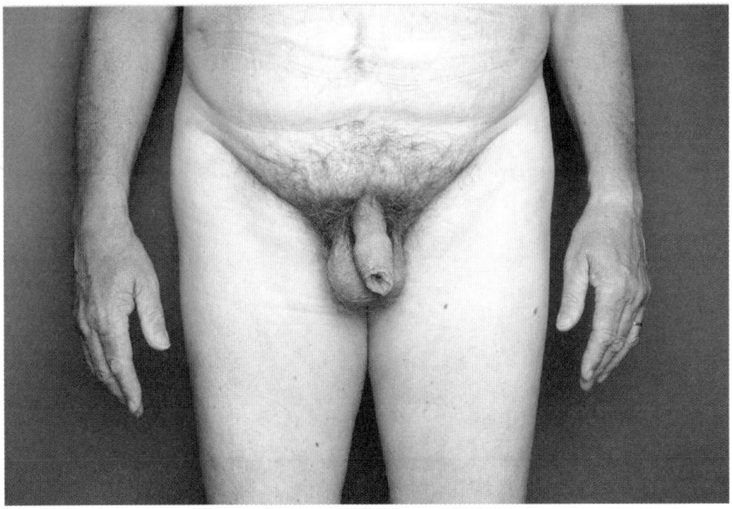

One night I got up to go to the loo, as we all do sometimes, and there was a tiny speck of blood. That set off alarm bells for me; I went straight to the doctor. The NHS has a wonderful system. I was seen within 48 hours by a specialist.

They put a camera up my penis. It is not comfortable. I have to have it done every year for five years. The first time felt excruciating, but I think the pain was partly psychological because I have had it since and it wasn't that bad. It's not dignified though, you lie down in front of people with your penis out, and they put a camera up.

The cancer was confined to the bladder, but they also found mild cancer in the prostate. It would just have been monitored if that's all I'd had, but, while they were in there, they might as well get rid of it. When I found out I had cancer I closed my business the following day. It was crystal clear to me that my focus was on getting better.

I had the operation robotically and had a new bladder constructed from the bowel and intestine. I just have one small scar. Incontinence is the big problem with bladder cancer. The doctors warn you to set your alarm for 3am every night to empty your bladder. Touch wood, I never had an issue. I'm lucky I haven't had any problems. Although I wasn't worried about the potential side-effects, I was worried about the cancer. It's very simple, you have two choices: one is going to kill you and the other is, hopefully, going to keep you alive.

I met someone who had the same operation and he mentored me through it. It was so helpful to know someone had been through it and survived. It's partly why I decided to run a prostate cancer group when the nurses asked me. They had no members and no funds, so because I have a commercial background I took it on as a business exercise in a way. I wanted to make it successful. I am keen that people become more aware of cancers. The side-effects of prostate cancer for men are terrible.

I was staggered at the first meeting. There were about ten guys. They were very candid about erectile dysfunction and incontinence, all these taboo subjects that we'd normally feel uncomfortable about. I was motivated to make it more successful because it was clear how much everyone was benefitting. The more guys you have being open, the better.

We also bring partners to the groups. Initially the men were against it, because they didn't want to talk about these issues in front of them, but, of course, your partner knows if you've got erectile dysfunction and incontinence, so it's silly to pretend they don't. About 80 per cent of partners come along now. It's still completely open and honest.

The support group has made me more open. It's changed me. I wouldn't have taken part in *Manhood* before the support group. I want people to be more aware. I want them to react quicker. One of the things I have learnt is that a lot of the men reacted very slowly. When I saw that spot of blood, I didn't hang about, but I know there are men who will be producing quite a lot of blood over a period of time before they do anything about it. More awareness will create more action.

Prostate cancer is getting more awareness now, it's getting closer to breast cancer awareness. I think there has been a lot more activity in the last couple of years. Prior to that it was very poor. Breast cancer kills a lot of women, so it was very important to raise the awareness.

I'm happy for my children to know I am taking part in this, but not my grandchildren. They are really quite special to me. I have eight grandchildren. You have a responsibility for your own children, and they are a 'task' in a way. You bring them through life. It's a job. When grandchildren come along, they don't carry that baggage. They are these wonderful little things you can have a relationship with, but without any angst.

My grandchildren did know I had cancer, but some were told late. My daughter didn't want her children to know at the time. They were going through exams, and she was thinking about that. There might have been more to it, but I didn't have the energy at the time to investigate it. It's no secret I was disappointed, I wanted them to know. She brought them to see me in hospital about two weeks after the operation, but we never talked about it. I didn't know what they knew. We had always been a very open family and, suddenly, at a time of crisis, we were talking with caution. It was bizarre. I would have preferred openness.

The relationship with my daughter has evolved since I had cancer. We are less close. I don't get uptight about it. I did at one time, but I don't now. It's life. The most important thing is that there is no disconnection. We don't have a bad relationship, it's a different relationship. I'm probably closer to my sons.

My wife has been remarkable. We've been married 37 years now. She is very supportive. We're a team. I hope I'd be as good for her as she was for me.

I spend time with guys who have been impacted much more than me. It's changed their lives and sometimes their relationships. I see myself as very lucky.

Sixty-six years old

“I turned into a hairy beast”

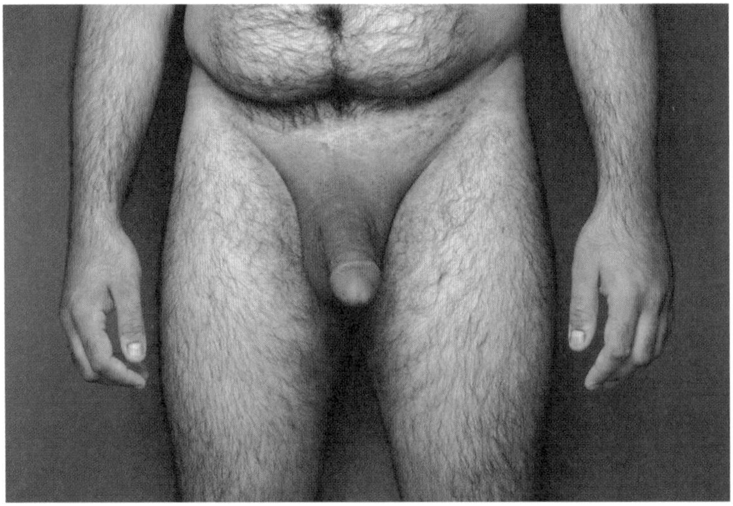

I’ve struggled to come to terms with my body. There are conflicting messages from society here compared to society back home in terms of cultural values about the body, being a man, and responsibility.

I was circumcised and most other boys weren’t. I don’t have a problem with being circumcised. I am Muslim, and circumcision was the practice of the Prophet, so I think it is a requirement to be circumcised. I don’t know any Muslim men who aren’t.

I didn’t notice my penis before puberty. After puberty it felt like I couldn’t get away from it. Erections all the time, at random times, with no inkling of why.

When I was 11 my body was more developed than everyone else. By that age I already had a beard, pubic hair, hairy armpits and my voice was breaking. Everyone else was a child, but I had turned into a hairy beast. The amount of hair... It was way too much! No one teased me, which I am thankful for. It was more I had my own internal battle with it, the pressure came from me.

I was shy and embarrassed about it. I didn't come to terms with the changes till much later on. I am OK with my hair now. Beards are in, which is great! I take advantage of that. The last time I was clean shaven was two years ago. Having hair in various places is OK and it's expected, but there is an invisible line – if your hair crosses it, it is too much. My hair is everywhere. There was a time when I didn't want that, I wanted what was normal: hair on my chest but not on my back, a beard, but not hair going up my face.

I remove my pubic hair and armpit hair for hygiene, otherwise I have a lot... I feel like I can smell myself two hours after a shower if I don't. I don't know if anyone else would be able to smell me, but I would be aware. I also like removing pubic hair for sexual reasons. My wife says she likes it too.

Here you get sexual education at school and there is more openness, compared to back home where my family are from. Back home someone from your family will talk to you the day before you get married! More commonly you learn from brothers and cousins over time. I never had 'the talk' with my dad. That doesn't mean he's a bad dad, he's a great dad – I think it was just assumed I would find everything out somehow.

The culture here is open. The culture from home wants everything to do with sexuality to be behind closed doors. I think a middle ground would be better. People I meet from home seem to have repressed feelings that they don't know how to express in a safe way. You are either a holier-than-holy civilised man, or a pervy serial womaniser. In South Asia there are a lot of problems with rape culture and women are very heavily controlled. The women know it's not safe for them to go out by themselves in non-developed areas, so they don't.

Women are seen as the property of the men, but I think this is more cultural, it's not from the religion. In the earliest times of Islam, women and men were equal and women had their own businesses. Now culture says that if you can't control your woman then you are not a real man.

My wife and I both grew up over here. I like to think we take values from the culture here, but also from our religion. I don't tell her to cover her hair; she only does that when she prays, as that is the religious requirement. I don't try and restrict her movements. If I want to go out with friends, or go for a run, it is only fair if she does that as well if she wants. If she doesn't feel like it would be safe in a certain area to go out on her own, then it is my role as a man and husband to be there to protect her. I don't know if it's a primal thing, or an ego thing, but it does feel good to look after her and my child, it does satisfy me. As a father I feel like the protector and provider.

Babies associate the mother with food, because of the smell of milk, so sometimes if my daughter just needs calming down, I can hold her to do that, and it makes me feel useful. I only see them at weekends at the moment, because in our culture the mother and baby stay with the mother's family to be looked after for a period of time. It makes me feel useless during the week that I can't be there. In this country the family is nuclear – mother, father and children. Back home the family unit is bigger and you look after each other more. This is the time when I have to take a bit more of a back seat. It's just one way to do things, I guess.

In the whirlwind of emotion during childbirth it was my job to be a rock. I am satisfied that I was. I remained calm. It's almost like the English stiff upper lip. As a man you almost have to be devoid of emotion, or at least not let the emotions ruin you, so you can be strong and calm.

As a man I have always been confused about this. We are brought up to think that women cry, and women get upset, but men don't. Men have big strong muscles and don't get emotional. Before marriage I used to be able to brush things off and show less emotion. Since getting married I have needed to open up to emotion. I find that hard because as men we are told to have a cool, calm exterior, never cry, brush things off. But you need to have emotion. When people suppress emotion it bubbles up in other ways. Opening up, in marriage, has opened up the gates. It can also feel overwhelming. I think I didn't develop the ways to deal with emotions by brushing them off when I was younger, but it's changing now.

Twenty-seven years old

"I had a threesome when I was training for the priesthood"

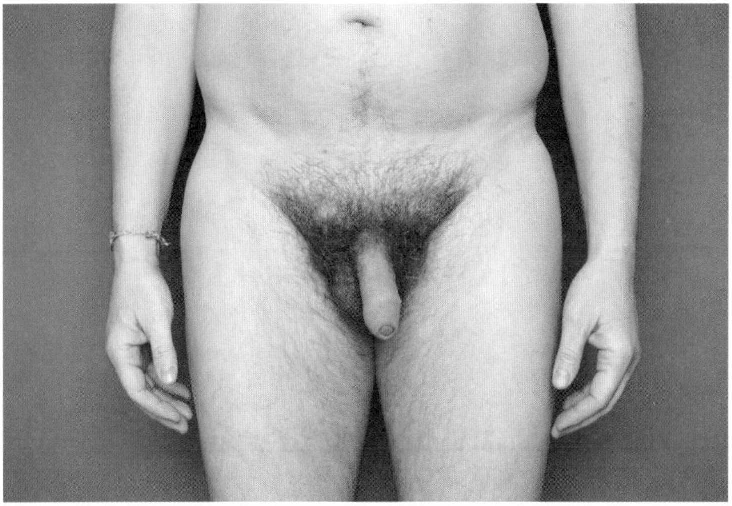

I am the fifth child of six children, and I was the first boy. My father was quite absent because he had to feed eight mouths. At one point he had three jobs to put food on the table. I was a very shy and quiet little boy, scared of adults. I didn't have male friendships.

I had a close and very over-binding mother, and a lot of female influence around. There was too much oestrogen I think. But also, to be fair, some of my sisters were quite full on and tough, and it wasn't all fluffy and pink.

There was an occasion when my clothes were dirty and my mum

put the first thing she could grab on me, and it was one of my sister's dresses. My father came home and went ballistic. This was kind of a motif growing up.

As a boy I knew that I was gay, and very attracted to the male. It would have been seriously dangerous to be gay: I was in a very hostile environment, in the family, the local environment, the school, the Church. When I began to realise I was gay, I was terrified and went into hiding. I believe I was taken into hostage psychologically by homophobia. I've moved away from the Catholic puritanical obsession with sex and homosexuality. When I told my dad I was gay he was pissed off, because he was watching Columbo and it was one of his favourite programmes. 'Gay? You're gay? I'm watching Columbo!' He showed his acceptance by giving me money to travel with my partner.

I acquired a brother when I was four. When he grew up it became apparent that he had a bigger dick than I did. I also saw my dad's penis once, and in my imagination it was huge. At the time I thought his was huge, and mine was small, and I thought they would be fixed like that forever. I didn't realise mine would grow. A wee part of me thought he would always have power over me, be bigger than me, more powerful, and I would be inadequate. I have spoken to other men about this. We have all projected all sorts of potency and power on to our fathers.

My father had been violent towards me as a small boy. Because I was quite a shy, quiet, sensitive boy who was comfortable with female company – I had no option as there was so many of them in the family – he would mock and ridicule me for being a sissy. It took me quite a while to really assert my authority and aggression with my father. I did it in a way I regret. I really bawled at him and shouted because he was treating my mother badly. He was devastated, really quite hurt. That was when he experienced my masculinity, and a bit of aggression and defensiveness of my mother. Nothing physical, just shouting. And I had a wake-up moment: 'I'm an adult. I'm a man, in the same way that my father is a man, and now he is recognising that.'

I remember being in a maths class at the time I was entering puberty, and I had one of those permanent erections. I thought, 'Fuck, how long is this going to ruin my life for?' It was strong and demanded my attention, but was draining at the same time. As a 13 or 14-year-old I would look forward to the day when it wasn't going to be in charge of me.

During my prime, I had no worries about my potency being taken away from me. If I was in bed with a sexual partner I would be erect the whole night; it wouldn't matter how many orgasms I had. That felt good at one level, it was an incredible energy source. My penis has had a great career. I've had a lot of sex and I'm pleased about that.

I am in mid-life now. The reduction in potency and fewer ejaculations have been quite a significant loss. Physiology drives it, it's never been psychological. I am kind of OK with how it is now, but often it feels a bit flaccid and sorry for itself. My penis can be a bit mournful and regretful. The mind is willing, but the flesh is weak.

My penis is quite moody. There are times when I look at it and I think, 'Well you are obviously feeling relaxed and fulsome, so this is a good day for you.' When that happens I feel quite content with it. But there are times when my penis is a bit sorry for itself, a bit shrivelled. I was worried about the cold this morning!

I trained for the priesthood. I took a vow of chastity, which technically meant I couldn't get married or have a sexual relationship. I managed that one year out of seven. I was in my prime when I entered the religious order. It asks the impossible of young men. People want to master it, but it's almost impossible. I had a lot of sex and, in fact, I had my first threesome when I was training for the priesthood.

I still have friends who are priests. They are sexually active and live double lives. That's how they survive. The majority of priests are gay. If the church were to become a 21st-century organisation, not a medieval one, it would have to provide homes for married couples, for husbands and wives or, if it was really modern, for same-sex couples. It would cost a lot of money. Control, property and money are the factors behind it.

I'm going to enjoy being a bit irreverent... To a lot of the senior people in power in the Church, their concept of God is the equivalent of a dry pea: a small, arid, ungenerous concept of God. I'm a theology graduate. Modern-day theology is very smart at being able to deconstruct religious texts and see them in context. They were never intended to be universalised across cultures, across the globe. The idea of holding on to 2,000-year-old practice, that Jesus only called men, is bunkum. It doesn't make sense.

One of the things that made me unordainable – aside from the celibacy and chastity – is the Church's relationship to women. It has a very ungenerous stance. I met women who felt called to be priests, and would have been wonderful priests. The Church can say what it likes about Mary, the Mother of God – it is oppressive to women.

My recollections of sex with women are positive. I like putting my penis in a warm, moist vagina. I've enjoyed women's breasts. Sex with men has been more like being in a gymnasium – more physical, thrusting, primal. The difference for me was that I needed sex with men, and I didn't need sex with women. That might be shifting a bit... I really love women. There is a rising awareness in me of missing intimacy with a woman. I have to have femininity in my life. My partner is 100 per cent homosexual and has zero need to have sex with women.

I don't have any children and that is a source of grief and loss for me. I think I would be a good dad. It's not impossible, it could still happen, but I don't think it will.

Fifty-four years old

“I would rather lose a leg than the ability to have sex”

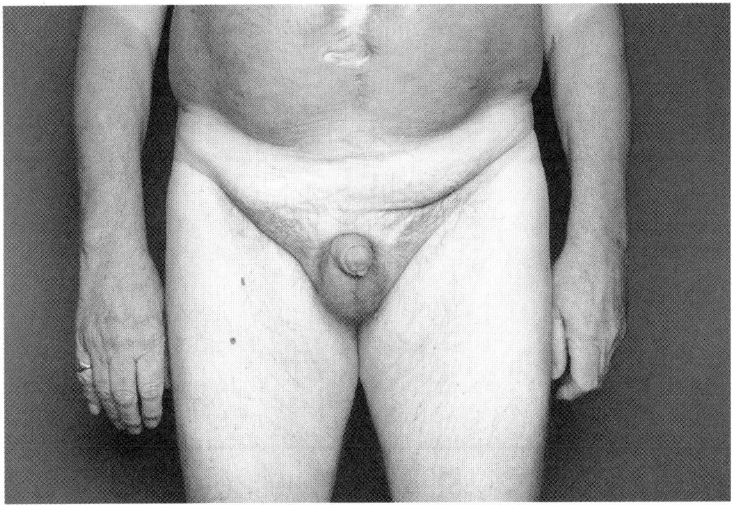

I used to wonder what it would be like to be told I have cancer. It was devastating. I’m hoping to be cured. When I’m the other side of it, I’ll be able to talk to men who’ve also been diagnosed with prostate cancer and tell them that no matter how awful it is, they will come through the other side of it and be OK. What happened to me is exceptionally unlikely, one in thousands.

My PSA went from 2.4 to 6.9. That’s an indication something is wrong with the prostate. My wife and I went to the oncologist together. He gave me a brief ‘finger up the bum’ examination. He said the prostate was a bit enlarged, but in his view it wasn't sinister. I asked if he would be worried, and he said he wouldn't be worried at all. He referred me for an MRI and a biopsy.

When I went back to see him for the results there was a Macmillan cancer nurse there, so I knew it wasn't going to be great news. They discuss the options with you, but it's your choice: surgery, or surgery and radiotherapy. It's a mind-blowing situation. You go on the internet and start looking things up. The internet is a terrible place to look things up about cancer. Apparently herbal tea and cannabis oil can cure all cancers!

The logical choice for me seemed to be surgery. I wanted it done as soon as possible, but I had to lose a stone in weight first. They prefer you slimmer. That was easy. You don't want to eat when you find out you have cancer.

I had keyhole surgery, performed by robot. The doctors sit at a keyboard. There were three anaesthetists. You sit on the edge of the bed, lean forwards, they put a needle in your back and they tell you to get back on the bed as quick as you possibly can. Within seconds your whole lower back and legs are numb, red hot and paralysed. Five hours later I woke up and it was done.

Within a few days I felt well. But six days after the operation I had terrible stomach cramps. I had a terrible night. The next day I phoned an ambulance. It turned out I had bowel adhesions. They said it was very unusual. I was operated on the same evening, through the same keyhole ports. Even after the operation it never got better; the pain was even more intense and my stomach was tight as a drum. Another few days later I had another operation, but this time they cut all the way down, took my bowel out and put it all back in again.

During the operation they squeeze out your bowel then put it back in like it's supposed to be. Once they handle your bowel it stops working. They said it would be three or four days till it worked. They told me I would have terrible wind, then it would turn to liquid. They were right, but I'll spare you the details!

As far as I was concerned, I'd had cancer and they'd taken it out, but replaced it with a massive problem in my bowel, which overtook any thoughts of cancer. My whole concern was getting over the huge surgery to my stomach.

Then three months later we go back for a check-up and once again I'm ushered into the consultant surgeon. My PSA had gone back up and

I required salvage treatment therapy. Only 5 per cent of men require it. All these figures are rubbish if you are the one it happens to.

I had radiotherapy every day for six and a half weeks, which was targeted to miss my bowel. Now I'm in limbo, waiting for the next PSA test. And it will go on.

Alongside the radiotherapy I am having hormone therapy, which effectively destroys my testosterone and turns me into a menopausal woman. I get very hot and sweaty and have put weight on around the waist. I have been very bad tempered.

In general terms I'm the same as a year ago: I eat the same, drink the same, tell the same stupid jokes. I still play tennis. But sex is a complete and utter no. It doesn't happen. It can't happen. The nerves which make the little fella stand to attention are removed. They said in all probability it wouldn't work anymore. The doctor gave me Viagra, but that doesn't work. There are other alternatives, which I am going to pursue.

I only have half the bladder control I used to have. After the catheter was removed, every time I moved, or coughed or sneezed I wet myself. Anything you do makes you wee. You have to wear things to take care of it.

I used to say I would rather lose a leg than the ability to have sex. And I still would, as long as it's below the knee. For the time being my wife is entirely happy with the situation. We have other things to worry about. She says quite a few of her friends don't have sex anymore and they are happily married. My wife says she is fine and would rather do without. If it still worked she would also happily go along with doing it. I think she's happy. Otherwise we'll have to get a bloke in! *(laughs)*

I've got a fantastic wife. She has been amazing throughout the whole kaboosh. Obviously some people manage to go through cancer without someone, but it's difficult to imagine how.

Prostate cancer is one of the big cancers for men and it's a big killer. What people don't realise is once you've had surgery your penis might not work anymore and you might be incontinent. At least my bowel is alright. For now. Losing that would be the cherry on the cake. Well, it wouldn't be a cherry, it would be a chocolate log. *(laughs)*

People talk about fighting cancer. It's nonsense. Cancer fights you. The doctors fight the cancer and you have to hope they win. That's how I see it. If you don't believe they are going to cure you, you may as well jump under a lorry. I'm not going to do that, I enjoy life too much.

Sixty-six years old

“I haven’t seen my children for ten years”

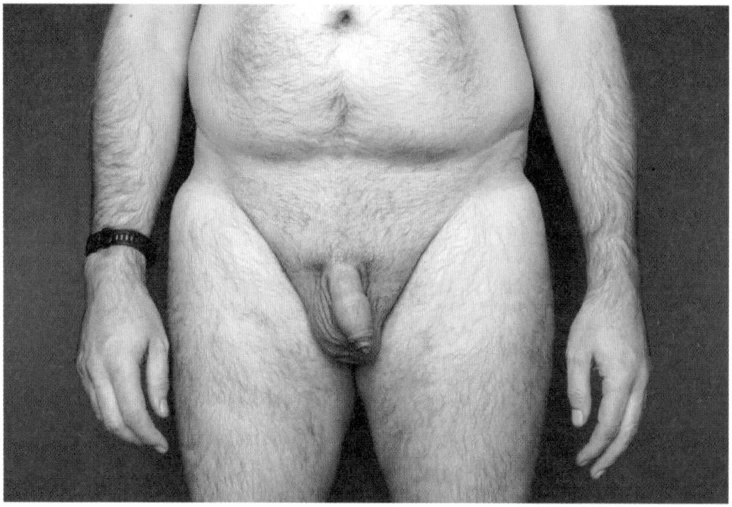

My penis is remarkably normal. Sometimes I would like it to be bigger, of course.

You hear about young girls growing up with expectations about how to look, how to have sex, how to perform... but those expectations also apply to young men now.

I teach in senior school. I’ve noticed a real change in how young men look after their appearance. They still go through the smelly, unwashed phase, but they hit the stage where they are into their appearance much earlier than my generation did. There is a lot more willingness to style their hair, there's more pressure to wear labels. I heard a young man say his coat cost £600. I can't imagine my parents would have spent that much on a coat when I was that age. There is a lot of pressure for kids to show that their parents are rich and there's a lot of judging going on.

Girls can be easier at school, not because they are perfectly behaved, but if they misbehave it tends to be more subtle. Boys go through more gross and showy misbehaviour. It's easy to not even notice whether the girls are doing well or not, because of dealing with boys who are playing up. Teachers have a hell of a lot on, and there is a limit to what you can do. So you deal with the obvious problems first.

There are also fewer fathers around now. I didn't have a dad around when I was a kid, and I felt different. Now it seems unremarkable. I remember thinking it was my job to look after my mum when I was seven.

Men take a far more active role in childrearing now. I very much enjoyed it with my own children when they were younger, but I haven't seen them for ten years now, due to what you might call call an 'implacably hostile first wife'. They are 18 and 17 now.

I look back on that relationship as abusive. I was isolated from my friends and family; she didn't want to see them because they smoked. She was a wife I couldn't please. I didn't earn enough, but I also wasn't home from work early enough. I was under pressure in lots of areas.

I had no control over how money was spent. I had no control over my relationships outside of the marriage. I was permanently shattered. I'd come home from work and the children were handed over to me. 'There, it's your turn now.' The advantage of that was that I had a very close relationship with them when I was at home, and I loved that.

I ended up exploring internet porn. I did some things that are not like me, and I haven't done them since. I put some sexual pictures of my wife on the internet without her knowledge or consent. I don't seek to justify it, but I think I was trying to exercise a measure of control.

After all this she suggested I was looking at child pornography and had my computers investigated by the police. The investigation was solely because of my ex-wife's allegations and I was completely exonerated. Despite nothing being proven, it affected the divorce and custody. When I wasn't found guilty of this, there was another accusation, and then another.

She had once told me that if we ever split up I would never see my children again. In court it felt like the relationship with the mother was paramount. My ex-wife was automatically believed and it was my job to disprove her allegations. I think judges come from a certain background and experience of life and they don't realise how much more involved men are these days.

In the end I agreed I would only see my children at a Contact Centre. A week later she moved and didn't tell me where. That was illegal, but unless I could find them I couldn't do anything about it.

I did find them and for a brief period I could at least send birthday cards. Then they moved again. I don't know exactly where they are now. The children were young when all this happened. As they get older the children's opinion is, rightly, more and more taken into account. I knew how controlling my ex-wife was and how difficult she would make it if they were ever asked if they wanted to see me. I didn't think they would be able to go against her. I decided there was no way I would put them through that. At the last contact I had with my son in a Contact Centre it was obvious he had moved and changed school, and was not supposed to tell me, so he lied to me. It was horrible. I had huge sympathy for him.

I completely understand that the courts have to play it safe to protect children and be absolutely sure that there isn't an issue. I don't think it applies to my situation. My computers were investigated forensically. The investigation took over a year. That must have shown there was no evidence.

One of the problems was money. I was paying the mortgage on the house, rent and my own legal counsel because I didn't qualify for legal aid, even though she did. I think if one party gets legal aid, it should be available to both. I couldn't keep going. At some point you have to cut your losses.

I coped by holding on to the belief I would see my children and be a father again. I could only do that if I looked after myself. I have always provided child maintenance, month after month. You hear about fathers who are angry about paying maintenance, and I can understand it, but I think it's a positive thing. It's the only bit of parenting I can do for them.

Being a father means constantly learning, through the experiences of my own children, the divorce and being a stepfather. I am constantly looking at myself and reflecting. It means giving my best all the time. You have to persevere when it's tough. It means never giving up.

I do believe I will have a relationship with my children when they leave home. There is something about your biological dad. Even if my mother, understandably, said horrible things about my dad, I thought, 'He's my dad, I love him.' I hope that my children feel like that about me.

Forty-five years old

"I had more female friends than men friends"

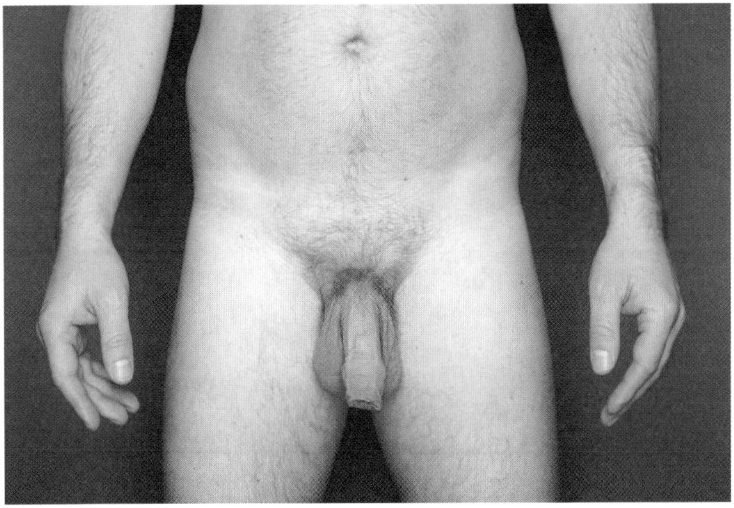

My mum and my auntie used to call my penis 'Chappie' when I was growing up. 'Oh look, little Chappie's out.' I didn't mind when I was little, but when I got to about seven it used to really wind me up. When my auntie used to come round she'd go, 'Oh, how's Chappie?' or whatever, embarrassing me. We used to have a dog and there was this really horrible, cheap dog food that smelt of fish called Chappie. So I got reminded of this every time I offered to feed the dog. *(laughs)* For some reason, my sister's vagina was called 'Sarah'.

What do I call it now? Cock. Cocks and cunts.

I've been complimented by women. I've heard, on multiple occasions, that I've got a nice cock. Not too big, not too small, just the right size, nice and pink, clean. It's a Goldilocks cock. Goldicocks.

There is something I want to speak about in regards to paedophilia and men. It's endemic in our society. I don't read newspapers and I don't watch the TV, but I go into the gym and Sky News is playing and somebody else is a paedophile. As a man I could get sucked into feeling, 'God, I'm a paedophile.'

A girl of 15 can be very sexually mature, very sure of herself deep down, but she's illegal. A 21-year-old can be very much like a child, and yet she's legal. But we have to have the age of consent in order for society to function.

Many men find some 15 or 16-year-old girls attractive. Yet we get branded... I get this feeling that it's not OK. I'm not OK, because that makes me a paedophile. So I get branded with the same stick as the evilness of child rape, which is a completely different category.

If I see an attractive young woman, I'll look at her because that's how I'm hard-wired. But I feel like there's something happening at the moment in our society, and especially within the media, that it's something that I'm meant to feel ashamed of, that I'm a fucking paedo. That's the message I'm getting. It creates self-hatred for men.

I want to talk about what it is to be a man. I think as a boy growing up, to be a man was to be strong, to be hard, to not cry. I'm sure you've heard this before. And then I was told that wasn't OK, that I should be softer. And so instead of finding inspiration from elders or from real men, I looked towards women and I had lots of female friends. In fact I had more female friends than men friends. Sometimes men were unsafe, as far as I was concerned.

And so the journey into manhood has been about allowing authentic male parts of my self-expression, the different elements of what it is to be a man, the power, that sense of direction and strength. If I use those elements to project my shit, my anger and aggression onto someone else, that's not OK. However, if I use my power and my strength to heal and to love, I'm still allowed to be a man, but the direction is towards love and not fear. And that's really important for me.

It's about time men got the support that we need. And that doesn't come from a place of being like a woman, or being more effeminate, it comes from a place of being OK to be masculine. We've demonised the masculine, it has to stop. This is the masculine, the feminine, the men and the women together, fighting the patriarchy. And actually it's not even fighting, because fighting is what is wanted of us. It's about just saying no, all of us together, as one, just saying, 'Not anymore. No more. Fuck you.'

Thirty-eight years old

“It looks small in its flaccid state”

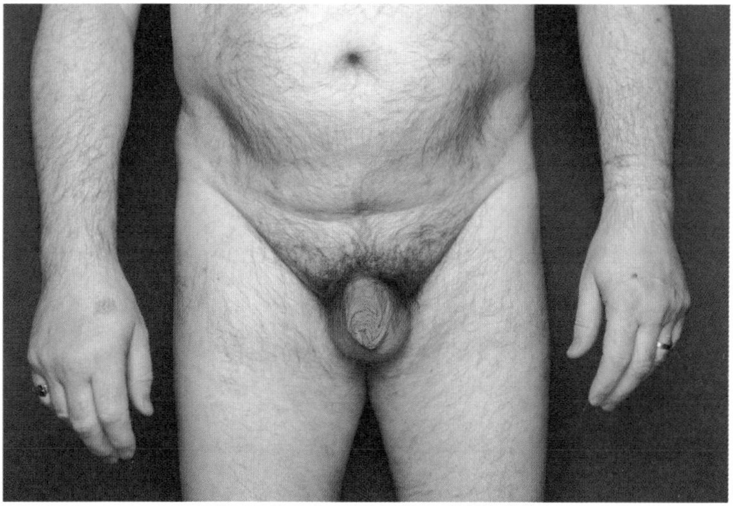

I remember seeing my dad walking from the bathroom to the bedroom wearing a very short dressing gown and nothing else and going, ‘Bloody hell, that looks big’, and then looking at mine and going, ‘And that looks very small.’ So I’ve always had this kind of inferiority complex. Feeling inferior made me feel a lot less confident around women. I was quite old when I lost my virginity. I have been married three times and none of my wives have complained, so...

I’ve had good relationships with all my wives and I think that I’ve proven that it works to their satisfaction and to my satisfaction and therefore it's not the issue that it was when I was young. I'm older now and have slowed down a bit sexually too, it's not as important in my life as it used to be.

I got married at 27. The fact that somebody, somebody much younger than me, was attracted to me and wanted to be married and all the rest of it helped me overcome my insecurity. It was a reasonably short-lived marriage, but my confidence grew.

I didn't know how to be married. I didn't know how to be a husband. Her father was very old-fashioned. We had to be engaged before I could take her to meet my parents, so we could stay away for the night together. And we had to be married before she was allowed to live with me. I think we both had a very romantic and idealised view of what marriage would be like and, of course, it wasn't like that. It wasn't that we fell out of love but... just irrational. If we'd had more experience, we could have stood back to take a look at things and maybe we would have carried on and had a long and happy marriage.

I've always been looking for a long-term relationship. I've never been interested in one-night stands. 'Is this somebody I could be in a relationship with?' has been a more important question than 'Can I get my leg over?' That makes me feel different from many men.

I'm not a big strong macho man in any way whatsoever. I'm not the guy who goes down the pub every weekend or goes to watch football matches, things like that. I've never really been involved in that sort of lifestyle. The closest was probably when I was in my 20s and would go to the gym or play squash. I'm not a big strong macho man in any way whatsoever.

I have a daughter, she's just coming up to seven. I don't want to be the father my father was. My father was a very good man; he made a huge difference to lots and lots of people's lives. He was a head teacher, he helped set up youth clubs, lots of activities, he was involved in Rotary clubs, things like that, but his focus was very external to the family. That's what I don't want to be.

I want to be there for my daughter. I was 52 when my daughter was born and at the back of my head it's like, 'OK, basically how old will she be when I go?' I want to make it as late as possible, knowing that there's a chance she'll be in her 20s or 30s when I go. That's a disadvantage of being an older dad. But on the other hand I have a more flexible lifestyle, I'm around a lot more. So I take her to school every morning, play with her every day, read stories to her at night. She sees a lot more of me than I saw of my dad.

Like most dads, I hope she meets someone who is going to look after her right, who is going to treat her properly. Someone she's happy with.

Fifty-nine years old

"I love stag dos"

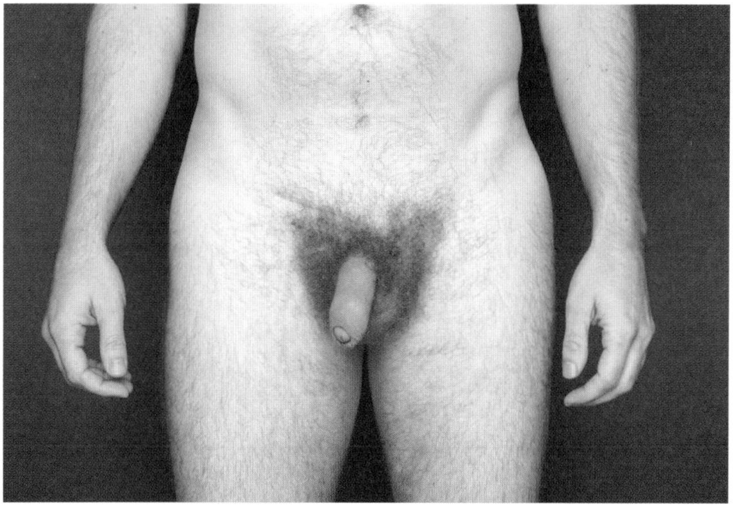

Some of the blokes I play football with are proper geezers. If they knew I was doing this, they would think it is the most ridiculous thing. Normally penises are comical and ridiculed, or sexy crotches in pants in ads. I don't know how we've got to this point. I mean, animals are naked, why are we so weird and nervous about it? I think as a bloke you desperately want your penis to be big enough. You worry that you won't satisfy a woman because you're not big enough. That's a huge thing.

I have a scar. When I was 11 I had a problem with one of my testes. Your balls can go up and down, and one of my balls went up and wouldn't come down. So that ball is now sewn into place. You know you can dress to the left or right? I have to dress to the right because the ball is sewn in the middle. It was the scariest thing in the world at that age having an operation on my nether regions. It looked very prominent before puberty helped me out. I was very conscious of it in the changing-rooms at school. At that age you look at other lads' penises to see how you measure up. In the end it turned out to be quite cool to have a scar.

I lost my virginity when I was 17 to a girl I'd seen several times on the bus. I saw her one night in a horrendous local nightclub and ended up going back to her place. I was very conscious of my scar, even then, so I tried to sort of cover it and not make it obvious. I desperately didn't want her to ask, 'God, what's that?' Actually, no one's ever said anything.

I don't remember too much about it, except it was pretty terrible. I was so nervous to be 'good' that I couldn't get fully erect. It was an underwhelming experience for both of us, certainly for her.

There was no one else in the house. About 8 o'clock in the morning there was a banging at the door, it was her stepdad. She'd forgotten she was supposed to go to her grandma's funeral. She was like, 'Oh my God, you have to get out of here, he'll kill you.' I'd been awake 30 seconds and I had to throw on clothes and run downstairs. He could see me through the frosted front door. 'You've got someone in there with you!' He couldn't get in, I think she'd bolted the door. I had to go out the back door and climb over the shed to get out the garden. I'd been awake about 40 seconds at this point. I was absolutely petrified.

I don't want to come across as too much of a lad – I'm quite a nice guy these days – but in my youth I had my moments. There was this one time I went back to this girl's house, and there was a tremendous amount of blood when we had sex. I was trying to be a nice bloke about it, saying I didn't mind. She was really embarrassed about it, and didn't understand how it happened. I cleaned myself up and was having a piss, and there was still lots of blood, and then I realised it was me! I'd torn my banjo string *(frenulum)* and it was hanging by a thread. I opened the door back into the bedroom, and she was 'Oh no, I'm so sorry,' and I said, 'It's not you, it's me,' kind of like we were breaking up or something, and we burst out laughing.

What had we been doing? I guess it had been a bit rough. I googled it afterwards and it's normally through rough sex. I was incredibly worried, but I didn't go to a doctor. It got bathed quite a lot, gentle caressing, checking it's OK. It healed.

I love stag dos. It's like being in your early 20s again: you've got no worries, you're allowed off the leash. You can eat pizza for breakfast if you want. Blokes are quite lazy and gluttonous: we just want to eat and go to the pub and laugh and laugh and laugh. I can't wait for stag dos, a whole day or a whole weekend of having a laugh!

You hear that men go on stag dos and have sex with prostitutes and don't tell their wives, but the reality is very different. I've been on about ten stag dos and I've only known one guy have sex with a prostitute. Not to sound too wishy-washy, but I can't see how it's attractive or a turn-on if the woman doesn't really want to do it. The whole point of sex is that you both want to do it. That's the attraction, and if that isn't there, I don't get it.

I think men's bodies are portrayed in a similar way to women's bodies in the media now. Not as much or as often, but it's the same thing. You only have to open up a broadsheet newspaper or a magazine and you see a close-up of David Beckham's crotch. I don't think there's too much talk about how women's bodies are objectified, but I think there's too little talk about how the same is done to men.

You can't help but be affected by it. I'm pretty comfortable with how I look, but I'll stand in front of the mirror side on and think, 'Yeah, I should probably go for a run.'

My girlfriend is a staunch feminist and has a following on Twitter. Some of my friends pick up on her writing and give me a gentle ribbing, just in a light-hearted way, the way blokes do. The weird thing is, it's made me much more aware of feminism. I've realised we are all more judgemental than we think.

She's had some horrendous comments and messages online. You just have to think of these people as keyboard warriors. I think they give her a tough time because they're struggling with changes in equality and society and they are venting their anger.

Thirty-five years old

“I got severe vertigo”

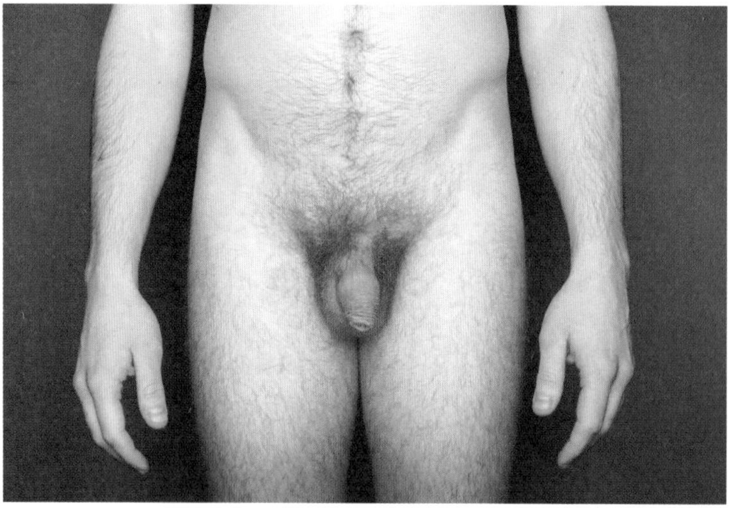

Part of connecting with masculinity is being able to accept and not feel shame. I thought this project sounded cool and I wanted to do it, but part of me felt a little bit uncomfortable, which made me think I should do it. Exploring the resistance is interesting.

I think masculinity is really challenged in the world. You ‘must’ be masculine. Masculinity gets so twisted and condensed and toxic.

Here is an aspect of femininity for me: the woman talks, because she wants to talk. They talk and talk and talk. It’s not for a reason. The reason is the talking. The man talks because he wants an answer. When making love, in my opinion, the woman wants to connect to God. She is having an act of love because she wants the man to connect her to God. The man's job is to do that, to have the consciousness that penetrates and connects. The woman has the power, and the man is the bridge that channels that power to the source. For me, the masculine doesn't have the power, it has the direction. When the two meet it's a fire and water locomotive. This is my experience.

My relationship with my cock has been interesting, it's changed a lot in the last few years. I went through a period when it was 'The cock and I', a disconnected thing. The cock was a device to give me pleasure and a way of disconnecting from reality. It used to be something that was in the dog house and I would bring it out every so often. *(laughs)* Over time there has been integration. I worked on my relationship to women and to sex and that improved my relationship with my cock. I now have a real love for my body, and my cock is part of that. Right now I feel really great about my cock.

I used to find life very overwhelming and I used sex to shut down and escape the over-sensory stimulation of work. At that time my girlfriend was doing the same thing, and it became an addiction for us. After that relationship ended, it was porn. Then I got really ill. It was nothing to do with my cock as such, but it's when I realised my life needed to rotate, and that is when my relationship with women really changed.

It was about four years ago when I got severe vertigo. My head had to be perfectly straight all the time, not a degree off, otherwise everything would spin. That went on for months. The health care team didn't know what to do, what would happen to me. I didn't want to leave this world, but it felt like that could happen. Just thinking about it now, it's so overwhelming and scary.

My belief is that working 70-hour weeks for 12 years caused it. I had to change the way I was. I think it was caused by trauma. In my case, there was a fear of survival. I grew up in Russia, and there wasn't enough money. I grew up with the fear of not enough money, and not being good enough, not being capable enough. Those fears drove me to work harder. A poor relationship with myself, and the world, and feeling unsafe, led me to work really hard. Being a man, using the tools available, being hyper-masculine.

I went to see a cranial osteopath and he sorted me out in two sessions – after thinking I was going to die! I realised there was something going on beyond science, that I didn't understand, and it was the beginning of my spiritual journey.

My questions were around purpose and integration. What is a healthy way of being? What is a happy way of being? I went on to do some healing courses, nutrition, shadow work, energy work, I went to the Esalen Institute, I got into something called DARE, Dissolve and Resolve Emotion, a pure form of energy work, like Reiki, but supercharged. It's blown my mind. I am a practitioner now. It's really advanced energy work, and now I can project and manage energy in my everyday life. Then I got involved with Constellations work.

Now I'm in a place where I have a really active business life, but at the weekends and in the evenings I have this other healing stuff going on. Unbelievably, the two are starting to integrate. I apply my energy work in business meetings. I feel like I am at a crossroads of finding integration.

In sex I am really vulnerable. When issues come up I have used sex to cover them. There was an occasion when my ex-girlfriend and I were kissing for ages and then, as I was about to enter her, all this stuff came up for me. I started wanting to say to her that I love her and she's the best thing that's ever happened to me, but I knew that wasn't really me talking, it was slimy and clingy. It comes from me being vulnerable and being afraid that women will leave me. I realised that all this lovely stuff I say comes from when my mum left me in the UK at boarding school when I was 13. I cried and my ex-girlfriend just held me. I realised that when vulnerability comes up I can choose how I deal with it.

I realised I really didn't like our sex though. I found her really frustrating. She wanted me to go down on her for hours and I was like 'I'm tired of this, I just want to have sex.' It challenged me because I thought I should really be able to do that, but on the other hand I was exploring my boundaries – 'What do I want in bed? And if I want the same thing all the time, what does that mean?'

After being together for three years my sex drive just disappeared towards her, it just evaporated. I had a big choice: do I split up with her and recreate this with the next woman, or do I explore this and try and make it better? I tried and tried, went deeper and deeper and kind of got some answers. I wanted to open up to love and sex, but I was exhausted. I knew I didn't need to go any deeper and we split up. It was frustrating, because I find her attractive and it was the best relationship I've had.

Thirty-one years old

“My partner was an escort”

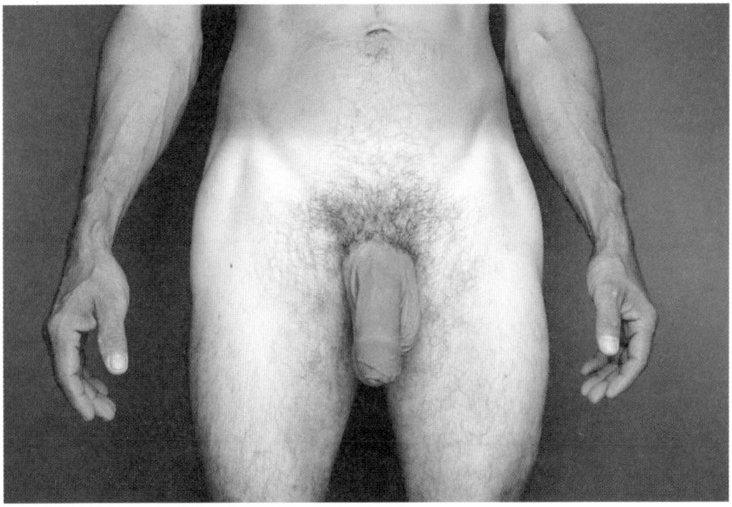

My cock is my favourite subject. It’s every man’s favourite subject! Every man likes to talk about it. But if you were a man with a very small penis then maybe you might be embarrassed about it. I am happy with mine. It’s a decent size. No matter what they say, every man has measured his cock. Erect, mine is eight inches long, with a six inch girth.

I watched a programme about a man with a micro penis and it was one and a half inches when erect. That’s unthinkable. It’s not even a penis anymore.

With the prevalence of porn, men have an unrealistic target. I don’t think men are honest with each other about penis sizes. Because of male bravado you wouldn't want to say if it bothered you. If you did come out and say you were worried about size, you'd be called 'John Small Cock' for the rest of your life down the pub.

I have three sisters. Women take so much time coordinating their nail varnish to their belt, and their handbag to their jewellery. Believe me, men do not think, 'Wow, she's coordinated three things!' We haven't even noticed. I think women dress for other women's approval. Men use drinking, being silly, or fighting for social standing.

Women definitely look to check out men's cocks. It's been proven in research with laser-tracking glasses. Men look at face, tits, minge, face. Women look at face, chest, cock, face.

My partner was an escort. It caused a lot of trouble between us. It still causes problems, really, even though she doesn't do it anymore. When you're having an argument you know what to bring up to really piss the other one off. It's hard for a man – even though you know it's only sex – to fall in love with someone who you know is going to fuck someone else. We met on a dating website, we can both view sex as just sex, and she has to be of that mindset to do that job. It got to the point when I would stay in and look after the kids so she could go out and do it. What annoyed me most is she is a very clever lady and has a degree, along with student loans she needs to pay off.

She's never going to say whether she enjoyed the sex or the cocks. I never asked her. I'm sure the reality for sex workers is that you're faking it. It's going to be life's flotsam and jetsam, your 18-stone car salesman.

I went on a job with her once. She visited this couple, right cokeheads, who work in the city. They wanted my partner to tie them up and whip them, just gentle, light stuff. Then the woman wanted a bit of bi with her, but he wasn't allowed to fuck her. She said it was a really easy night. They asked if she could come again and bring a male along for the woman. So she asked me if I'd like to do it. I said, 'Is she nice?' My partner said, 'Yeah, you'd fuck her all day.' It was great, the woman was lovely, early 50s, really good-looking, massive tits, looked after herself, spent all day at the gym. I got paid a couple of hundred quid. He wasn't that attractive, he was overweight and had a small cock.

It was funny, very amusing in some ways, but in other ways it was quite boring. I was banging the life out of her and looking at the plastering. My partner and the guy were having a conversation on the other side of the room.

I arrived, we talked for 20 minutes, and she went upstairs to take a line of coke. She then got a pack of cards out and said the one who pulled the lowest card had to take an item of clothing off. I thought we might as well all just take our kit off. Of course, I pulled the lowest card! So I'm standing there naked while no one else was. *(laughs)* Then she went off and came back in suspenders and everything. She wanted to dance, and I am not one of life's dancers. My partner was really trying not to belly laugh. She tried to get me to dance all the time and I wouldn't. I said a flat no, but she said she was paying me and I had to. She insisted she would teach me. I thought, 'What have I got into?' So, I'm naked, and she comes up behind me and says, 'It's like a clock face, we move from 12 to three, to six to nine.' It wasn't dancing, it was like a slow hula hoop! *(laughs)* My partner and I still laugh about the 'clock dance'.

Then the partner said, 'Right, let's get down to it.' He was paying £400 an hour, and he wanted to get on with it. The woman sucked us both off. I struggled a bit, because I was thinking my soft cock was bigger than his erect cock. It wasn't sexy, my mind was on that. Eventually he moved away a bit. Her and my partner had a little bit of a play, and then I got on with it. I gave her a bit of oral sex. I bent her over the kitchen table. While we were actually having sex my partner came over and said we only had five minutes left. No pressure then! Women are so tricky... She sounded like she had an orgasm, but I don't know. I asked her how she wanted it to finish and she wanted me to cum on her tits. Then we got dressed. 'Nice to meet you,' and off we went.

I won't judge anyone who does sex work. If I could do it, I think I would. Being a plasterer I kill myself doing very physical hard work for a couple of hundred quid. I get no pleasure from plastering, and I'd get a bit from sex work. I don't want to fuck the 18-stone woman. We could both earn a lot more money than we do now. There's probably quite a market for a couple doing it together.

I wasn't sure what I'd talk about today. I'm quite 'buildery'. As men we're told not to talk about feelings. Women are bred to be caring and talk. If men share they might get called a cry baby for the rest of their life.

Forty-three years old

"My body epiphany was the first time I ejaculated"

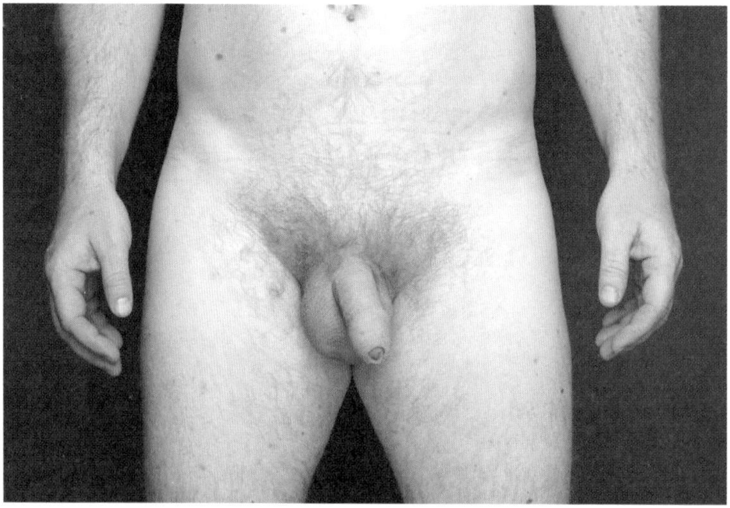

I call it a cock or a penis. I've been re-owning it and bringing some more sexuality and clear masculinity in recent years. We've had a good, long-term relationship. If my penis could say one thing to me, it would say, 'Let's play!'

When I was younger I would push against the skin as a form of stimulation to masturbate. It made my penis lopsided for a little while. When I first masturbated I didn't know what was going to happen. I'd do it with a full bladder, that felt like more of a turn-on. The first time I was going to ejaculate it felt like I needed to wee so I ran to the toilet, and what happened was a complete shock. I think I'd been told stories about ejaculation, I just didn't know what was going to happen. I imagined the seed coming out as more calm.

I did a course when you had to remember what your 'body epiphany' is, and that was mine – the first time I ejaculated. Your body epiphany moment is the first time you feel really embodied.

I had a Quaker upbringing. My parents had a journey in understanding their own sexuality. I was given quite a healthy space. My dad was particularly open about sexuality, there was an acceptance and lack of guilt. Quakers were very much about feminism and the empowerment of women.

I spent my youth being quite conservative really. I didn't have anything to rebel against. I'd go out with my friends and drink cider when I was about 15! I didn't do any drugs. I didn't visit a prostitute despite being curious about them.

I think the effect of testosterone is very distinctive. When men are around women they are attracted to, it increases their testosterone, which makes them more attractive to their partner. Just being around women – not having affairs with them – will make men more attractive. If a woman holds space for a man to flirt with other women, it doesn't mean he will leave her.

My feeling as I get older is that couples need to accept each other for who they are. Ideally we should love our partner's joy, be it in work, life, or their connections with other people. I once had two relationships at one time, but I think depth was lost. I was clear after that I wasn't looking for multiple relationships. I don't see the point of that.

There is something basically different in men and women. I have struggled after babies. I have two children and looking back I felt my testosterone go down with each baby. I think men need to be free to find that testosterone again, and that doesn't mean having affairs. I don't want to drop into stereotypes of what women might need, but maybe it's safety. I can create that, but not all the time. Ultimately the sense of safety has to be found within, as does the sense of freedom. You can't get something in a relationship that you haven't found within yourself. That's where pain comes from in relationships.

I like to make a conscious choice to orgasm and ejaculate. I like to talk about when I will orgasm. Just the reassurance that there is space for my orgasm means that I am less likely to snatch at it. Then I won't orgasm until it's time. I started doing this with people I was having casual sex with. Even the first time, I would say, 'When would you like me to orgasm?' Some women liked it, yes. Some though had very subtle ways of trying to create my orgasm. I think they were fundamentally trying to test me, make me orgasm. Men love seeing women have pleasure. I think some have seen it as a challenge to make me orgasm. There is an unconscious challenge to make me lose control and orgasm.

Now I am on a journey of trying to orgasm but not ejaculate. Orgasm and ejaculation are not the same thing. Sometimes I have sex or self-pleasure, maybe for an hour or two, without orgasming. Or I apply pressure against my prostate to stop ejaculation. Or to relax so much that I don't orgasm. The second is very challenging to do, and I've never managed it during sex. It takes a lot of relaxation of the body, but I have done it during masturbation.

Forty years old

"My limp penile size is now 50 per cent smaller"

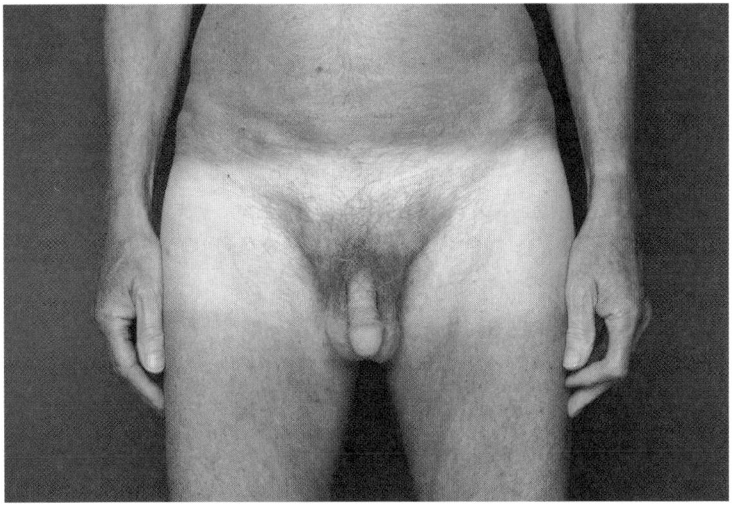

I used to be an anaesthetist, mainly in urology and gynaecology. I've seen more naked bits than the average man in the street. What you see is just part of the job.

I had to have a major operation for the prostate cancer, which comes with three downsides, one of which is incontinence. I was totally incontinent, although that's been fixed now with an artificial sphincter. When I had the operation my granddaughter was coming out of nappies – that really hurt in a strange way.

I used to go swimming at the leisure centre and there are communal changing-rooms. I didn't want my incontinence treated with bags, because my ego couldn't cope with people seeing that. I just used pads in pants and went through millions of them. It was very, very important to me to look normal in front of other people.

The second downside is that you lose penile size. The surgery takes away the support from the inside. My penis was average before the surgery, but my limp penile size is now 50 per cent smaller than it used to be. I'm a doctor and I've worked with urologists, so everyone assumed I knew everything and nobody warned me about this.

When you are told you have cancer you just want to deal with it. Incontinence, reduction in penis size, blah blah, they are less important. But perhaps we should be talking a little more about it. If someone had told me I would lose 50 per cent of my penis size, would it have stopped me from having the operation? Probably not. Who sees your limp penis? Very few people that matter.

More of a problem, the third downside, has been that surgery interferes with the physiological function of having an erection. There are three tubes in the penis that become engorged with blood and give you an erection. It is easily affected by surgery and radiotherapy. You will often end up totally impotent. That's quite hard to live with, especially if you're young.

There are drugs which can help you have an erection, but they only assist, they don't give you an erection. If your nerves are totally cut, as many men's are, then these drugs don't help. You don't lose sensation though. I learnt very quickly that you can have an orgasm with a limp penis. It's different, it's strange. You don't produce semen, it's a dry orgasm. In my case the orgasm would squeeze my bladder and I would wee all over the place. My wife was brilliant about it and we used to laugh. It was like a rampant hosepipe to be honest.

After 18 months I could get spontaneous erections. I have to assist them with Cialis. One of the blood-filling spaces doesn't fill, so I end up with an erection which is hard against my tummy. The penile head also doesn't fill with blood. So I have a soft head on top of a stiffish erection. I haven't been able to have penetrative sex since my operation. I can still have an orgasm though, and in a strange way it is more intense.

I've been through all of the treatments for sexual dysfunction. Mercifully, I have some nerve function. One of the treatments I have tried is injecting hormones directly into the base of the shaft of the penis. It's very important to get the dose right. Unfortunately I had an erection that wouldn't go down. It was embarrassing and incredibly painful. All of the time, because of my background, I was thinking of patients I had known, who had never been able to have an erection again after an experience like this. After a couple of months I tried an injection again, but the same thing happened. Fortunately I had early treatment and I am OK. I had to be aspirated. They suck the blood out of the penis. It takes about 20 minutes. I'm as well as can be expected now. I left everything alone, and in time I was able to get spontaneous erections.

We have mutual masturbation. Sex has to be more planned because I have to take a tablet, which takes 30 to 60 minutes to work. Sex is a very important part of my life and ego. I think I'm fortunate that I can have some form of sex life.

I feel concerned about what would happen if, God forbid, my wife died. No one else is going to look at me, a mildly emasculated man, as a long-term partner. Would it be unlikely I would find another partner, especially with the sexual dysfunction?

We used to do hysterectomies at the drop of a hat 20 years ago. Some people would sail through it. But it's not always straightforward and there are minor inconveniences. Some women would say they felt like less of a woman and you'd think, 'Well, what are you talking about, dear. We've taken away something carcinogenic, now get on with your life.' I can understand how they felt now. I don't need my prostate or seminal vesicles at this age, but it's not as simple as that. It's a good experience to see life on the other side of the fence, it makes you a more caring individual.

I'm someone whose glass is half full, not half empty. I fill my life with things that make my life feel good. I do talks now for Prostate Cancer UK. My wife says I like the sound of my own voice!

Sixty-eight years old

"I'd be wildly different if I'd had a good father figure"

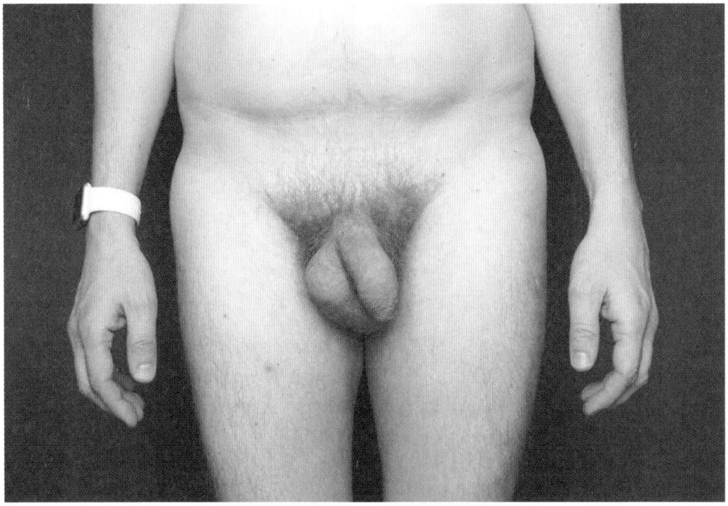

I wanted to support this project because my wife is in *Bare Reality*. I didn't even need to think about it, my immediate response was to say yes.

My earliest memories of my penis are feeling uncomfortable in the showers at school. I didn't know if my size was adequate, or if I was small. Even at the gym now I choose a cubicle, I don't change in public. I sometimes struggle with confidence. But I'm not micro-small, I feel blessed that I haven't had to worry too much.

My foreskin is quite tight. In the first few years of sexual activity, it was quite painful to get the hood back. Without knowing anyone to ask, it turned me off sex to a certain point. It would stress me out. I didn't know what was wrong.

I'd go back for another experience, and I'd orgasm, but it did hurt a bit. In the end I saw a doctor and he said it was very tight and I might need to consider circumcision. I didn't want to do that because of the discomfort and the healing time. A little baby won't remember, but... I used lubricant and it got better on its own. It's been fine now for 10, 15 years. You have to be persistent.

I don't really have a dad. I was born in the Ukraine and my mum and I went to Australia when I was five. My dad drank too much and she divorced him. Then she married another Ukrainian. We never got along. He wanted me to do maths and science, but I was more into arts and design. All my weekends had to be spent doing work around the house with him, rather than seeing my friends. He was verbally abusive, but not physically. If I didn't do my homework every night I had to write things out or stand in the corner. As soon as I turned 18 I left home.

My half brother and sister, his children, don't have anything to do with him anymore either. I think he's very lonely now. Lonely and stubborn. My mum and I are quite close. She eventually left him. She's a bit of hard work too, but in a good way. A bit fierce and Slavic. She's from a different world and mindset.

When I got to 25 I realised there was no point being angry at him, it's just who he is. I don't hate him. He was trying to do his best, in his way.

I'd be wildly different if I'd had a good father figure in my life. I would have had someone to talk to about sex, maybe gone on camping trips, someone would have shown me how to shave my face. I wouldn't have partied as hard, maybe saved up for a house. I try not to think about it.

I want to be nothing like my stepfather. My wife and I are much more 'loose' with our son. There's no bedtime – although my son is a nightmare about going to bed now – and we don't discipline him too much. We buy him what he wants. We're only going to have one though. We love and like him so much, we don't want another one, although it would be nice for him to have a friend at home I suppose. He plays with Lego non-stop. Sometimes that worries me a little bit! My brother is autistic, so I worry it could come through.

I take him on adventures – camping, castle hunting, big walks. He can do what he wants in his life, maths or art, whatever he wants. I think I'll be able to talk to him about anything, we both will. He can talk to me or my wife about sex, anything.

My son looks at my penis when I walk around naked. He's quite focussed on it. No one walked around naked when I was growing up, it was a very different environment.

When I was growing up I liked art, and didn't do sport, I was in the territory where people might think you were gay. I had friends who thought that about me, but I knew I definitely liked girls. I liked very masculine movies about war.

I've never had big muscles. I think men feel more pressure to be big now. Internet porn has skewed perceptions about body size. All the men are muscly now. Everyone I knew in Australia used to watch internet porn.

I haven't used porn for years. My wife wouldn't like it now and so I wouldn't out of respect. I don't have any need. Sex is quite minimal at the moment; we have a young child, and we're tired. There isn't a big sexual aspect to my life at the moment.

Thirty-nine years old

"I think the penis is beautiful"

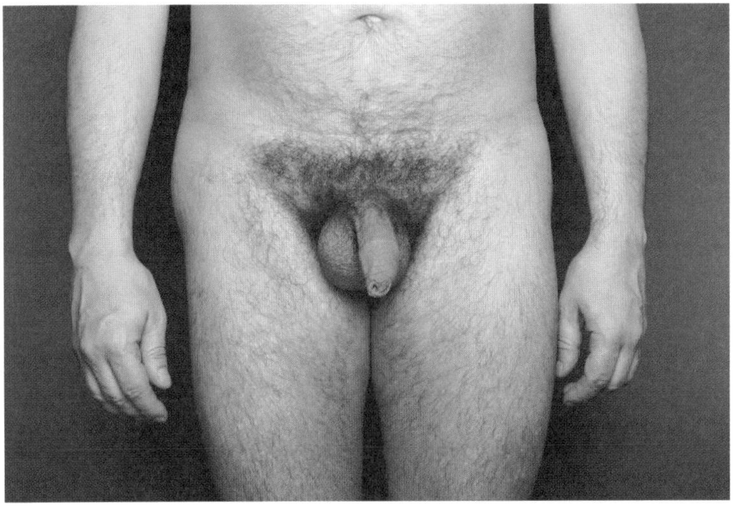

I am a performer, writer and poet. When I perform my poetry sometimes I choose to be naked.

I do a lot of my performance work naked because I write about sexuality and intimacy. I am often billed as 'The Naked Poet' because I am the only one in London. I'm not doing it for the sake of it, there is a consistency between what I say and how I present it. Poetry is intimate and personal so, in a way, the natural way to do it is naked. It adds a vulnerability. Although some people see the body and then have a reaction and they can't hear the words. Very rarely, someone leaves the room.

When I first started performing I would start naked, but I learnt that people react to the nudity and can't hear anything I say. Some people take a while to get used to it. Now I start dressed, they get used to me and my words, and they decide whether they like me. Then I get naked and they can make their judgement again.

When I am performing all the blood goes to my head because I am concentrating and my penis is smaller. People judge that and think I am small. Only rarely has anyone said anything about my penis size during the performance. I have had a comment that it is too soft and small. When I saw photographs of myself performing I thought it would be nice to be fuller and bigger! But it's not the point of why I perform. I'm not a porn actor, I'm not a sex worker, I am using my body as a tool to communicate. I don't have to have a massive member!

We live in a male-dominated society. There is a heterosexual male dominance in art. For instance, in most art galleries, most nudes are of women, but created by men. Women have been brought up to fear the male body, to have the averted gaze. Heterosexual men are not interested in the male body and women are taught to fear it. If you go back to the art of Ancient Greece there were penises everywhere. We are so used to hiding it we feel like there is something wrong there. Dolls have no bits. Penises are erased – it is a mutilation.

I'm OK with mine, I like it. I think that in general the penis is beautiful. Of course, some are more beautiful than others, just as with eyes, noses and hands. I like a proportionate penis, not too big or small. Actually, I like a variety of penises! I tend to prefer them uncut, but cut can be very beautiful too. I like an average-size penis, uncut, nicely proportioned scrotum, with lots of nice black pubic hair. Or blond. I'm not fussy! I like pubic hair a lot.

Men's beards are fashionable now. There is a reverse trend because a man might have a fantastic beard and then everything else is shaved. 'Come on, you're selling me something and then it's not there!' It's bizarre when people shave their pubes. They have this idea that it's cleaner, but it increases your risk of sexual diseases and infection. We've been sold this idea that we have to be clean and 'beach ready'. But everyone is ready, and there is a purpose to hair. I think it is a shame that women have to shave their armpits. But imagine all the products that are sold because of just that?

It's a real thing now about shaving the body. Not all men do, luckily, but many do. I like men to be men. One of the things that separates men and women is that men have chest hair, so it is disappointing for me when a man is hairy, but I know he shaves. It also makes adults looks infantile, like children. I think the trend comes from porn. When women shave their pubic hair they look like young adolescents.

In my opinion the majority of people don't mind nudity, don't complain and don't care what the laws are. It's a small vocal minority who are against it. I would like it to be more normalised. It would be good for people's mental health. And a lot of the things we are sold are based on making us feel bad about how we look. So there is an economic interest in us being covered up and feeling bad about how we look. I think anorexia has something to do with it as well, although it is more complicated than that.

Toplessness is not as common in the UK for women as it is in the rest of Europe. There is no equality between men and women around the upper part of the body. It doesn't make sense logically. Different cultures treat breasts differently. Here in the UK you are very unlikely to see a woman with her top off in a park. You wouldn't see a topless woman in Hyde Park. Even though it's not illegal people would probably complain and the police would come. Whereas in Spain, where I am from, there would be no issue in an area where people are sunbathing.

But genitalia, especially male genitalia, are still taboo. I can't imagine the reaction if you put penises on the cover of this book. Some friends and I went swimming in the river. We were all topless, the men and the women. I decided to be naked, which for me is the equivalent of a woman being topless in terms of social taboo. Women showing their boobs was lovely, fantastic, but the feeling of a man showing his penis was very tense and uncomfortable.

Forty-nine years old

"My son is going to have a hurdle that I didn't have"

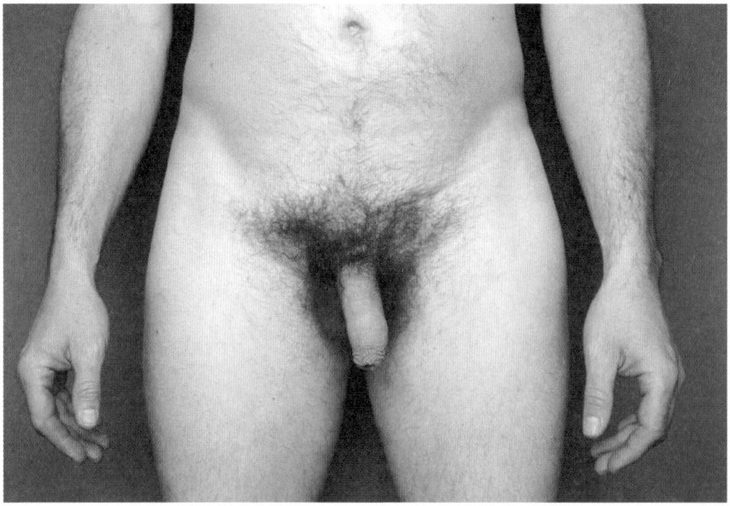

My wife talked me out of asking men I know at the gym to take part in this. One friend was up for it, but his girlfriend vetoed it. She owns that champ now, it's not for sharing. *(laughs)*

My wife wouldn't have stopped me doing this. I think she thought it was a 'classic' for me. Not that I expose myself normally! It's just me doing another wacky thing. But when I spoke to her about asking other people, a look came across her face that suggested she had more reservations than she had voiced. She's definitely glad this is anonymous.

I'm very happy with my penis. It's never been a source of embarrassment; I've never been shy about it. I fit the cultural stereotype of a nice body. I'm a gardener so I keep fit. Over the winter I wasn't getting much exercise so I joined the gym.

The first time I remember being conscious of showing my penis in public, I must have been 11 or 12, in the showers at school. I remember pulling on it a bit, getting a bit of blood into it, trying to give it a reasonable showing. I remember a kid who had a small penis would get laughs by putting sweets in the end of his foreskin, spinning a negative thing into attention.

Sex education can't have been very good at my school, because I remember playing with myself in my room at home, and being shocked and scared when I came for the first time. I went downstairs to my mum and dad, who were watching TV, to tell them what had happened, to ask if it was supposed to happen. *(laughs)* They were dead embarrassed and basically ignored it.

Nowadays I guess kids see everything on the internet. I think that's not a good thing at all. Partly because discovering little bits of porn is titillating. If it's just there in all its myriad forms and vivid detail on the internet, I think that spoils porn and must corrupt early sexual experience. I think it should be harder to access porn. At least it would make it special!

I like porn. I always have. I remember finding a mag at a train station. It has its problems, and people get addicted to it. I think it's similar to violence on TV. I think it's terrible that they'll happily show horrific violence in films to teenagers, but they won't show boobs or sex. To me it's the other way round, you should not show violence and you should show sex. Our indulgence in violence is not healthy. Maybe we have so much violence because we're puritanical about sex.

This project is only capturing one state of the penis. I think that's significant. Some people will be growers and some will be showers. You'd be straying into different territory, but I think you should photograph erections.

I had a massage the other day from a beautiful young lady and I was worried I would get a hard on. But because it was so contextualised it wasn't sexy and I didn't get an erection, so I think it would be hard for people to get an erection in this situation.

I wanted to take part in *Manhood* so I could mention hypospadias. It's not much talked about, but it's quite common. It's where the penis is attached to the testicles. My son has it. There are operations for it, but it's a big deal. There are Facebook groups for parents. My son is going to have a hurdle that I didn't have. I'm actually proud of my penis, whereas he is going to have a stumbling block to get over when he first gets naked with a man or woman. His is fused pretty much all the way to the helmet. He's had one operation, which went OK, but he's going to need another one. It's tough from a parent's point of view. Penises are so linked to our psyche. Language says it all, we call a penis our 'manhood'.

We don't think about it a lot because he's only two, but we have bridges to cross. We want to do our best to make him love-orientated. I'm sure he'll suffer for it emotionally, maybe be taunted, but we have to give him the resilience and strength to deal with it. There are also risks with the surgery, there always are, which is another worry.

In some cultures the penis is highly thought of and displayed more, a symbol of power and fertility. We still have Victorian repression and reserve, cultural taboo. We are a product of our environment. What's good about this book is that the more you talk about something, the more everyday it becomes and the freer you are.

I think that something that is lacking in our culture is a rite of passage from adolescence to manhood. In tribal cultures there is always a rite of passage for women and for men. We don't have that in our culture. The Scouts are good for that, and Youth Leaders. I can see that a lot of young men struggle with the feelings they get from testosterone. As a young man, you feel you are supposed to be someone that people should look up to, but we're not told how to wield our power and earn that respect.

There is a power in manhood – the male is more powerful than the female. But that power is a soft power, and it's not about dominating; it's about driving ahead, not pushing down. We don't seem to have good role models in popular culture.

Having a son and a daughter has really inspired me to be the best person I can and explore everything. I want to be the best I can be and give them the tools to be the best people they can be.

Forty-one years old

"I've liberated myself"

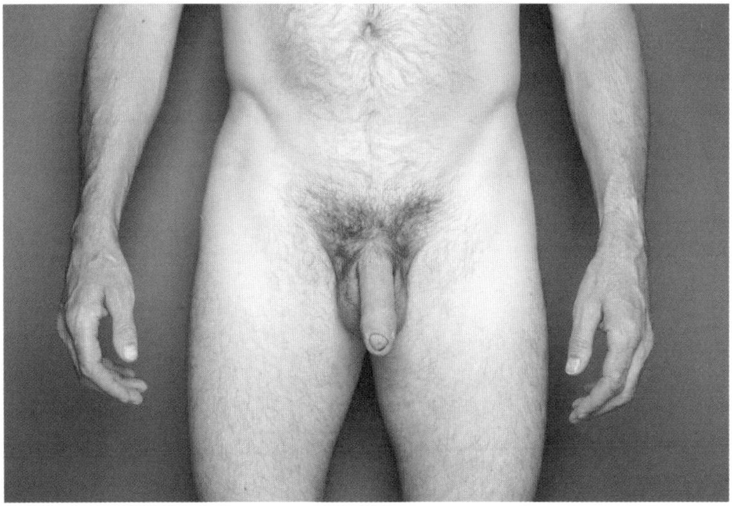

Up until eight years ago my relationship with my penis was not good. It was the source of insecurity and affirmation that I was not good enough. I always had this unconscious belief that I was too small, which fed into a feeling of inadequacy in my whole life.

I never had any complaints from women, it was all psychological, inside my head. A lot of fear emanated from the school showers. When you're anxious and scared everything contracts. If I had given myself a quick fluff I would be semi-erect and then I would be open to being labelled as gay, which was the worst possible label that one could have been given at that point. Thank God things have advanced now. Well, I hope they have. I haven't been in a school changing-room for a long time.

I'm taking part in this to help educate young men that air-brushing is just as common in the schoolboy changing-rooms as it is in the glossy magazines of today for women. Boys airbrush in the changing-rooms with bravado and talk and comparison.

Also my sex education predominantly came from porn, where everybody had huge cocks and that formed the basis of terrible insecurity. The other misinformation porn peddles is the pounding, speed and power. Faster, friction-based sex has its moment in a love-making process, but there is a huge spectrum that is not portrayed in porn. There is an awful lot of Viagra in porn. And also the men selected for porn movies are selected primarily because they aren't your average men, they have abnormally large penises.

Youngsters need to be able to reference honest cock sizes and shapes. I think as well as this project, what's screaming to happen next is showing flaccid and erect penises. Young kids with smaller flaccid penises need to see that it doesn't necessarily reflect the size of erect penises. That will potentially take away a lot of bullying.

Because I felt inadequate, basically because I thought my penis was too small, I also developed macho behaviour, aggressive behaviour. I now realise that something I did a lot was attack others before I was attacked. How would I put it? I developed a more superior, grandiose, false way of being to cover the fact that I felt insecure. And I suppose, yeah, fast cars and lots of money could enhance that sense of superiority.

I stopped drinking 11 years ago and I've gone through a whole process of conscious development. I've looked in depth at what was causing me to live a life of bravado. My body image, relationships and love-making have completely changed. I now experience sex with feeling, heart-centred, heart-connecting, feeling the whole body rather than just the genitals. Emotion merges with physical sensuality. Once that has been experienced the old friction-based pounding concept of porn seems ludicrous.

Part of my personal process was to stop arousing myself with images and arouse myself with sensation and feeling and connection. In other words, being present with a person and staying in the moment rather than fantasising about something that's not real. Porn is not real in any way, shape or form. And the more you really listen to it, the fakeness is so blatantly obvious.

I got into Tantra and also started training in the field of sexuality. I trained as a sexological bodyworker. Through that work I realised that I was perfectly average, normal, nothing wrong at all.

I work with people to help them overcome blocks. The blocks could be from anything, such as religiously-induced shame, religious indoctrination, or trauma-based, rape or incest, or around physical scars, scar tissue. I'm really interested in helping people liberate themselves from negative belief systems that are not even their own in a lot of cases. I feel cautious talking about it, because there is a lot of shame-based bigotry.

I liberated myself over the last eight years so I'm a good person to be able to help other people liberate themselves.

Forty-nine years old

"It's really hard to be a man sometimes"

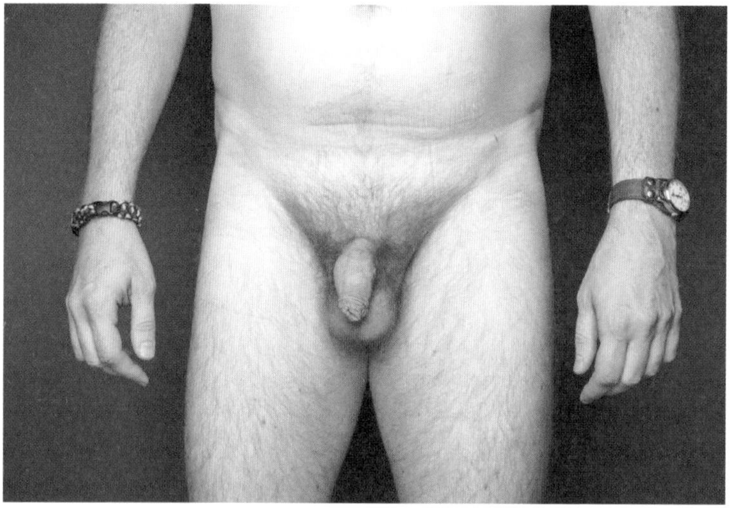

I had the world's biggest mental breakdown. During this time I started seeing the work I was doing as wrong. I had to give it up because it went against my principles. It's funny, but I never thought I had principles. I thought if I was offered sufficient money then I'd do any job.

I was working for a publisher that made brochures about army recruitment. I would go to army bases and interview people. If I was working on a brochure about officer recruitment, I would interview an officer about leadership, that kind of thing. I became more and more interested in what made them tick, what was happening in their lives before they joined the army. I felt like a father confessor to a lot of people. I spent a long time with them and they would open up. I was made party to some things that were really disturbing. They were people with Post Traumatic Stress Disorder. I realised that the idea of the army that I was selling didn't really exist. It's like putting sand in an axel. It runs fine for days, maybe weeks or months, but eventually it breaks. The final straw for me was a young man telling me he imagined he could see dead bodies at a petrol station at home, after he came back from Afghanistan. I was selling something to people I would never do. It was just bollocks.

Masculinity says you don't talk about stuff. If you have PTSD you are locked up with it. People with PTSD kill themselves to remove themselves from the pain. It's part of the price of being male.

I've been right up to the edge of suicide. I've been minutes away from doing it. I've been sufficiently close to not judge anyone for it. It gets too much for some people. I'm happy to talk about when I was suicidal. I think it's important.

After leaving that job I felt like I didn't have a role. There was an anguished search for how to make money. That search is ongoing – I sporadically make money as a writer. I had relationship problems. Why didn't I just take myself out of society altogether, because I was so fucking useless? Near where I lived there was a railway line. My plan was to stick my head on the railway line and be decapitated. It's important that people understand that suicide ideation doesn't come just once. Once you've had the thought it doesn't go away. I think I will always be aware that suicide is there.

I'd like to say it was thinking about my loved ones that stopped me doing it, but it was just cowardice.

My ex-girlfriend tried to take an overdose once. I stopped her. I went for a wee and found her in the bathroom with a box of paracetamol. I did all the things you're supposed to do. But then, afterwards, you have to be in the house on your own. It felt like suicide was running close to me.

I'm not spiritual in the New Agey clanging bells and finding angels way, but I found God. After the breakdown I needed something to repoint my compass and I found an evangelical church. It was very much about emotion and very little about thinking. They would worship for half an hour with very euphoric songs, arms in the air, giving it for Jesus, then you'd hear a sermon. You go away from the church feeling you are on fire for Christ. Your language becomes the same as the people around you. Instead of saying I was thinking about something, I'd say, 'This is on my heart.' If something happens, it's because God is good. If something bad happens, it's because you didn't pray hard enough. It was like a cult. I was involved with it for a couple of years, very much on fire for Jesus, very unbearable, very mad.

Then, bizarrely enough, I got called for jury service. I thought, 'I can't do this, I'm mad.' I told them I had major depression. They didn't care, I had to do it anyway. I didn't think it was a great idea. Jury service is quite intense, so it made me take a break from the evangelical church, and whatever hold they had over me waned. I decided not to go back. I had already been baptised by this point, full immersion, blah blah, fucking mad.

I contacted a United Reform Church vicar for some advice. She said, and these were her words, 'That's fucking mental.' So I went to her services and they were 100 per cent less mental. I'm not sorry I experienced all of it. It was interesting. But I'm fucking glad it's over.

It's really hard to be a man sometimes. I'm 6ft 3in and I look like a rugby player, but I'm just not that big bonking guy. I cry at stuff. I have cuddly toys in my bedroom. Ten years ago I thought I had to apologise for that, but now I'm OK with it. Society is changing. It has left men without a value system. I don't think feminism should rewind, it's great, but there needs to be a way for men to say it's hard for us, that we hurt. That should take place away from feminism.

When you get single-sex groups of men you can pretty much divide the IQ in half. I went to a 'men's weekend' with the church. It was all cigars around the fire pit. Not me at all. Men need single-sex groups, but I'm not remotely interested in the ones I've seen.

I wasn't sure I could talk about this... It's about sex. It's embarrassing, but liberating to talk about it. I have had mild transvestite leanings ever since I went through puberty. I went through the whole of secondary school wanting to wear what the girls were wearing. OK, let's call this a moderate transvestite leaning.

Stuff that you wear day to day is dull. It's a uniform. I'm not remotely interested in make-up but I like a skirt and a nice top. If I had my time again I would be a women's shoe designer. Women's shoes are gorgeous. Airing that idea at my school would have got you beaten up.

Growing up in a mining town and going to a really fucking violent comprehensive school was lonely. There was a guy who was kicked until his kidneys split. Someone had 'scab' gouged into his forehead with a compass at school because his dad was a scab. I want to go back in time and give my

13-year-old self a hug. He was so lonely and so confused and so sad.

My big passion is tights and hosiery. Putting on panties and tights feels brilliant. I have a girdle and stockings. I really like wearing a suspender belt. If you are wearing panties you can see your penis bulge and pull them down and masturbate.

Because it feels sexual, I don't know if this is classic transvestism. I do feel comfortable wearing women's clothes to sit around and watch TV, but I also like to wear women's clothes and wank.

I think wearing women's clothes is linked to surrendering power, being voluntarily disadvantaged, because femininity is seen as disadvantaged. It's about being passive. Wearing high heels, spending time putting on suspenders and stockings, is about being passive. That's where I want to be.

My current partner is understanding. The best sex I ever had was lying face down on the coffee table being abused. Being at the whim of someone else is incredibly hot. I'm not sufficiently clever to know whether this is about power and the patriarchy, or whether I just enjoy it.

I like having a cock and balls and I'm happy to be a bloke.

Forty-three years old

“It would be silly to die of something preventable”

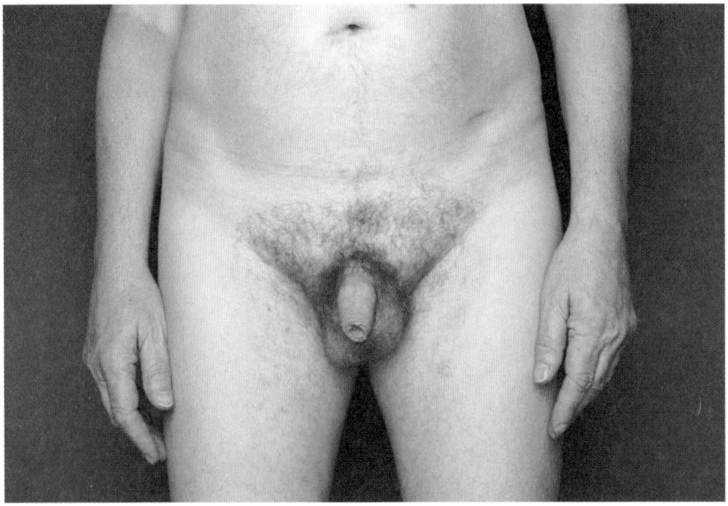

The conventional wisdom is that men don’t like to talk about things, and that they are suffering and even dying because they don’t talk about this part of their body. It’s good to be less inhibited and talk about this part of our lives.

I don’t know how true it is that men don’t talk though. I go to a cancer support group occasionally. Some men don’t shut up, they just keep yakking. Others don’t want to talk at all.

My father had prostate cancer. It didn’t kill him. I’ve always been aware and felt it would be very silly to die of something preventable if you didn’t have your eyes open. I've had my PSA checked all through my life at company medicals.

My PSA jumped around a bit and so I had a biopsy. They found a possible precursor to prostate cancer. Then the PSA jumped right up and I had another investigation. They recommended I took the prostate out. I thought about leaving it and opting for active surveillance, but in the end, with very good advice, I had a radical prostatectomy. That is the gold standard for living the longest, but there are side-effects. You can have urinary incontinence, sexual dysfunction and there are other unpleasant possibilities.

When they removed the cancer it wasn't actually as serious as they thought, which was a bit of a disappointment! We knew it was relatively small, about the size of a pea, but it was a less serious grade of cancer.

In terms of healing, it has been better than I expected. Sexual dysfunction is still a problem, but I'm no good to anyone dead, so we have to live with that part of it. I've had erections, but I haven't been able to maintain them. I have sexual dreams and occasionally wake up with erections, which is a healthy sign. Drugs like Viagra have had no effect on me at all, they just made me feel queasy. Apparently that's not that unusual. Things are going in the right direction, albeit very slowly.

I think about 40 per cent of men are not able to get an erection by normal means after a prostatectomy. I also think my penis looks a bit smaller since the operation.

My wife and I have adapted. There is no diminishment in our relationship. We keep trying. It is the second marriage for both of us, we didn't have our children together, and this is our first big challenge. You can still have a normal loving relationship, holding each other, being kind, being loving.

One positive is it's not going to kill me. Yesterday I had a little bit of backache. Now, if I hadn't had it taken out I would have wondered if the cancer had spread. My hypochondria would be worse.

It's amazing when your child is passed to you and you realise there is no one but you two to look after this little person. Family live close by. I have just become a grandfather. It brings back a lot of memories. The little boy is so like his father when he was a baby it takes me right back to that time. Seeing his little smiling face is so uplifting. It really feels like this new life has given me new energy in my own life.

Sixty-six years old

“Find the king”

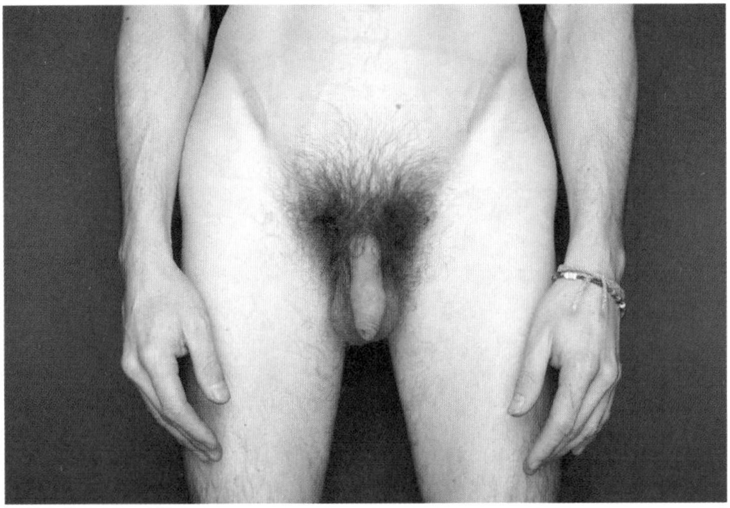

I definitely felt nervous about taking part in this, but it seems like a really good opportunity to support people who are coming into self-acceptance and loving themselves. I’ve been through my own journey of that.

I feel very grateful for my body. I’ve got a very healthy body and it’s never needed a lot of maintenance. I am always physically fit and well. Despite that, until I was 24 I didn’t like to be seen naked at all, even with my partners; it was like get undressed, move to the bed in boxers, and get in the bed quickly.

I was at a festival and a friend persuaded me to use a naked sauna called Lost Horizons – it travels around to different festivals. You don't have to be naked, it's 'clothes optional'. Part of me wanted to keep my boxer shorts on, but I also, for the first time, just wanted to embrace being naked and express myself. So I did. And I did naked yoga. It was a completely liberating experience for me to be naked in that collective space. I was with maybe 50 other people all just being naked and enjoying it. There's something so liberating about being naked.

So, nudity is a new and beautiful thing for me. It's about being free of restrictions, not telling myself that I'm not beautiful enough, not perfect enough, that I don't look good enough, or that I'm being judged by others. It means I don't tell myself that my willy isn't big enough, or it's a weird shape, or I haven't got enough pubic hair. Not listening to that voice is liberating. Being naked means I accept myself.

I'm not at 100 per cent acceptance, but maybe at 98 per cent. Definitely really high.

I had a massive transition in my life when I embraced my nudity. I got asked to work as a part-time pixie! I'm paid to go to events to entertain kids with bubbles and music and glitter and silliness and unicorn races and parachute games and hide and seek – all the beautiful, fun, creative things that come from playing with children in that environment. I embrace my inner child.

It's never too late. The reality is that your inner child is always there, it just takes some listening to, or some time to really feel into what it is. I was a very playful child. Actually I could be quite a brat. I think I was just crying out for attention.

My dad is the epitome of a man who doesn't show his emotions. He doesn't like to hug. I do hug him. I forcefully hug him. I'm like, 'Come on, dad, give us a hug.' But probably nine times out of ten he'll say, 'Oh, I'm not a good hugger.' He doesn't know how to show his emotions. I feel that when men come together and talk we can integrate our emotions and then be true in our actions as well.

I think it's wonderful for men to try and find the king within themselves. He's the graceful king, the king of honour and truth and justice, not of ego, domination and power. Being in touch with your inner king can bring you peace. I implore men reading this to talk to their fellow men, share and be honest. Find the king.

Thirty-one years old

"I use nudity as a metaphor for honesty"

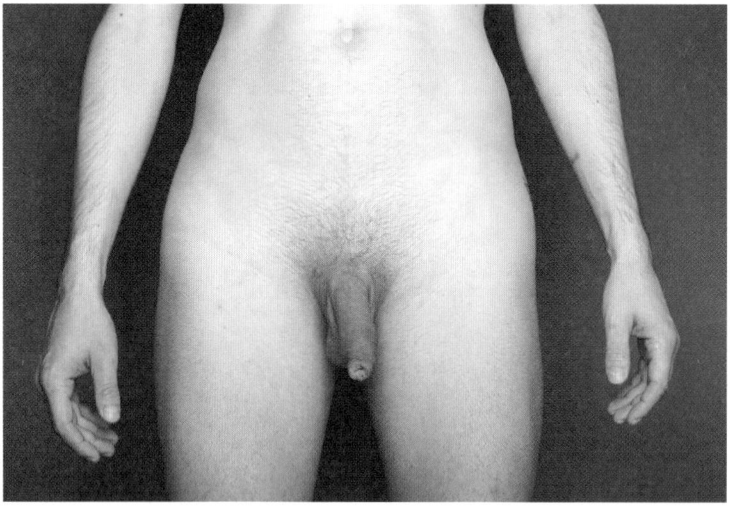

I feel good about my penis. I never had the typical worries in puberty, I never worried if it was big enough.

I produce daily nude self-portraits. I use nudity as a metaphor for honesty and transparency. Nudity is always somehow charged with multiple layers of meaning. An art dealer told me I should describe my work as post-pop conceptual realism. *(laughs)* What's that supposed to mean? Art speak always sounds pompous and deep. You have to speak that way if you want to be part of the art world. I studied philosophy and I have no idea what art dealers and curators are talking about.

I set out to take a daily photograph as it challenges me to think of a concept every day. Since this is about total honesty I should tell you that sometimes I take five self-portraits a day. Sometimes I skip a day, but it averages about once a day. The best ideas are the ones where I think, 'Oh no, I can't do that, that's too much, too crazy, too whatever.' Those are the ones I have to do!

This work has helped me to be more self-confident and also more vulnerable in everyday life. Being naked in photography helps me to be less shielded in life. I find it easier to admit my shortcomings and when I make a mistake.

I thought about having erect penises in the photography. Erections are totally frowned upon in life-modelling. You're an object to look at and depict, but a non-sexualised object. The common definition is that an erection makes a picture porn. But I felt that an erection was called for in some of my self-portraits. An erection can symbolise a sense of power, and sometimes I want to use that. Sexual power can be a surrogate for actual power. I didn't want to exclude erections. They do exist, so why not show them?

I have to get into a sexual mind-frame to take an erect self-portrait. I am more in my head, funnily enough, for the photo.

My partner used to be a photographer and has no problem with the project. She is honest and probably gives me the most unkind feedback! She tells me if something isn't good enough.

I mostly have a positive reaction to the work. People think it is 'brave' for some reason. I made the mistake of reading the comments under an article about my self-portraits and one man said I did this 'just to get a date.' *(laughs)* Yeah, let it all hang out to get a date...

I was depressed, very down, when I first had the idea to take self-portraits. Being creative kept me busy, motivated me, and was one of the main factors in coming out of my depression.

I think that my creativity is linked to my work as a life coach. I like asking questions and finding meaning, understanding what deeply resonates with us. I can help people discover themselves. My nude self-portraits are a metaphor for facing my own truths, not just on the surface but on a deeper level. I stand naked in my own truth.

I want to understand life in a deeper way and experience it intensely.

Forty years old

"My penis is a tiger"

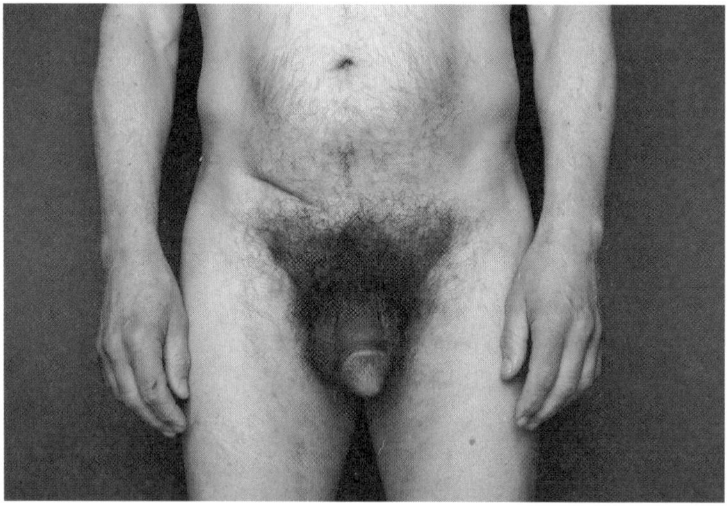

Normally I'm quite shy, especially when it comes to my sexuality. I'm an artist and I recently started painting abstract female nudes. I think passion, sensuality and sexuality are becoming more important for me. I'm getting in touch with them instead of avoiding them.

I like my penis. I certainly feel very comfortable with it. It's been a wonderful part of my life. I understand from women that it's a nice size.

I have always called it my penis, but recently I have a new name for that part of my body. My partner and I describe our respective genitalia as tigers. Tigers tend to be solitary creatures, roaming around the jungle until they meet one another and then something happens, if they are male and female. They really love to be with one another and in one another and around. It's natural, harmonious, and at the same time passionate and wild. And then, you know, it goes back to being a solitary tiger for a little while.

I am Jewish and circumcised. I didn't really think about it until I had my son, and thought, 'Oh well, he needs to be circumcised,' just as a part of being a boy. But the mohel, that's the rabbi that does the circumcision, didn't want to do it because his mother's not Jewish and therefore the boy is not Jewish. He refused to do it. So I thought, 'Oh, OK, well maybe that's not a bad thing.'

I didn't really have a choice when I was circumcised and maybe I would like to have had. He can choose to have it done if he wants, but I don't think he will. I'm OK with being circumcised. My parents did it automatically as part of their culture.

Is sex better for me because I'm circumcised or not? Is it better for the woman or not? Jews put forward these sorts of arguments for the advantages of circumcision, but how real is that?

For the most part, I think I am a very involved, caring parent. Sometimes maybe too involved, but that is probably over-compensation for the lack of involvement of my own parents. My father, you know, he came from a very wealthy German Lithuanian family and was brought up by a nanny. He married my mum when he was in his 50s so he was an older father and very involved in his business. He was completely detached. He thought bringing up the children was my mother's business, but she was hands off because of her upbringing. Nannies looked after me and my brother, but essentially they followed Dr Spock, you know, the famous American paediatrician, to the letter. Basically that involved leaving the child alone to do what they want, which, in many ways, was wonderful for me. However, as I grew I up I realised this was very different to most of my friends. So then I didn't feel normal.

Many people were inspired by the book that he wrote on how to bring up children, but they probably had some kind of instinct that said, 'OK, if your child is crying, or doing this or that, you really need to intervene', and they probably did that instinctually, but my parents didn't have that instinct. I was brought up strictly according to the book. Spock wrote an apology several years ago for the damage his book caused and published it in many newspapers.

Fifty-nine years old

“My first kiss was when I was out with my gang”

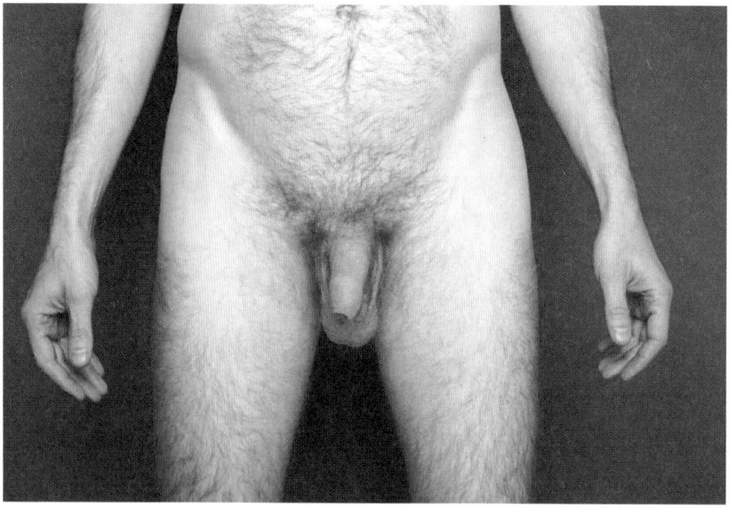

Where I went to school the male teachers were a bit strange. They were a bit pushy about you getting naked for showers, and some of them would shower with the lads. Looking back it was a complete no-no. One of them always used to scratch his balls in class and you'd see his pubes. I think it was deliberate. When I think back it makes me feel a bit angry that he got away with it. He was sort of flashing to us, I guess. Back then things were different, there was corporal punishment, all kinds of things.

I got strapped when I was seven, for some minor infringement. I think an older boy had told me if I threw jelly it would bounce up, and I fell for it. The psychological torture, the waiting, was worse than the physical pain. Getting strapped was just a stinging really. I was strapped three or four times, from 7 to 14. It was a Catholic school. I think a Catholic priest is more likely to do damage than a man who has permission to have a normal sex life. If you're not supposed to have sex, or masturbate, where does all that energy go? Or maybe certain types of people are drawn to being priests.

The old way of bringing up boys, the socialisation of boys and men, whereby you are not really supposed to express your feelings much, ends up with men doing odd things, and those energies can come out in other ways which are unhealthy, in violence, or sexually. It's more acceptable for women to express themselves emotionally; they are more integrated, more whole. Men are more fragmented and disconnected from parts of themselves. I express myself artistically. If I didn't I would go mad. Talking and expression are a big part of healing.

I'm from a very big family. You had to shout the loudest to get what you wanted. I made a choice early on not to do that. That was the wrong choice. The right choice would have been to try harder. It was inevitable I didn't get what I needed. I became more introspective. I lived in my head in a bit of a daydream world, distant from reality. I slipped into a big depression that affected me from 17 to 21. It wasn't particularly treated or managed, and it wasn't public. I was suicidal at times.

When you go through puberty and adolescence you just hope you are going to come through it a 'man'. The town I grew up in was a very white, working class, northern town, a dole town, not much work. There were lots of fights. The talk in schools was who's the 'Cock of the Year', who's the hardest. Which lad could beat up any other lad in the year was a constant conversation. People had a bloodlust for fighting. It was the early 1980s and there was a lot of gang fighting. Being physically strong, being a fighter, being big: that was valued. Being creative, intelligent or academic was not valued.

My last fight at school was when I was 14. I won the fight, but it was laughable. I didn't land a punch, but I got him on the floor, I didn't want to do it, but I was lining up a kick to his head and he went, 'No!' There was an audience; people had literally come to watch a pre-arranged fight from 4pm till 5pm on a particular field. He was the better fighter and had landed punches on me, but I had got him on the ground and he'd given up.

We used to go out on the streets a lot and it was all about tracksuits and trainers and having a little gang. My first kiss was when I was out with my gang. We came across a gang of girls and one of the girls shouted over, 'Hey you! My mate fancies you!' And then I realised it was me. I can't remember how, but in the next few minutes we were down the side of a chip shop and I had my first kiss, which was amazing. I remember getting a girl's tits out somewhere in another alley. Sounds charming, doesn't it?

That set a pattern of being passive with women. When I try and chase a woman I don't feel confident. I normally have a heads up from them or their mate that they fancy me, then I go in knowing I am probably going to do alright.

I had a relationship with another girl and she was quite cool. She was more experienced than me. We used to go to her house at lunch time. She wanked me off for the first time, which was good. I was excited, but also scared and anxious about losing my virginity. I hadn't read the leaflet with the condom. I thought you stretched it over your penis, but of course you don't, you roll it over. I remember just fucking it up and losing my erection. Later I read the leaflet, and I thought, 'Oh my God, you dick, that's how you do it!'

I've only had one true one-night stand but I had lots more opportunities than that. I'm not ruthless enough to do it. Yeah, it's like being ruthless, it's like a game; you may have to make the circumstances go your way. I've never read a pick-up artist book, but apparently that stuff works. The motivation is to get laid with a large volume of women.

If I can't get an erection it feels horrible. I feel numb, nothing that the woman says could help. I would want to be anywhere except there. It should be said, the vast majority of the time I have been fine. But obviously, you have to take responsibility for your issues, and it's my issue. I've had some therapy for it.

I waited for an adolescence that didn't really happen. I ended up being relatively tall and hairy, but very skinny. As soon as I went through puberty I started to slowly but surely go bald. And that's who I am. I'm not the physical man I would ideally have chosen to be.

I'm now a middle-aged man and much more comfortable with who I am. I've worked on it, I've had some counselling over the years. I work full-time, but the artistic stuff is more important to me and how I value myself.

Forty-eight years old

"It's a source of delight and fun"

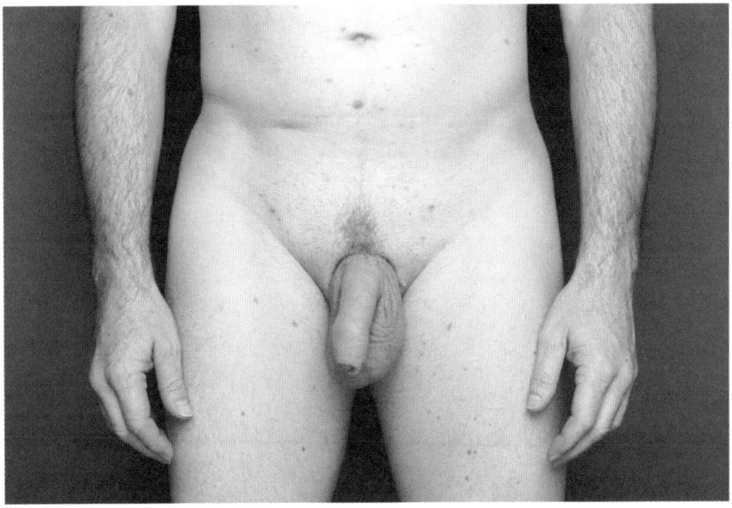

I love my penis. I have a good, healthy relationship with it. It's also an enormous source of pleasure and gratification. There is no way round that. I have a great sexual relationship with my girlfriend and my penis plays a significant part in that. I enjoy having a penis. I've always been quite sexual, as far back as I can remember. It's been quite an adventurous journey. My sexuality is an important facet of myself and my life. It's good to indulge.

My penis is a source of delight and fun. I have an abiding memory of being on a long car journey when I was four or five, and I drew with biro on my penis. This was discovered by my parents and the source of some hilarity for them. It's an example of the fun relationship I have with my penis.

I identify as bisexual now. If you'd asked me ten years ago, I would have identified as heterosexual. There came a point in my mind, where it didn't feel true anymore. I took a conscious decision to examine it and address some of what turned out to be a significant amount of shame about that. My partner is super supporting and loving and interested and I have a safe space to talk.

I'm more interested in women. I've never fallen in love with a man, but I have fallen in love with women. I don't find myself perving at men in the street, but there is a sexual interest at times.

If you look at young people today, there is a narrative about gender fluidity. There is an ease with which young men are flirting or kissing, in a way that perhaps women were doing about ten years ago.

There's no point having any anxiety about the size of my dick. No point. There is a pressure to conform and have a better body shape. Young guys get that much more than men my age. I can't invest too much anxiety in that. I keep myself fit and healthy and I feel good in my skin. That seems more important. Of course, it's also important that I look good naked, let's not underestimate that!

I was repressed when I was younger and had a difficult time expressing myself emotionally, because of where and when I grew up. I had feelings but didn't know what they were as a young man.

I've done lots of self-development work and therapy, a crazy-paving journey to some kind of adult state. I did quite intensive therapy for some years; workshops, groups and followed my intuition and heart. There was a lot of work to do. I'm quite in touch with myself now and I can be honest about what's going on with me. In the last five years I have learned to be more vulnerable. I don't mean in a weak and collapsed way, I mean I own and share parts of myself in group space or with a partner. That's been very liberating. Learning to be vulnerable started with my first therapy group about 22 years ago. It was terrifying, but I wanted to learn what was on the other side.

I grew up in south London with my mum and dad. It was the 1960s, but they weren't part of the 1960s generation, they were part of the 1950s generation. How many of my friends and peers were supported in the way I support my children in being who they are? My parents were mad and repressed, and driven by the ego and unwilling to look outside of their conditioning. Those terms weren't even really known back then!

I have a girl and a boy. How do I parent them? They think I'm a great dad, but they are still of that age. I like to encourage them to have fun, I'm not a pushy parent. My boy is very in touch with how he feels and I encourage that. My daughter is a bit more guarded about sharing what she feels. I will try and just feel into what I think she is feeling and suggest it as an option for what I think is going on. She'll go, 'Dad you are a genius!' It's very sweet. I think it's important that as fathers we step up. There is something in the ether at the moment, in the collective, where there's more discussion about self-development. Twenty or thirty years ago that would have been leftfield. It's difficult if we get stuck without a full range of feelings.

Fifty years old

“There I was, a naked man with a wheelbarrow”

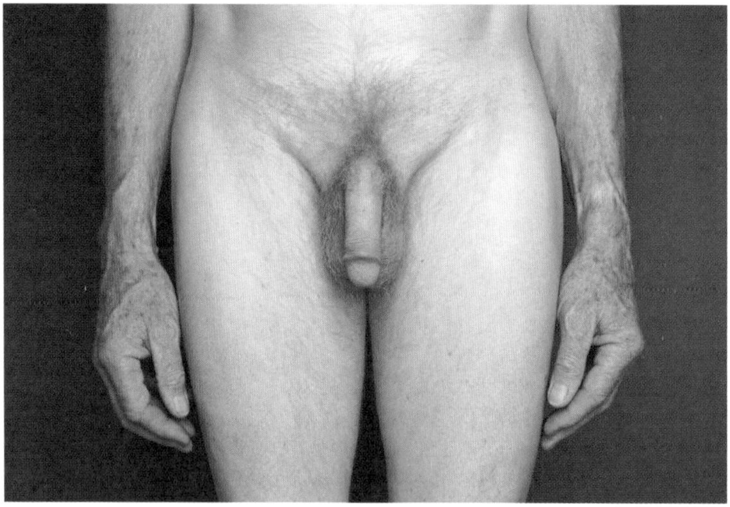

Your penis is a big part of your life as a bloke. Luckily, I’ve never felt inadequate in any way.

I’ve gone with the flow all my life. It seems to be working so far. I’ve been lucky. I just missed National Service. It probably would have done me good, but I’m glad I didn’t find out! And I also went to college just before you had to pay. I’m not a macho sort of man. I don’t go to the pub and drink with the lads and I don’t go to football matches.

My father would go to the study when he got home and eat his meal in there. Later I would be allowed to go in and say hello. That was late 1940s, early

1950s. Our relationship wasn't extraordinarily wonderful, but it was fine. He would take me on train journeys, and take friends and me to play cricket. Boy stuff.

My wife, children and I used to go on boat holidays. We had a boat for 44 years. We'd all strip off and skinny dip in the river, which was rather nice. The funny thing is another boat would go by, and you'd be under the water hanging on to the ladder and realise how clear the water was! It was very English and eccentric. I live on a boat now.

Unfortunately I became a widower. I have since got more into naturism and joined British Naturism and a local club. I often pop into the club. Taking your clothes off is something I like, but it's also about taking off everything you need to do. It's about being relaxed and free. I like the sun on me and I enjoy skinny dipping.

I think the human body is too sexualised and we should be more relaxed about it all. If you think about young people sending naked photographs on the internet, if the naked human body was more normal, they wouldn't bother, would they? If you could see bodies more easily it wouldn't be such a big deal.

I go to the club all year round, but if it's cold then I'm a great one for the sauna. I was doing some gardening at the club in January and I found if you take a wheelbarrow of earth up a hill over and over, you do get warm. I ended up stripping off, in January. Three men from the gas board came over, and there they were at the top of the hill, all wrapped up, and there I was, a naked man with a wheelbarrow. They must have thought I was bonkers.

I looked for evening classes in the local paper for something to do, but there wasn't anything I fancied. There was an ad for life modelling though. I think my wife would have been very amused. I actually heard from a different college and it was for sixth-form girls. I felt nervous about that and had to draw up reserves of courage. I survived. Actually, they were wonderful, and it wasn't uncomfortable, they were perfect ladies.

I make some money from the modelling, which is great because I am retired now. I can earn from £12 to £25 an hour, and I can work two hours or a whole day.

My wife was an artist, I used to model for her. She used to draw me and model me in clay. I still have the art. Our relationship was wonderful. She never nagged me to be ambitious and get more money. You hear from other guys that they had problems with their wives wanting them to be more ambitious. She was fairly easy-going. We had a good relationship and I miss it.

Seventy-one years old

"I don't think marriage is designed to last long"

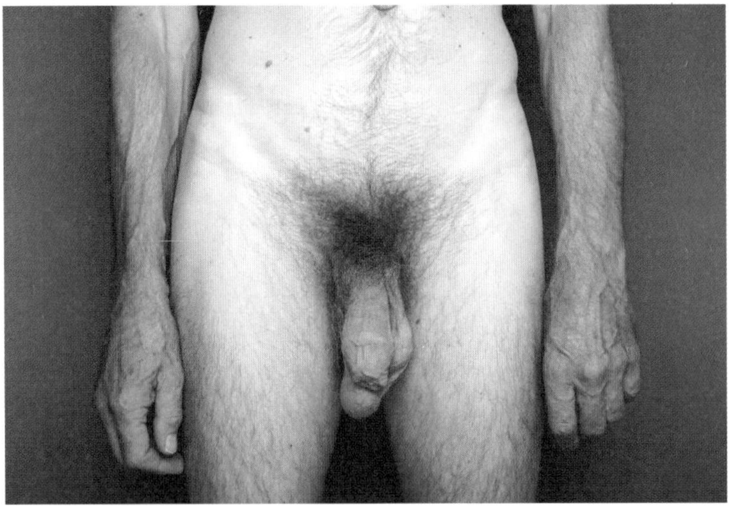

I like my penis. I am quite sexual, so I consider my penis a significant part of me. I enjoy masturbation and I like my own relationship with my penis and I like making love.

I like body practices, but for a long time I didn't recognise that as a need. I came from quite a closed-down family background. Unlike many men I wasn't drawn to sport. My work was in IT so I was in a 'heady' career path. I was repressed in my physicality in general. Yoga was the first thing I found. After yoga I got involved in dance practices.

I have two sons who are in their 20s. They were quite sporty. I learnt a lot from observing them. They had greater confidence than I did. Maybe if I'd been more confident I would have got into sport as well. I felt like my weakness would have come up against male power in sport and that frightened me. I was quite weedy and nervous.

When I started yoga a long time ago, I was the token male presence in a group of women. Then I found a class that attracted more men. When I started 5 Rhythms there were a lot more women than men, but that world has expanded considerably and there are more men now. I also joined a choir which was mainly women, but the man that led the choir started an all-male choir, which I now belong to as well. That's brilliant for me because it gives me an opportunity to explore my relationship with men in a team, but not competitively. The mixed-sex choir and the all-male choir satisfy different needs in me. I like them both.

I think I used to be overly drawn to female company because I was frightened of the male. Now I am more comfortable with men and I find there is an enjoyable robustness in male company.

I am now in another sexual relationship. My marriage has become 'open', although the situation is complex. There is quite a lot of tension around it. My wife had a relationship for a while too. I'm not sure she wants another one now. At best it can be rather lovely being in two relationships, but it can create conflict.

We were young and immature when we got married. We have been good home-makers and parents, but as individuals we have evolved quite differently. Our sexual energies are very different. I think sexual energy can decline in a long-term relationship. Fundamentally, I don't think marriage is designed to last long... Once the woman has adjusted to the menopause I don't think there is much difference in sexual drive between men and women. Men take hormonal hits too. I think people go off the boil when they are together a long time.

In the modern world, given more leisure time and longer retirement time, and all that's on offer for people to explore, I think it's unsurprising that relationships change. My father and grandfather lived quite narrow lives compared to me and my generation. I've had ten years of not having to work.

I was really aware I just wanted to fuck another woman, basically. I don't know how much was not having sex with my wife and how much was the urge to have sex with another woman. That a woman wanted me made me feel really good and potent. I stopped feeling good about myself as a husband, but I felt good about myself sexually.

My wife and I stay together for a number of reasons. When I started to seek other women, our children were in their teens. I wanted to be a responsible and good father. I think that was valid. It could be described as a cop-out, of course. We have a nice house together in the suburbs and it works quite well – I can have the security and go out and explore. My wife is not as adventurous as I am, so it's less ideal for her. But she knows I wouldn't want to be more contained.

I don't want to recreate another married situation. My ideal would be more of a tribal situation where we don't have to live in such a binary way. That's why I like choirs, they are a community, a tribe of sorts.

Strength is an interesting feature of being a man. I think I have strength. This can apply to being a human though, not just a man. I like male humour. I notice from being in mixed groups and men's groups that the humour is more sharp among men.

This is a cliché, but I am good at DIY; I can put up shelves. If I come across a man who can't do DIY, I think, 'Come on, you could learn!' My greatest delight is to be practical and creative. My lover and I have just finished tiling her basement. I really enjoyed figuring out how to fix tiles to a damp wall and using the free tiles that were available in a creative way. We came up with a practical, artistic solution together, but the actual building was all me, and I associate that with my maleness.

Sixty-five years old

"My penis is linked to quite a lot of sadness in my life"

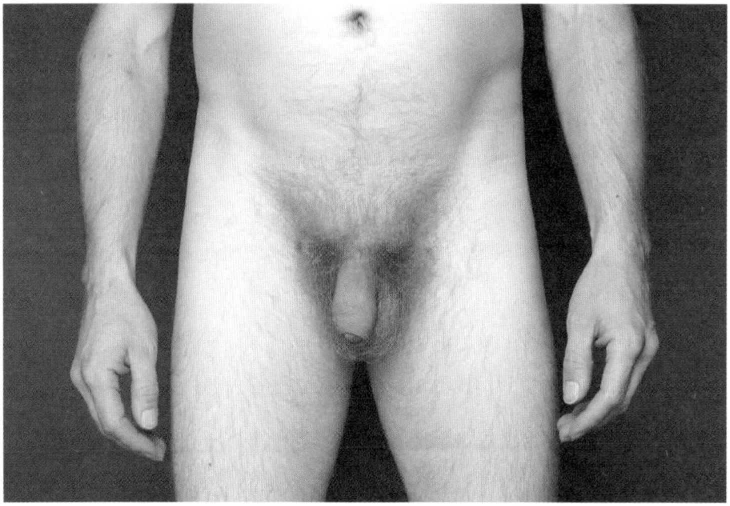

I quite like my penis. I think it's one of my better features. As penises go, it's a nice one. If it was a factor I could enter into a beauty contest it would contribute towards my score somewhat. I like mine more than most.

Not that I think that a flaccid penis has much to say about itself; it's just a willy. They all look fairly silly when they are flaccid. That's not the essence of penis. It isn't the way it is so it can be flaccid, it's the way it is so it can be erect. In a way, a flaccid penis photograph misses out on what the penis is all about. What is there that is really defined by the state in which it spends only a very small part of its time? It's only erect for a few hours or minutes a day. Okay, maybe not a few hours! *(laughs)*

It's not a great exercise to wallow in feeling sorry for yourself, but despite what I said about my penis being one of my better features, no one has taken an interest in it for some time. So when I think about my penis I feel sad because of the missed opportunities throughout my life. I haven't spent much time in relationships. Not through choice, but because of insecurity, issues of trust. So my penis is linked to quite a lot of sadness in my life. What is sad about missing out on sex is missing out on love.

A soft penis is seen as vulnerable, but a hard penis isn't. I don't understand the link between penises and aggression. People gravitate towards this idea as a truth, but I don't know if it is. It's reminiscent of the dilemma that women and girls are presented with: being a good girl or a sexy girl. You can have a hard penis or be a good man. To get an erection a man needs to feel safe, so an erect penis is still vulnerable.

I think the association of an erect penis with aggression really encapsulates something about society's tragic attitudes to male emotions. If I have an erection it is because I want to show someone how much I love and desire them. Where is the aggression in that? I see passion, but I don't see aggression.

I had a difficult childhood. In terms of sexual relationships it has meant that I have issues with trust and intimacy. I've been growing more aware of this recently.

My mother was on the autistic spectrum. Her feelings were all-powerful and all-consuming to her. You might as well spit in the wind as have your feelings acknowledged. She wasn't cruel, but she was emotionally abusive; she was a toddler in a woman's body. When a toddler doesn't get what it wants, the whole world falls apart.

It's a bit like having a parent who's an alcoholic. You have to be the adult in the relationship. Your parent is a source of instability, not a dependable source of soothing and nurturing. My life wasn't all bad; some parts felt safe and stable. The bedtime routine was fairly safe and peaceful. The morning was dreadful. During the day the world could end, over something related to me or not related to me. My feelings were invisible and her feelings were overpowering.

To admit to anyone that your mother has had an effect on your potential to have sexual and romantic relationships is a very unpleasant and disturbing notion. All the most frightening, disturbing and dangerous men have had abusive relationships with their mother.

Norman Bates, for one. It hasn't made me a worse person, but it's left a mark in terms of how my life looks. It's hard to allow someone to see you if you think they might see something like that.

I've had lots of therapy and I have a much better sense of it all now. It's difficult to take the risk in starting a new relationship if you are already standing on unstable ground.

We men grow up from toddlerhood, certainly from the first day of school, knowing that violence is always an option. Wherever we go, we have to be prepared for violence, it's part of our role. Man-on-man violence is a fact of being a man. The need to avoid that violence is ingrained into every aspect of man-to-man etiquette. Little boys are obsessed with violence for a reason, because you might get into a fight.

As an adult I am not interested in violence in any way. But there are still occasions where there could be an altercation, or a situation where you think, 'Should I run? Should I fight? Should I look like I can fight?' And it's actually quite hard work. It doesn't necessarily involve feeling afraid, because you don't show fear. If you show fear, bad things happen. Fear is an emotion you have to hide.

I almost got mugged a few months ago. A man crossed the street and walked towards me. I had a backpack on and I couldn't get away. I thought 'OK, this is not a good situation.' I made myself look as big as I could, and crossed the road so we would pass on the cross and he couldn't stop me. He managed to slow me down enough by asking me directions. It was bullshit, the whole thing was sketchy, I spotted it 100 yards away. But I had to not feel afraid, or it would have showed. So some of the stuff we criticise men for is actually adaptive, rather than maladaptive.

I think we should hold people to account more for how men are talked about, just as people are held to account more now for how women are talked about. It's quite common to dismiss men's feelings as fragile male ego. Men's feelings are trivialised.

Women, rightly, are concerned that girls and women have anxiety about the appearance of their vaginas. I agree that it's tragic that women are concerned. I think vaginas are all beautiful. It's shocking and appalling that women should ever have to doubt anything about how they look. Yet we laugh at men who are worried about their penises. That's not on.

Forty-one years old

“I love it when my partner holds my cock after I’ve orgasmed”

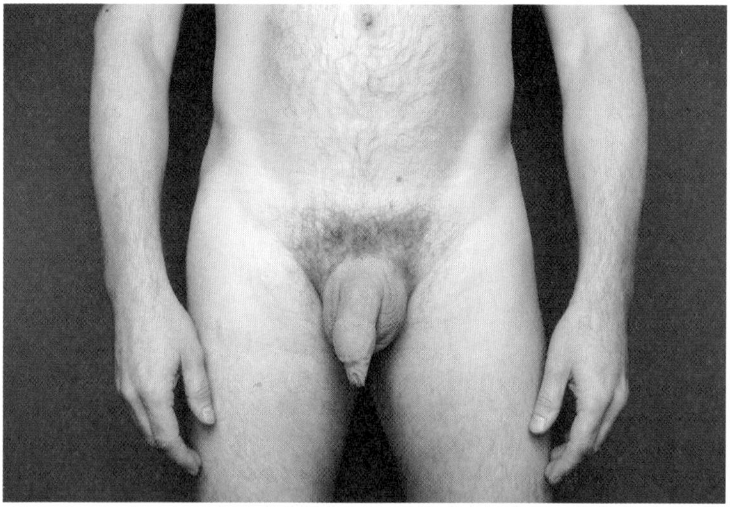

As a young man I had a difficult story about my cock: it wasn’t big enough, it wasn’t good enough. It was just a reflection of how I felt about myself in general.

I grew up with lots of sexual shame, body shame, the normal middle-class British upbringing. Plain vanilla, straight sex was the only kind of sex that was OK in the eyes of God. I knew that I wasn’t completely straight, that I was having same-sex thoughts and fantasies, and it was like, ‘Oh my God, that’s terrible. I’ll go to hell for that.’ In the 1980s when AIDS was out, I thought if I so much as looked at another man’s cock I’d get AIDS and die because God would know and then I would go to hell.

I had two monogamous marriages and didn't feel particularly sexually confident. After my second marriage ended I had a spiritual awakening. I trained as a psychotherapist and also got into Tantra. I wanted to understand and explore my sexuality more. Those two streams merged to form the basis of my practice now as a sex therapist. Through Tantra I have learned to become comfortable with my own body and being naked. I have done a lot of work on myself and my sexuality.

I think that in New Age spirituality there's a lot of relabelling of old paradigms and presenting them as new constructs, but actually they're just the same. So Tantra talks about Shiva, the masculine, and Shakti, the feminine. The masculine is meant to be present, consciousness and doing. The feminine is meant to be emotions and being. But if you think about it, these are just old-school 1950s principles of men being thinkers and breadwinners and women being emotional and staying at home. In sex the man is Shiva, penetrating, and the woman is Shakti, receiving. That's just a man fucking a woman, same old stuff with New Age labels on it.

When you watch movies, notice how much full-frontal female nudity is allowed, versus how much full-frontal male nudity is allowed. Sometimes you see a sneaky male bottom. Something about the male genitals is somehow more taboo than the female genitals. Maybe there is shame because we might get visibly aroused and we don't have complete control over when we get erect.

In a post-feminist world it also feels like men's genitals are somehow something to be ashamed of, because we abuse with them, or we impose our lusts on women. Like men are monsters, men are abusers, men are violators, men are violent, men are responsible for war and all these things, but men are also responsible for loads of wonderful things. There's almost an apologetic feeling, like, 'I'm sorry I've got a cock.' I think this emasculates men. It cuts our balls off. A certain element of feminism – not feminism as a movement, but elements within it – might have wanted that.

I hope we get over this whole male/female divide thing because we're all human beings. It's divisive to have all these projections about what men and women do. None of it's helpful. We have to just experience each other in the moment and feel each other as human beings, divine beings, souls.

My relationship with my cock has evolved over the years. Like I said, when I was younger I felt embarrassed about it. I also have something called – it's a beautiful name, actually – pearly penile papules. They are tiny little glands on the head of the penis that can get a little bit inflamed. I felt a lot of shame and embarrassment about it. Now I'm completely at ease and peace with it all.

I absolutely love my cock now. I love the shape of it, I love the size of it, I love the straightness of it. I shave around my balls and I trim my pubic hair. I like the way that feels, particularly on my balls. I really enjoy my cock when it's not hard, as well as when it's hard. I just love that it's there and I very often lie at night with one hand on my heart and one hand on my balls or my cock, just to kind of hold it, cup it, talk to it and be grateful to it. I think that's probably a result of having done a lot of work on myself and my sexuality and in Tantra.

I love it when my partner holds my cock after I've orgasmed and ejaculated, like, 'Thank you, that was really lovely and we enjoyed that experience.' That feels really respectful for me. Very often, what I've experienced in the past is that once the cock has 'done its job' of ejaculating, then it's forgotten and discarded. The honouring and respect feels really important for me. I hold my partner and stroke her pussy afterwards as well. Once the intensity of the sexual energy has gone there's a space for something else – intimacy and connection.

I think this is a really important project. There's a lot of stuff about women's bodies, 'The Great Wall of Vagina', your *Bare Reality* breasts book, 'Free the Nipple' and Naomi Wolf's *Vagina*. I super-support all this stuff for women, but we mustn't forget that as men we also have our vulnerabilities around our bodies, our genitals and sex. That needs to be honoured and respected as well. It's very courageous for men to show their genitals in a vulnerable state.

Forty-nine years old

"I would like to be sexually promiscuous"

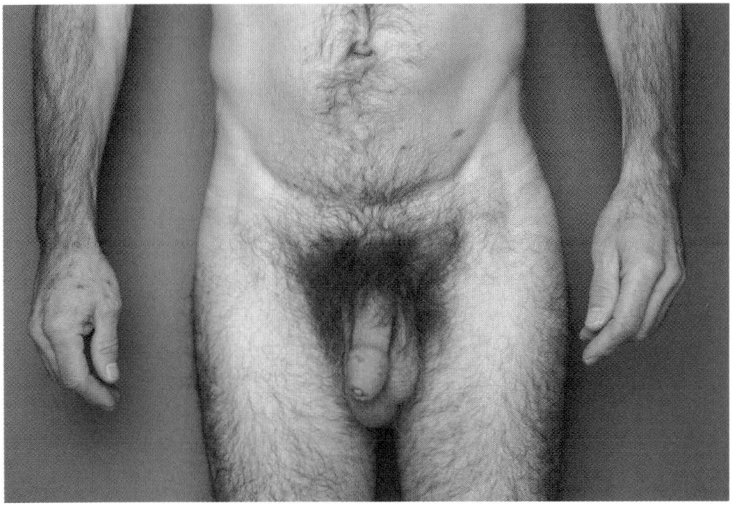

My penis and I are good friends. We're separate, but on an adventure together. I feel happy with how it looks, although of course it could be bigger.

I thought maybe I should have got myself back in trim for this photograph. I haven't been on my bike for three weeks. Then I thought, 'Hang on, it's only my penis, that's completely separate!' as though it's not part of me, a separate entity. That said, it defines me; it is part of me. I very much feel male. It's been a very important, huge part of my life since puberty.

It does get in the way, and gives an impression of having a mind of its own. It's wayward and demanding, but also an amazing toy, always ready to be played with. It's comforting to give it a squeeze.

It's average, it isn't big or small. It has a thousand different forms. The penis I hoped you'd photograph is the one on a warm sunny day, which is relaxed and warm and comfortable. That's the one I like for public display purposes. It's a bit chilly today! I'm very accepting – my penis is what it is and I don't feel insecure about it.

A penis is untidy, generally. It's not attractive like breasts are. But rationally, why would anyone want to see it? I think deep down many men do want to flash, but would any woman want to look? I think it's something primeval: 'This is what I'm able to do.'

I am very sexually driven. I think about sex a lot of the time. It is always there, deep down. The penis has its own mind: 'Would I like to, or would I not like to?' The penis is the chimp side of us, 'Let's get on with it, let's do it, let's have fun. Blow the consequences.' The more rational human side of us dictates how we behave in society.

Given the opportunity, I would like to be sexually promiscuous, but for all kinds of reasons I am relatively controlled, if not completely saint-like. I find women extremely attractive, women of all shapes and sizes. It's a warm, wonderful thing seeing a beautiful woman, it's not always just wanting them. It isn't just the pure sex act I am interested in, it's something more complete and full, it's a communication, a shared intimacy. Sex is communication. If I am trying to solve a problem in my relationship – I am married – I use physical contact. Sex can be a great way to resolve conflicts and diffuse things.

I am attracted to other women. I am open with my wife about that. She is aware that I might like to explore it, but I don't, and we don't confront it. I think it's only fair if I feel like that, for her to feel like that too. I think it would be interesting. Why would she find another man attractive? Would it be because I am sexually inadequate? Hypothetically, if I were to have sex with another woman it would be to be wanted. To be desired is very attractive. It would be for a sexual adventure and to push boundaries more.

I find it much easier talking to women. Men don't talk to each other in the same way. It's liberating to talk like this. My close male friends and I have boring male conversations about mechanical things. We'll appraise the waitress across the room then go back to engineering talk. Safe subjects.

Sixty-one years old

“Between the ages of 17 and 30 I was impotent”

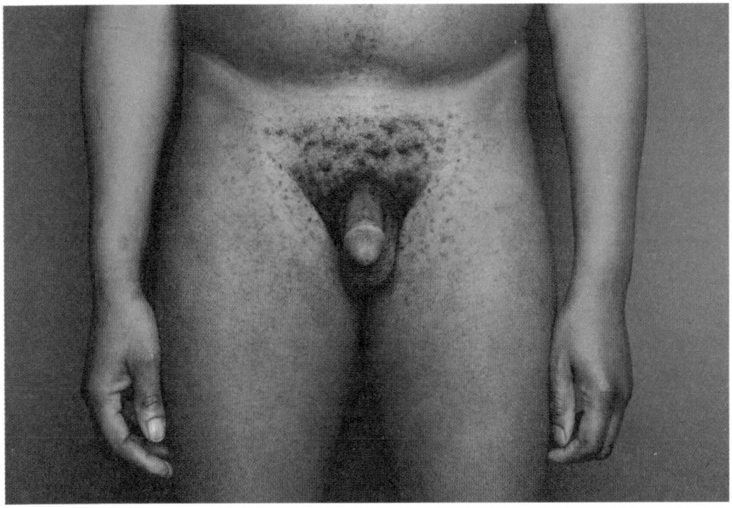

Because of my physical size I used to feel under pressure. I’m 6ft 7in, so people think my cock will proportionately be that much bigger. My penis size felt inadequate compared to my peers. It had such an effect on me that between the ages of 17 and 30 I was actually impotent.

My alpha male teenage friends were always talking about cocks and sex. They’d talk about fucking girls hard. My idea about sex then was making love, but back then there wasn’t such a thing as making love, it was all hard fucking. I couldn’t see myself slapping women and fucking them like that. I thought, ‘If women want that, then I am shit in bed.’ I thought there was no way I would be good in bed.

That meant I would either have one-night stands or long-distance relationships. There had to be no chance they could tell my friends how shit I was in bed. On the flip side my mates thought I was cool having these long-distance relationships.

I lived life just watching porn. I had this persona of being a ladies' man, but I was a wanker. I would literally just go home and wank.

Watching porn I could have a constant erection. With a woman I would only sometimes be able to have an erection, maybe 5 per cent of the time. I only had sporadic amounts of sex; maybe I would manage it on one occasion out of 20. I had one girlfriend for six months in my 20s. That's all.

My first erection that felt sexual was when I was eight. It was after watching a porn film. My brother was older than me and used to let me watch porn videos. When I was about ten, my friends and I would come home for the school lunch break and a group of us would watch a porn video at lunch.

I was a product of my mum and my four sisters. My dad was a real alpha male; he had lots of women, it caused turmoil in the marriage and he left to go back to Africa. My mum and my sisters didn't want me to be like my dad. Part of my impotency was because if I felt an urge towards a woman I thought I should back off. I was pushed so far down the feminine side that I was too far from my masculine side. Boys have the physical side. I was brought up not to be physical – and I was a big boy too. They were trying to protect me, but it meant I didn't recognise natural male feelings. I thought anything masculine was bad. That messed me up and drove me more into porn.

My friends used to talk about the sexual aggression stuff, and slapping. My sisters would talk about loving and caring – they failed to mention that sometimes women do like the slapping stuff. They weren't honest that women do like their hair pulled sometimes. They only told me the nicey-nice stuff. And that messed me up some more.

The first woman I made orgasm was the woman who became my wife. I was at a workshop, and the lie about who I am was feeling heavier and heavier. I was so sad that everyone there fell for the dude persona, and couldn't see I was actually a wanker. I stood up in front of the whole room and told everyone my story. When a woman hears a story like that it's sexually enticing. The woman who became my girlfriend and then my wife was straight over to me.

When I shared my story I was set free. I could have sex as a novice, without expectations, go with the flow. She orgasmed and I was still hard. Some of the things my friends told me when I was a teenager, about how women react when you fuck them properly, were true. When you fuck them properly they squirm around and say your name, and she was doing all that. She wanted me to pull her hair and slap her bum. I realised that some of that stuff my friends used to say wasn't a lie. 'Oh, so women do like this sort of shit!'

It took me three years to properly feel my cock. It's like it was frozen. It was like a dildo stuck to my body. It was so hard, but it didn't feel like I thought it would feel. After watching porn for years, when I was finally having sex, it did not feel like it looks. When you see men reacting to a blow job on porn, that's not how it really feels. Most of the time when I have a blow job I feel fucking bored. It's nowhere near as satisfying as it looks in porn. I think the body has memories. Touch has to thaw out.

I am a masseur and healer. My workshops give people a place where they can touch, where touch doesn't equal sex. In society touch is equated to sex. It's so fucked up. The word 'healer' means different things to different people. I have healing hands. Nearly everyone is in some kind of pain: physical, emotional, spiritual. I've had miraculous things happen. I am a conduit for healing, loving earth energy. Some people are more potent conduits for this energy.

As a masseur I have touched over 5,000 women. Last year I only had sex five or six times with two women. Right now I am a bit bored with women. I'm not feeling that excited about sex and intimacy. Because of what I do, I meet lots of beautiful women and powerful women, but we become friends. It's very rare that I get the hots for a woman. I'm not sure how long this is going to last for. I am optimistic to meet someone. I look forward to the playfulness, the dance.

'Big black bull' is a term for black men. Black men are seen as hypersexual. It adds pressure. People can be nudge-nudge, wink-wink, 'Look at the size of his hands, look at the size of his feet.' I've had girls make jokes about big cocks. Someone is history, gone to me, if they joke about me having a big cock. Any references to the big black man are not worthy.

I am lucky that I am born in a time when it is fashionable to be black in some circles. In another part of the world I might be in jail, at another time in history I might have been a slave. As far as life goes for black men in this world, I am a lucky black man. It's shit, but it's true.

Forty-eight years old

"Being submissive is new to me"

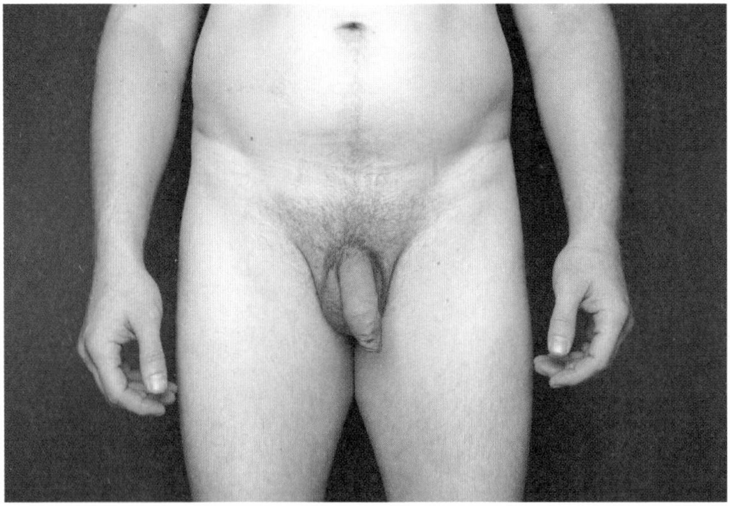

I've had a love-hate relationship with my penis over the years. I'm very much in love at the moment. It's taken me a while to realise that the ideas society puts on us about potency are bullshit.

Phallic things are everywhere: guns, skyscrapers, statues, guitars – so many things. The bigger the skyscraper, the more powerful the company is assumed to be. Size matters across everything. I think that, for men, these subliminal messages are baked into the system from an early age. I believe it is toxic.

Everyone is an individual. I feel there is an unfair amount of pressure focussed around the penis. I've never had any complaints about size, but I did worry about it. If you are unable to get an erection you feel like less of a man, you're not able to please the person you're with. It's a horrible feeling. And the more you try and make it happen, the less it will happen. I don't give myself any undue pressure now, I give less of a shit. I am very comfortable with the size of my penis now.

According to society, real men should be strong, the hunter gatherer, get married, provide for the family, earn money. We're supposed to get women and be sexually dominant with them when we're in bed. There's an idea that men take what they want from women. It's not right, it's unfair and it gets me riled up. Not cool.

I've been polyamorous for two years. I spend a lot of time trying to justify polyamory to people. We strive really hard to show to people on the outside that it's not all about sex, but basically, it is. *(laughs)* Safe sex is a must and I get tested every two months.

It's hard to break down ideas like jealousy in the beginning. There is a term called 'compersion'; it's a feeling of happiness from seeing your partner happy with someone else. It's the opposite of jealousy. We strongly believe you can be in love with more than one person at a time. The more you give out, the more you get back. If your partner is attracted to someone else it doesn't mean you are deficient. Polyamory is liberating, it strips away a lot of angst and anxiety and jealousy.

I've been in the room when my partner has had sex with other people. In fact I've been in the room when two of my partners have had sex with other people, in a 'playroom' at a sex party.

I have six partners at the moment. A lot of men I speak to would say, 'Fucking hell man, I can't even deal with one!' I don't see them all the time. One lives in Berlin, for example. Some are intense relationships where there is a lot of love. Some are more physical.

I'm what is known as a 'switch'; I can switch between dominant and submissive. It opens up lots of possibilities. I was dominant till I discovered polyamory. Being submissive is new to me. I am a big and powerful person. Letting go of the power and giving it to someone else is extremely liberating and extremely hot. I would say that the submissive side of things is for myself, and the dominant side of things is for other people. I like it when the other person gets off on me being dominant, but I don't derive sexual pleasure from it. The sub side turns me on.

I like 'pegging', which is being anally penetrated by a woman with a strap-on. The male G-spot is in your anus, it's basically like nothing else you will ever find. Any men reading this should give it a try!

I don't hold to specific aesthetics and stereotypes of beauty. My own self-image is about how I feel in myself, not how others see me. But I feel good when I am about 82 kilos, in really good shape, cut and about to strangle people! Professionally! *(laughs)*

I practise ju-jitsu, a submission grappling martial art. You wrestle to the point of pain; if the other person is better then you submit. It's about as close to human chess as you can get: you both know the rules and how it works, but you have different ideas about which moves you can accomplish. It's a way of developing your life and it's a good learning process. If you can't get out of a move, you have to submit. I have found over the years that it breaks down the ego entirely. Boxers and kickboxers tend to kick off because they are normally the hardest person in a room they go into. But ju-jitsu is called 'the gentle art'. It gives you confidence without bravado. You can win and you can submit. You learn from your mistakes. It develops your psyche as well as your physical form. Other martial arts also have a spiritual side, but they are more about personal glory. Ju-jitsu is like a family.

Martial arts are for men and women. Wing chun is a deadly martial art and it was developed by nuns. Who gives a shit what's between your legs? It's about the training and the ability.

Thirty-eight years old

"I'm around four inches erect"

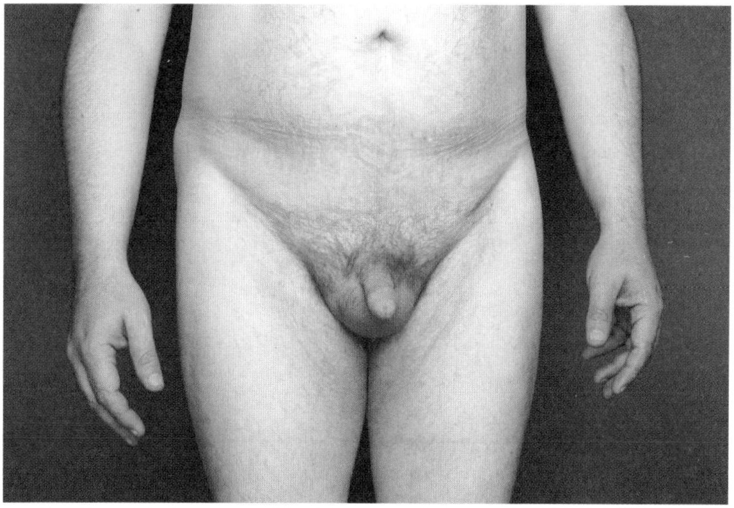

When I was a youngster I was quite shy, and by the time I was in my late teens I had developed a lot of body shame. I was never happy physically with who I was and developed quite a lot of penis-size anxiety.

I did very well at university, got a good job, travelled the world, became an IT expert, and outwardly seemed like a very successful and confident guy who was able to lead people. But on a personal level I spent years shutting people out because of my relationship with my own body.

There haven't been a large number of sexual liaisons in my life. When I was with someone I used techniques like making sure the lights were off before I was completely undressed with a partner, or getting into bed with my boxers on and only taking them off once I was in the bed to control and minimize vulnerable exposure. Coping strategies.

I think penis size matters way more to the owner of the penis than to anybody else. There were times when my penis was a contributing factor to a failed relationship, but the relationship was probably failing anyway. We're told all the time that size doesn't matter and that women don't care, but you know, I think some women do care. We all have preferences and it's our differences that lead to the success of the species. So I think it's fine to acknowledge that some people have a preference for larger penises in their partner. Not all of them, not most of them, but some do.

One of the things that has struck me is that there's an awful lot of small penis humour bandied about casually on television. I'm around four inches erect, and maybe 5 per cent of men are my size or less. It sounds like not many, but 5 per cent is actually one in 20. So most situations where you make a small penis joke there's somebody just a few feet away from you who is suffering because of it, and if people knew that then it would drive the penis size jokes out because folk are not inherently mean about their family and friends.

Very small penises – under three inches when erect – are medically diagnosed as a micro-penis. It's the only case in medical history that I'm aware of where we diagnose by statistic. Other conditions are diagnosed on the basis of problematic symptoms. There's very little that can actually be done after the diagnosis. It feels as though the major point of a diagnosis is so that we can sacrifice that 2.88 per cent of men who have a micro-penis and leave them in misery, and use this yardstick to tell everybody else that they're normal. *(laughs)* So if you go to a doctor with a 3½ inch penis and complain, he says, 'No, you're normal.' He does nothing for you. Maybe if your anxiety is extreme you get sent for therapy, which concentrates on adjusting your belief that you're not normal and convincing you that you are. It's really, really poorly thought through.

So I'm a poet, a performance poet. There's no room in poetry for something that isn't fundamentally believed to be honest and true by the poet. If the poet writes something duplicitous, that's automatically transfigured into not being poetry. I finally wrote a poem about my own small penis and I knew that once I'd written it I would have to perform it. Truth is a hard master; you can't be selective with the truth. Performing that poem was probably the turning point when I really started to get my penis-size anxiety issues in check.

It's been viewed on Youtube over one million times and was covered in the media. I get contacted by men who've lived their whole lives with these issues. I thought as well as being a slave to the truth as a poet, I kind of owed these people something. I didn't feel that I could just walk away from it and ignore these messages from other men who were thanking me and calling me a legend and a hero. I pulled together a special one-off performance evening, which was geared around acceptance, and I called it *The Big Small Penis Party*. I got half a dozen of what I consider to be the best poets in London who did some pieces around the theme, and they all decided they were comfortable with performing their pieces naked. I had naked ushers giving away free gingerbread little cocks and balls.

The Big Small Penis Party was covered on TV, radio and in newspapers in the UK and around the world. If you google 'small penis' it now leads you to very positive stories about my party and poem, not just to the exploitative websites that you'd expect. I feel really, really happy about that. It's a legacy of value, to my mind.

I did some heavy reading for research before *The Big Small Penis Party*. I found one documented story of a lad of about 17 who committed suicide because of his penis-size anxiety. But finding actual documented cases like that is incredibly tough, and I came to realise there's been no research into the relationship between male mental health and penis-size anxiety.

I think the hang-ups all come from secrecy, dating back to the mythology of Adam's fig leaf. As soon as you believe there's something shameful about yourself that should be hidden, you build a dark corner where all kinds of negative feelings and illnesses grow.

I got to the point where I thought, 'How can my wife love me when I'm wielding an unlovable penis?' Ultimately I could not keep pushing that aspect of her connection to me and her desire for me away. She might make some joke about penises, like, 'Oh, I love all dicks, me,' because we have a pretty bawdy sense of humour, but I'd have this little voice in my head that says, 'Yeah, all but yours. She can't possibly love yours.' She has definitely made me confront my own self-loathing. I still feel lucky just about every day that I've got a woman with such a smart mind on her. We're really well matched.

I'm nearly 50 now. What a waste, spending all those years hating something about myself that, no matter what, I couldn't change. We increase our miseries through darkness, secrecy and shame. This project is really important and I'm glad that it's happening.

Forty-nine years old

"I don't hate men, I hate patriarchy"

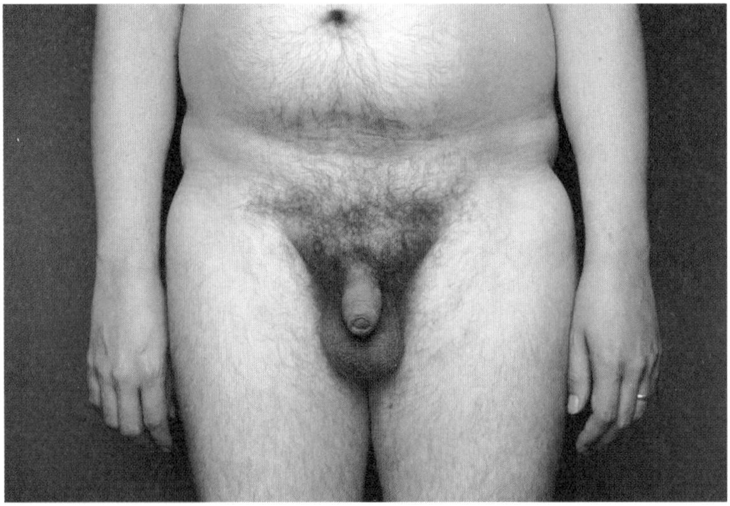

I was assaulted by a woman when I was 19. I was having a flirtatious relationship with a girl on my corridor at university. Then I changed my mind. I didn't think I was that interested in a relationship with her. I went to her room to tell her. She had finished with a boyfriend for me, so I think she had stakes in it 'working' between us.

She believed that by forcing herself on me I would change my mind. She was bigger than me and stronger than me. She held me down despite me saying 'no'. I didn't feel like I could push her off, because she was a woman. I don't agree with chivalry, but I do agree with the masculine code of not hitting women.

She forcibly gave me a blow job. Eventually I became erect and she thought that was me consenting. I couldn't come, so I was held against a wall and assaulted against my will for a fucking long time. In UK law I can't describe this as rape, but in my view it was rape. I did not consent to penetrate someone and I was forced into it. She was crying as well as seeming turned on. She wanted to get off, and I knew that, so eventually I persuaded her to stop and I semi-consensually went down on her till she orgasmed. I don't think she was prepared to let me leave the room until she orgasmed. This is a very different view of women's sexuality than we normally see. But it makes sense to me because I don't see that many differences between men and women.

When I was eight my mum and stepdad married. He was strong and stoic, but also soft. Before they married, when he hugged me, it made me feel safe. But when they got married he changed, it was like something clicked in his head. He had had a complicated childhood and had been hit by his dad with a belt and caned at school. He'd experienced quite a violent and rugged masculinity growing up. When he married my mum he was a teacher and having a tough time with the teenage boys, throwing chairs around and things. I think he had less patience with my 'boyness'. His anger was cold and measured. He gave you 'discipline'. You knew he was holding back. If he'd let it out he could have killed you.

I could hear their arguments; very adult arguments about sex, anger, masculinity. She used to hit him. One time he hit her back. That was a complicated thing to hear. They had this pact in the end where she agreed to be a 'good wife' and be meek. It didn't last; she was too tempestuous and she'd failed to be this 1950s idea of a housewife.

There was a year when I was kind of flashing. I'd wear a dressing gown and it would just 'fall open'. I was beginning to grow pubic hair and I guess I wanted recognition of moving into adulthood. There was also a sense of wanting people to 'see' me. We couldn't talk about our emotions, it was very quiet. I felt my mum didn't love me, so I think there was an element of some misplaced desire for her. I don't have time for Freud – he was a misogynist bastard, I don't hold with his theories – I was a child wanting to connect with my mother, but there was an element to it... I had a lot of shame around the flashing for years.

After my mum and stepdad split up we moved away. My mum had a nervous breakdown and spent a year drinking late into the night, a borderline alcoholic. One time I was trying to calm her, and she told me that men are evil and wrong and sick, and that every problem she'd ever had was as a result of men. She said 'Men are a curse, a cancer.' 'Even me?' I asked. 'Even you. You're a curse, you can't help it. The fact you are a man means you can't help but hurt the women in your life.' I have some sympathy. She had reason to hate men. And men can be fucking awful.

In theory, school should have been my safe space. But I was new, I had glasses, I liked reading books, I had acne. I was not the masculine ideal. So, I was bullied. I threatened to cut my wrists once in art class and everyone shouted 'Do it!'

So when I was 13 I felt like I hated men. There were complexities with my stepdad, my mum telling me that men are a curse, and being bullied at school. Now I know I don't hate men, I hate patriarchy.

I had a lot of anger, but I didn't want to show it and be what my mum had talked about, so I self-harmed. I would punch walls. I couldn't talk about it. I also had anxiety and depression. I could show other people empathy, but never myself. I wanted to stop existing, but I didn't realise at the time they were suicidal thoughts. It's only in the last five years I've been able to talk about my life. I've created a show about masculinity. I have said, in public, 'I have depression, I have anger, I'm a rape survivor.' I made the show to directly speak to men. It's very powerful when men cry when I am telling my own story in my show. It has changed me.

Men are ready to talk now about masculinity. It's coming out in loads of different ways and not all of them positive, like the 'Manosphere' and men's rights activism. There are a lot of men pushing back incredibly hard against feminism. But because of the changes brought about by feminism there are also men like me who are willing and ready to talk about masculinity. I don't have a very positive relationship with masculinity, but I am trying to change that.

I've had negative feedback online from radical feminists and men's rights activists. The rad fems are more polite. Men's rights activists called me a 'cuck'. I don't give a damn about being a cuckold, I have an open relationship! I have no problem with it, but they thought they were belittling me. I think they hate women, but they hate men too. The kind of insults they paid me were like the ones I had at school, about being gay, or being like a woman. I have a lot of problems with the 'Manosphere'. Men's liberation is the only answer – not men's rights, but liberation from patriarchy.

I have a funny story about my penis! When I was a kid I was lying in bed and rubbing against the mattress and got an erection, and I was like,

'Woah, this is magic!' I did that until I orgasmed. I went into school the next day, gathered all the boys together and said, 'I've discovered this amazing thing, and I am calling it "Simulated Sex"!' I'd had enough sex education, I'd been given hippy sex books, I should have known – but because I didn't use my hand, I didn't know it was masturbation. And everyone was like, 'That's wanking.' It was embarrassing but very funny. I was just young enough to get away with it. At secondary school I would have been destroyed.

I feel ugly, but I have never felt ugly because of my penis. I don't feel very in touch with my body. Sex is the only time when I get out of my fucking head and into a 'moment'. So I love sex. I don't have as much sex as I would like. The longer I don't have sex, the more complicated I feel, and the more I hate myself. I know I should be able to love myself without feeling validated by someone else's desire, but ultimately that validation is very important. It's weird, women are so objectified by society that they need to escape that, but for me and a lot of men we don't feel objectified enough.

Thirty-four years old

"I felt different"

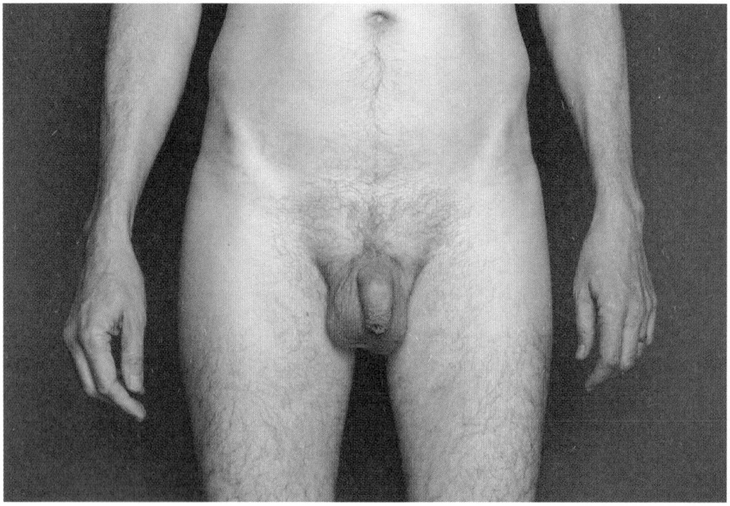

I want to say how average I am. My erect penis is average, or maybe a bit larger than average, but my flaccid penis is in the bottom few percent probably. That has had an influence on me. All my life I had the feeling that I wasn't a normal male. I now know that isn't right.

I was brought up in the south Wales valleys, in a mining town. Everyone played rugby. In the showers at rugby I realised there was a huge difference between me and the others, not just in terms of penis size, but also they had hair growing everywhere, their voices were changing and I was a lot thinner. I was even thinner then than I am now. I felt different. I used to take part in every sport I could, so I grew up as a typical male in that community, but I felt different.

When I was younger there was no reference point to show me if I was normal or different. In the parlance of today, I am a grower, not a shower. When I was younger I never knew if there was such a thing. All I saw were other men who had penises, which if they grew as much as mine... Well. This always affected my emotional and sexual life immensely.

There was another thing in my head. Although I was always attracted to females, there were people who called me gay because of my appearance. 'If other people call me gay, if I look like this, perhaps my instincts to find women attractive are wrong, perhaps I am gay?'

I was attracted to women and found to my amazement that women were attracted to me. But the thing in my head meant that when it came down to it I was nervous. I came close, but it wasn't until the age of 30 that I lost my virginity with the woman who is my wife. I am very happy with her. She is the first woman I fully made love to. We have two children and we are very happy.

So, in a way I am completely monogamous and always have been. It's not what I planned, but when I look back on it I think it is very good.

If I hadn't had those uncertainties, between 18 and 30, where would I be now? Would I be as happy as I am now? If I knew then what I know now, would I behave differently? Maybe I would have let situations with women unfold more.

I had to push myself out of my comfort zone to let people see my body in communal changing-rooms when I played sport. I have tried to deal with it, but even to this day I still feel different. I took part in the Brighton Naked Bike Ride and wore a sign on my back that said, 'Embrace your naked self.' I think I do embrace my body now, but not completely. There are things I could change about myself, but I wouldn't. I am content.

I worked as an accountant, but as a hobby I have been taking naked self-portraits for 30 years. It was only through that I realised that I am a normal man. I shoot myself in all sorts of states. I've shot some other people nude as well, on the back of them seeing my nude self-portraiture. I saw Mapplethorpe's exhibition in the 1990s and it gave me a feeling of legitimacy; even though what I did wasn't as technically perfect, it was aiming to do something similar.

I find the penis beautiful when I photograph it. If I find it beautiful to look at, do I also find it erotic? Yes, I can, but I am not attracted to the rest of the male. Men don't like to say that the penis is beautiful to look at.

Fifty-nine years old

“Britain’s manliest man”

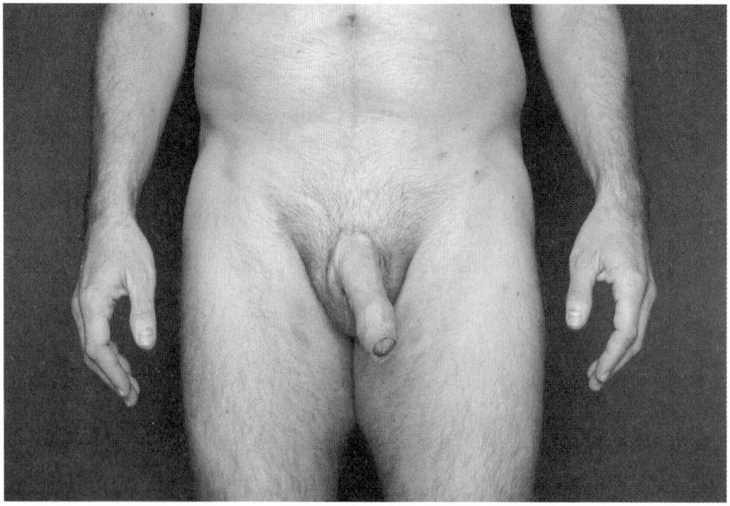

I came from a north-west working-class town. No one went to university, it wasn’t even mentioned. I worked hard at school, but I left when I was 16 and got an apprenticeship at Rolls-Royce cars. Then I saw Top Gun and that was it.

I thought only Oxford and Cambridge super brains flew planes, not people from my town. My dad encouraged me to check if I had enough qualifications. I had enough O-levels and my apprenticeship qualification counted as two A-levels, so I had the bare minimum. I went to the selection and bombed it – I didn’t have a clue and hadn’t done any preparation.

One of my biggest attributes is grit. So a year to the day I was there again. They'd given me some advice to research the air force and do some work with the Scouts. I'd done that, and I'd improved my maths calculations. Second time round I got through selection, but they offered me non-commissioned air crew, which means being at the back of a helicopter, or air traffic control commissioned officer, neither of which I wanted.

A year later I was back again. I'm now an instructor, and I know that one of the key attributes we are looking for is determination. They would have thought, 'Fine, go on then.'

I didn't pass the aptitude tests to be a pilot. Anyone can be a pilot, it's like driving, but they are looking for someone who could go on to be the equivalent of a Formula One driver, who would pass their driving test in five lessons, not 20. In hindsight I would have been an average pilot, whereas I've been a good navigator. It's worked out for the best.

It saddens me that we live in a world where we need the military. I just wanted to fly jets, to fly fast and low, not go to war and kill people. But that's the pay-off when you join; you have to accept that's what your life is.

War is a serious undertaking. It's horrible that it has to happen. I've been in Iraq, Afghanistan and Libya. The vast majority of things I've been involved in prevented innocent people being killed. I'm lucky that I don't have to lie awake thinking about what I've done. I'm proud of my role in the forces. I'm lucky, I'm not on the ground and I don't experience the blood and guts.

I've never been asked to do something I was morally against. We get the decision in the cockpit whether we let a weapon go. If we see innocent people, children, we can go home. We have a zero tolerance target for collateral. That's a bit different to some of the people we have been up against, who use fear as a weapon. We get a lot of briefs about morality and proportionality. We are trained as much on that as the flying.

I am an instructor at the RAF college for initial officer training. Some of them will be promoted above me very quickly. The stars I'm training now will be Squadron Leaders in seven years and I will be calling them Sir or Ma'am.

On Week 24 they have to call me Sir and jump however high I say. By the time they graduate they are junior officers and they can come and tell me what they really think. So you can't be an absolute idiot to them. I wouldn't anyway, I'm not in the militarisation stage, I'm not making them crawl through mud. I'm sitting in a classroom with them talking about leadership.

I've never been in an environment where we only train men. When I started, females had just been accepted as fast jet air crew. Honestly, I don't think of male and female cadets differently. If someone's good enough to do the job I don't care if they are man, woman, straight or gay. We've got great female pilots. Would that have been seen as a good career for a wife and mother just ten years ago?

I'm proud of the fact that I've changed my views. I was probably homophobic in my youth. In my town and the factory I worked in, that's how it was. Meeting someone gay would have made me uncomfortable. Now I have gay friends. I couldn't care less any more.

Being an officer and a gentleman are similar, which is why I was drawn first to be one and now teach them. It's about a set of virtues to live by, such as loyalty. This has existed for centuries, from the Spartans through to the Samurai code of bushido and our own knights' chivalry. There is a quote I like: 'Being male is a matter of birth. Being a man is a matter of age. Being a gentleman is a matter of choice.'

I'm very attached to my penis! We've gone through a lot together. I'm fairly confident that it's about average.

One day I was watching TV and my hand just wandered to where it does and I found a lump. Lance Armstrong is now this villain that nobody likes, but through his books I had awareness of testicular cancer and that probably saved my life. I knew that testicular cancer would be no big deal and I could make a full recovery.

I went straight to the doctor. I've been really lucky, I've not missed a heartbeat throughout the whole process. I was of the opinion that it was better gone and be healthy, than to worry about it. I approached it with quite a lot of humour as well. I made sure they drew a really big arrow on my right thigh to make sure they took the right testicle.

I was back in the cockpit, flying jets, within three months of finding the lump. I was discharged after five years.

Cancer didn't hit my manliness. I have a reasonably fulfilling and active sex life. Someone asked me if it's embarrassing only having one ball. By the time a woman's close enough to count them it's a done deal, so I don't really care. I don't bring it up beforehand. I might ask if she spotted anything different afterwards!

Before the experience you don't do awareness work, obviously, but afterwards you want to make sure no one else has it. I'm involved with a few charities now. I'm always preaching not to be embarrassed.

There was a competition in 2014 by a shaving brand looking for 'Britain's Manliest Man.' How ridiculous! But it was sponsored by Orchid, a male cancer charity. They weren't looking for looks, they were asking if you had a manly job, or a story to tell, or if you do work for charity, that sort of thing. I thought it would be an amazing platform to talk about testicular cancer, to talk about manliness and the number of balls I have. So I entered and got down to the last 40. Luckily, my story seemed to resonate and I won the popular vote. The other guys were fitness guys with ripped six packs.

The media tells us that if you are a spy, fireman or soldier, that is manly. My dad was the manliest man I knew. I realise now he hated his job in a factory. He only did it to support his wife and kids. What's more manly than that?

I'm a fast jet navigator, I've been to war several times, and if someone said I was less manly for having one testicle, I'd say, 'Have you been to war?'

It's good to be involved with this project. It wasn't easy though! But I do this awareness work, and I have to put my money where my mouth is. If the Spartans could go into battle naked then I can take part in this project!

Forty-five years old

"I felt constantly rejected"

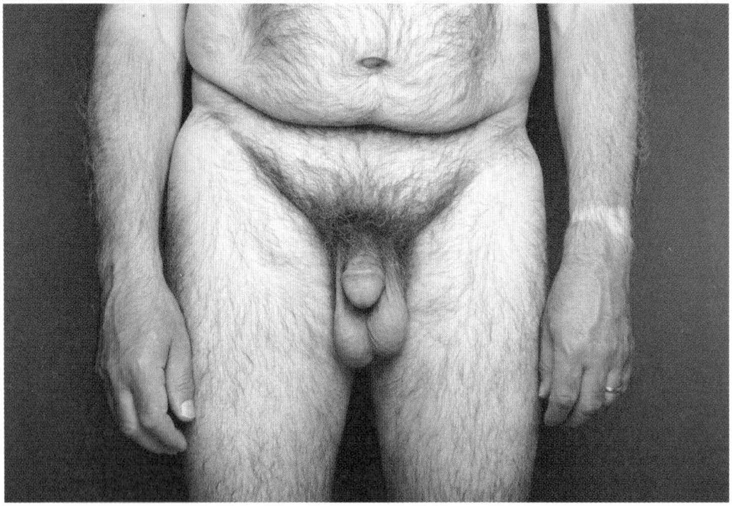

I don't like my penis at all. I feel quite ashamed of it. I would like it to be bigger. If I don't have an erection I feel inadequate. I'm annoyed I was born with such a small one.

I've been married for 24 years and we have two grown-up children. We had a good, healthy sex life for the first few years of our marriage. When my second child was born 20 years ago, my wife stopped being interested in sex. We made love maybe once or twice a year after that. I felt constantly rejected. There were a myriad of little excuses, being tired, having a headache. It used to make me feel emasculated and frustrated. The only way I could deal with it was masturbation.

I've always found masturbation very unsatisfying on the whole. Ejaculation would give relief, but I would feel ashamed of myself afterwards, as if I'd done something dirty. It is messy and you have to clean up afterwards, which isn't pleasant.

You need intimacy to keep a relationship going. Sex and intimacy aren't the same, but it's hard to keep intimacy going without the sex. I have to accept some of it is my fault too. We didn't talk about it earlier in the relationship and state what our needs were.

We had some therapy and were given 'homework'. I discovered that my wife wanted the touchy-feely stuff without sex, whereas I wanted the sex. The homework was that I would do the touchy-feely stuff and she would have sex. I did my part of the deal, but she still didn't want to have sex. There was no willingness on her part.

I have talked about it with close friends. Some people say there is a sexual contract of sorts in marriage. Women friends of a similar age who have also lost their sex drive say they still have sex with their husbands to stop them going elsewhere.

I feel angry and rejected. If my wife initiated sexual relations now I think I would be quite nervous. I struggle at home now, there is a negative atmosphere. I think the only solution is to leave, but I don't have the mental strength to do that at the moment.

I have had a lot of mental health problems in the last several years and I am on various drugs. I don't know if it's a drug thing, or a personal thing, but I now have erectile dysfunction. Occasionally if I dance up close to someone I can feel myself get a little bit hard, but that's about it. I slow danced with someone a few weeks ago; nothing happened that was wrong, but I felt a little frisson of excitement. If I was to dance with my wife I don't think I would feel that. So much negative stuff has passed between us now.

My mental health problems have lurked in the background of my life until they surfaced in my 50s. I developed OCD at school. I think it was a coping strategy, because I had no control over my life and I was bullied and teased. I was sent to public boarding school at the age of seven, which is ridiculously young. I found life very difficult. The whole of schooling was a horrible experience and scarred me. I am still scarred now. I don't look back with any fondness.

When I got to the age of 20 I decided to invent a new me – one that was confident and fun to be with. So I did, I built a different me.

Gradually this persona became part of me, and I became part of it.

Then as an adult I developed anxiety and depression. At times it has been low profile. Now it is right up there. I have lots of intrusive thoughts and rituals to do with contamination. Since becoming ill I have started to lose the persona I developed when I was 20 and gone back to the me when I was 12 and threatened to kill myself.

We used to have to write letters home every week and it was invigilated. If you wrote anything negative about school you had to rewrite the letter. Your parents thought you were having a wonderful time. The letters were completely and utterly meaningless. I worked out how to get letters home without the school knowing and I told my parents how unhappy I was and that I was going to kill myself. It was a cry for help rather than a serious plan. My parents were very worried and called the headmaster. He told them he would deal with it. I was called to his office. 'Your parents are very upset to have received this letter from you. There is no problem, is there? Now, don't do it again.'

Have people talked to you about wet dreams? They are really peculiar. You have a dream, not even necessarily a sexual one, but at some point in the dream you feel like you are weeing. For me, the ejaculation would feel like weeing in my pants in the dream. The first time was scary, having all this mess everywhere, I had no idea. We had very little sex education, and it was purely about the biology. Sex was just a funny word at school.

I think my father only talked to me once, very briefly, about sex. When I was 18 he suddenly said out of the blue, 'Well, you know what I think about sex before marriage, don't you?' I thought, 'Woah...' So I said yes. I used to joke later that I assumed he approved of it!

When I first had sex I was 21 and I had no clue what to do. I didn't know where to find her vagina, and I couldn't sustain an erection. We tried on that one occasion and then we never talked about it and never went to bed again. We went out for a few more months and then it was over. I didn't have sex properly till my next girlfriend. I've never really discussed sex with partners.

Sixty years old

"I might go through life without having sex again"

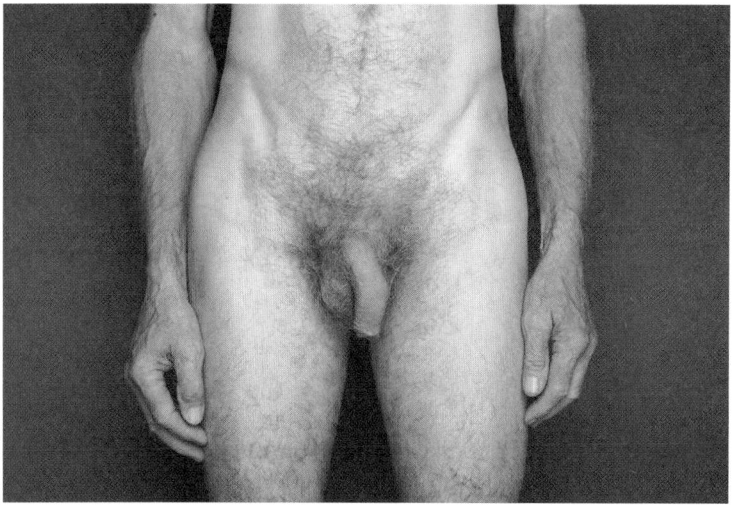

I'm a private person. I don't like talking about personal things, especially my sexual habits. I don't think many people do, unless it's to a very good friend.

My first time with a woman was unbelievable really. I must have been 18 at the time. I put a woman up for the night to help her out. I didn't really know her and I thought she would settle down on the floor, or that I would. It was quite a surprise that she took her clothes off, got into bed and snuggled up with me. I had such a hard-on, I was so excited. But I was also worried, because I didn't think she was the right person for me and

I didn't want her to get pregnant. Luckily I had some protection. I needed several condoms that night! It wasn't just one position, there were several. She had an amazing sexual awareness and knew what to do. It seemed like she had experience behind her, and she taught me a few things that night. It was an exciting time to lose my virginity, but it was tinged with anxiety about her getting pregnant.

She came back a second night because she'd left her handbag. I wondered if it might be an excuse. It was so tempting, but I said, 'No, I don't think we ought to.' I knew she wasn't the right woman for me. I wasn't that attracted to her.

I am currently divorced. I've been married twice. I've had lots of emotions over the years I have been sexually active. The first time I got married was really to pass on my genes. She didn't have as much sex drive as me, but she was very intelligent and quite good-looking. I was attracted to her and I thought she would make a good mother. It didn't feel as clinical at the time as it sounds now. I think that when she was interested sexually it was because she wanted children. I don't regret the marriage as I have three fantastic children and seven grandchildren.

When our eldest child was 16 my wife said she didn't want to make love to me anymore and I could find someone else if I wanted. I didn't want to go on like brother and sister.

More recently I have had a relationship where we were very sexually compatible. We've been with each other for about five years. We fancied each other a lot.

I get a huge amount of pleasure out of foreplay with women, as much as making love. It's not about the orgasm, it's about the path to it, the intimacy, the giving and the taking. Exchanging love is what it's about. The sensation goes after the orgasm. I love the build-up. Rather than going over the edge, my ideal is to make love for hours.

I'm a loving person. I have a huge amount of love to give. I don't want to be grasping. The last partner and I were very good with each other in some ways, but she was quite different to me. I'd love to find somebody who is loving in the same way. I don't think I have ever found anyone who is right for me. But I have a hurdle to climb. What I haven't mentioned is that my last partner had genital herpes. I didn't find out until it was too late.

She told me to go to a sexual health clinic. We both had the full set of tests. I came out with no problem, nothing at all. She also had no problem. We both had a clear bill of health. But they don't screen for genital herpes. I wish I had asked the clinic if there is anything they don't screen for, and to tell me what to ask my partner. I think we should be made aware of what a difficult thing genital herpes is to deal with. I assumed she didn't have it. I would have thought she would have told me. She didn't tell me until we had made love a number of times.

There isn't any treatment. That's why I'm in a bit of a hole. It's like having a cold sore. When it came on there were blisters on my penis. The first flare-up was very painful, and didn't look good at all. Quite off-putting. Devastating. She was distraught because she didn't realise it affected people like that. She wasn't half as distraught as me.

She wasn't quite the right person for me. If she had been, I could have spent the rest of my life with her and then it wouldn't have mattered. I have missed her though. I miss the closeness, and also the fantastic sexual experiences we had. She is otherwise diametrically opposite to me in attitudes and life. A few times I thought I could live with her and we could get on OK, but I'd get to a stage when I'd been with her for a period of time and want out. Then I'd be out for a period of time and miss her. There's been a lot of coming and going. I think she loved me. *(cries)* We haven't communicated for about six months. I think she's fed up of me coming and going.

I don't know quite what to do. The only thing you can do is wait. You are less and less likely to have an outbreak over the years. You have to just leave it to heal itself. I could go back to the clinic, but I don't have any hopes. Gonorrhoea would be better than this; at least you can do something about that. Condoms help, but they don't completely protect. I haven't had symptoms for months, but every now and again it can flare up. When you don't have a flare-up it's alright, but there is still a bit of a risk to your partner.

Very few people would want to take the risk with me now. I might go through life without having another sexual partner. I am devastated. I would like to be sexually active and I have lots of love to give. I think the only person I could safely have a relationship with would be a woman who also has the genital herpes virus.

I hope my story helps other people. I think people should ask their partner, outright, face to face, if they have herpes. I know it's difficult.

I feel like I have gone down into a hole and there is no way out. I just have to accept it and do the best I can. Who knows what will happen in the future. But I am positive. I have had a fantastic life so far.

Sixty-five years old

“I wanted her to feel the power of my cock”

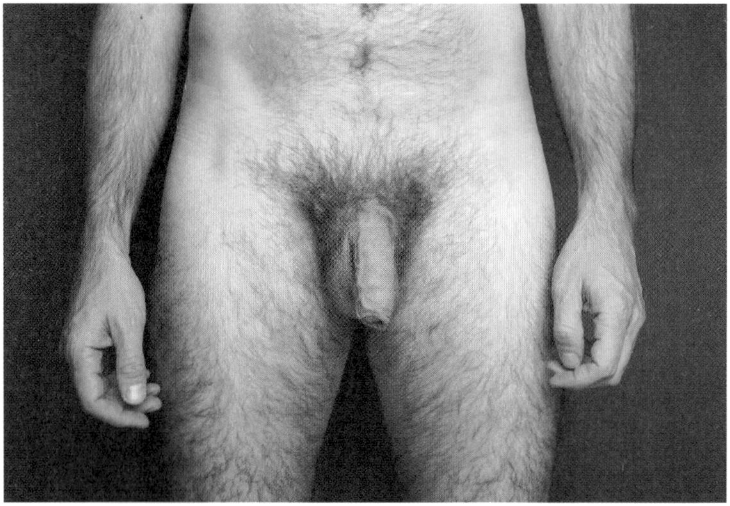

I use the word penis. Cock has more of a sexual connotation. I’m embarrassed to use the word willy, it’s a silly and childish word. I used it when I told a friend I was doing this. I’m ashamed to use it because it trivialises it, although it’s to take the edge off.

I love the idea of having a fucking massive schlong. A beast. Today I asked my girlfriend to hold my cock before we had sex. I wanted her to feel the power of my cock. I wanted to be powerful.

What I think of my penis has changed over the years. I learnt to masturbate really young, accidentally. I was at boarding school and we all used to shower in a big cubicle together. There was a guy who looked semi-circumcised. I really wished I'd been circumcised, I preferred the look. I used to pull my foreskin backwards and forwards to stretch it, to look the same, and then I got aroused. So, yeah, I used to do that fairly regularly! I didn't think it was anything to be ashamed of. I used to do it in bed, and my roommates must have been able to hear me jiggle around in bed. I didn't know it was a thing. I was only 10 or 11.

As a teenager you wonder what the average size is and how you compare. I measured, regularly, just to see if it was still growing. I was obsessed with knowing whether my penis was average or bigger. When I was a teenager I thought I had a really small penis to look at when it wasn't erect. I remember going to see my older brother and saying I was worried about it. He said we all had big penises in our family. I insisted mine was small, so he asked to see. 'Yeah, that's really tiny. What is it, four or five inches when it's erect?' Actually it was seven or eight inches when it was erect, so he said not to worry. Also, much later, he taught me to masturbate and I had to pretend not to know, so I didn't spoil it. He showed me how to put a condom on as well.

My penis isn't 100 per cent straight when it's erect. I didn't know if that would be a bad thing. I was worried it was because I had masturbated when I was young! That was a big thing for me in the relationship with my penis. I found a book by my mother's bed called, *Everything You Wanted To Know About Sex But Were Too Afraid to Ask*, and read about this thing called 'bent nail syndrome', where the cock bends to the side. Some people can be so badly bent that it does cause a problem. Once I started to have sexual relationships no one minded. Girlfriends told me I had a very nice cock. And in the end, it's what you can do with it that matters.

But I am aware I am talking around this big lump in my sexual experience, which happened when I was at boarding school. I suppose my first sexual experience was with two guys in my cubicle. I've almost never told anyone this. We'd take it in turns to pretend to be girls and hump each other in the missionary position. We were going through the motions, and we were naked, but there was no sensuality and we didn't orgasm. We never mentioned it to each other afterwards. I'm not friends with those boys now.

I was 18 when I first had sex. She was 23 and I met her at a party. She sucked me off in the orchard. We met up a week later and had sex. At 18 you can do it over and over again. She brought herself off by rubbing herself on me. By the end of the night my dick was pretty raw. Then we spent a weekend together and we must have done it 10 times. She rubbed herself a lot. She felt like a much older woman at the time, so it was pretty cool, a big badge of honour.

I went through a phase in my late 30s when I felt my libido decrease a lot. That really worried me. I've always been a bit of a tart when I'm free, not when I'm in relationships. It came to a point when I'd get girls into bed and I wouldn't want to have sex with them. That really bothered me. Now I realise I don't want to fuck people for the sake of it. My cock knew that before I did. My libido has gone down, but my maturity has gone up.

There was a woman who I had God-like sex with; she jumped me, really went for it. She was the first person who deep-throated me and that was pretty amazing. The sex was wild and I was able to make her come easily, over and over again. She was very loud, but not in a way that is fake. I've been with girls who make the porn star noises and it seems fake, but she was so passionately connected with her body. It made me rise up and be more animalistic and God-like and have sex hard, and soft, and not come quickly. She was the first woman who ejaculated on me too. But although we had this incredible sex, I couldn't be bothered to spend time with her. She was fake in every other way. I think she was always trying to impress me, and to be what I wanted, which made me despise her.

There have been times I've been ashamed of my manhood. I had a girlfriend who was abused as a child. I felt bad having penetrative sex with her. I've always been quite good with fingers and my tongue, and that was enough for me. I didn't want to fuck her. When I did have sex with her I felt bad about it, like I'd taken something from her. It must be so different to penetrate and be penetrated. Being penetrated must be more personal. Maybe I'm wrong.

I'm now with a girlfriend who is gorgeous. Sex wasn't amazing at first, but as the love and the trust has grown the sex has changed. She is quite young and her libido is much stronger at times. It worries me that I won't fulfil her and satisfy her. We've grown together in the two years we've known each other. I'm not having any problems in that area, although I haven't reached her levels of libido. I get aroused often enough because of the love and trust between us.

So, I'm very happy with my penis at the moment; we have a very good relationship, in terms of how it works mechanically and being connected to my emotions.

I don't like to think about what being a man means. We're not just men and women, we're human. I do feel like a man, of course. You don't get many women my size and shape. If I hold my woman in bed I am very aware of the difference in our size and my role as the biological protector. There are different ways of defining feminism, but it's our role as men to be feminists. I'm not individually responsible for violent and abusive acts carried out by men the world over, but we do all have to acknowledge things have happened.

In a world much less comfortable than ours, it's men who fight to protect women. I hate the fact that human society is violent, but when the shit hits the fan, and when people cannot get on with their neighbours, it will generally be the young men who will fight and kill each other, to protect their women and their food resources.

I wondered if men might fantasise about taking part in this project, having their photograph taken. Maybe I'm projecting, although I think some men will have fantasised about it. When I'm with a human being, you, now, and I respect you, I don't want to have sex with you. But in my imagination, I'm going to take my clothes off and be photographed, and there is room for objectification and fantasy. I created a fantasy around this. In the lead-up to this there have been moments where I've wondered if something sexual might happen in this room today. I wondered if we might do an erect shot as well as a flaccid shot, and how we would effect that. I wasn't sure whether to go into this, because I didn't want to create any discomfort in this room now, but I think these thoughts would occur to any heterosexual man.

Forty years old

“I feel happier when I get to share it with people”

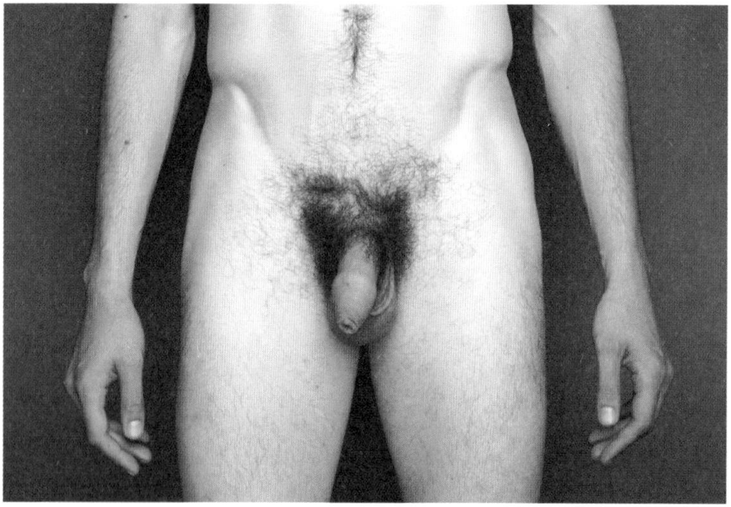

As a child my relationship with my penis was joy and playfulness. I literally used to play it like a guitar and pretend to strum it. As you grow up you are told not to show it and wear clothes more. It goes from a feeling of playfulness to shame and vulnerability.

How do you know what a good size penis is when you hit puberty? I had two friends who used to measure their penises and talk about it. It was quite a concern for me. American films like American Pie talk about penis size and add to the insecurity.

Throughout school and college and university I was terrified to expose myself to people in case the boys judged me and thought my penis was smaller than theirs, or the girls thought I was inadequate. Not wanting to expose yourself for fear of humiliation becomes the norm.

When I first realised I could masturbate and ejaculate that was a wonderful time of my life! It was incredible and insane to discover I could have that pleasure, and it was private and it was mine. But at the same time I had this massive shame that I could be discovered doing it.

No one ever said I shouldn't masturbate, but from a religious perspective I wasn't sure. I believed in God until I studied philosophy when I was 15. I remember not wanting to masturbate on Sundays because it was the Lord's day.

Last year I started experimenting with psychedelics. I read about how they can alleviate depression. Having gone through two depressions myself I thought I'd try magic mushrooms. It was literally one of the best experiences of my life. I made huge jumps in my understanding of myself and stripping away negative filters. I'm not as afraid of things anymore.

I used to be scared of how women would perceive me when I was naked. No one has ever said I look horrible naked or have a small penis. I think that taking mushrooms helped me erode these fears. Fear of being naked and fear of sexuality are used to control us. I think if we lived in a world where people had more sex we would be more relaxed and there would be less violence and horrible things. And yet sex is such a big taboo.

I feel more comfortable with my penis these days. I feel happier when I get to share it with people. The more comfortable I am naked, the better the sex and the whole relationship goes, because I'm not trying to hide anything, the insecurity is gone. The first time I couldn't get it up was when I was stressed about lots of areas of my life. I felt less of a man. The idea of manhood is so tied to the ability to have sex.

I want to be even more comfortable about my penis and talking about it. Taking part in this is a step in that direction. Initially I felt reticent and fearful about taking part in *Manhood*. I thought, 'How can I expose myself to the world?' I've been trying to think about where my reactions and beliefs come from. I think we are conditioned from an early age. It's almost like we are told to hide and repress our sexuality. How can the means to reproduce and create pleasure be something to be ashamed of?

I think the next stage in my life is to be more honest. I think I'm one of the most honest people I know; I'd only tell a white lie to not hurt someone, but I want to get to the point where I can be as honest as possible. I worked out after a relationship that didn't go anywhere that I don't want to be in a relationship. I couldn't handle it. I'm very committed to my work and I would drop the ball in the relationship all the time. This girl clocked that I would always be busy with work. She confronted me with it. And I thought it was interesting. I need to be more honest about it. She put a lot into the relationship and invested herself in it for three months. So I told the next girl I met that I didn't want a relationship. After a while it was obvious she was giving more to the relationship than I could, and I had to tell her that I couldn't do it, even though that meant I had less access to amazing sex, and intimacy and amazing conversations.

Next I have to be more honest with myself about what I want. I don't want a relationship at the moment, but I know I want intimacy. I don't think I want a traditional monogamous relationship because it consumes my life. I don't want to just have sex, I want to have intimacy and great conversations. I want to have my cake and eat it, which is stupid. I see how happy my parents are and I think I want it one day, but not now.

My parents met years before they got married. My father was a priest and my mother was a nun. They were both from Spain, from very Catholic families. As a priest and a nun they both used to whip themselves and tie that wire thing round their legs. I read about that in a Dan Brown book and thought it was some crazy shit, but my dad said they all used to do it back in the day. They left the Church to get married.

I was brought up religiously: baptised, communion, confirmation. I used to pray every night. Church every Sunday. My dad became an armchair philosopher and quite critical of the Church and didn't mind that I stopped believing in God. They didn't stop believing in God, but they had been missionaries in Africa and questioned what that had really done for Africa. My dad ended up supporting the liberation movement and my parents were very conscious. I'm very inspired that two people fell in love and did what they did. I think it's beautiful.

Twenty-eight years old

“It’s a bit like a badly-behaved uncle at a wedding”

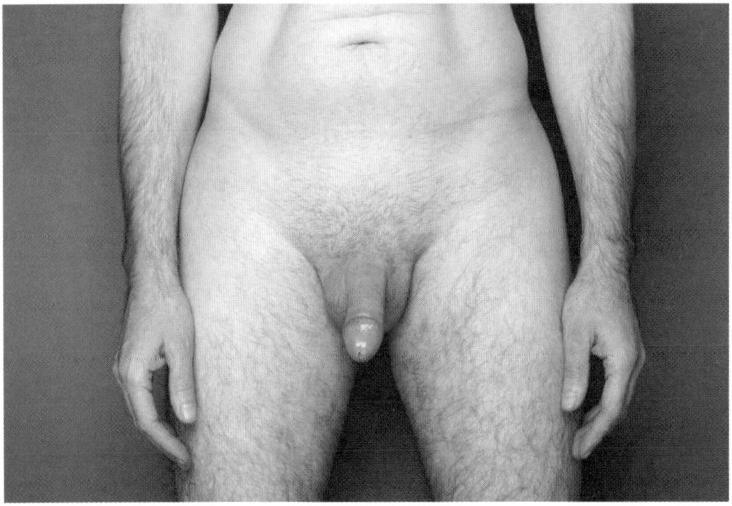

I would define my relationship with my penis as one of acceptance. I am 52 years old, and with age comes acceptance of all sorts of things: your body, the ageing process, the life you lead, the house you live in, the job you have, the money you have or don’t have. I have come to an accommodation with my penis. It’s not tiny. And anyway, it’s the only one I’ve got.

I’m happy with it and accept it. What I would say about it, it’s the one part of my body that hasn’t grown up with me. It’s a bit like a badly-behaved uncle at a wedding. I’m a grown man, I know which knives and forks to use, I can choose wine with reasonable confidence, and I can move in all kinds of social circles. The rest of my body understands that, but my penis has a mind of its own. You would think by this age you would have control over your penis, but it will still have an erection on the London Underground for no apparent reason. Skinny dipping can be a problem. Sometimes I've been halfway to the water and found myself with an erection. A penis can betray you. I wish I had volume control over my penis. Maybe one day it won't be like a badly-behaved uncle, but more like a grandpa on a chair who can't get up anymore!

I take my penis for granted. It's very good at going up, less good at coming down. I was ever so slightly anxious about the photograph for *Manhood*. I was worried I might have an unwanted erection. I bet other men have had them. They haven't? Ah. I would have been absolutely mortified if I'd been the only one!

Penises are masters of disguise; they can appear in many forms. My wife is not obsessed with her vagina, lovely though it is, but men are obsessed with their penises. My penis can be appallingly small if I jump in the sea, to the extent I can't even look at it! I wanted it to look normal for the photograph today, like it looks most days when I am relaxed, not like I've just come out of the North Sea.

I do think penises and testicles are untidy. My penis is fairly average when it's down. I like it best when it is erect. I like the look of it. It looks, dare I say it, almost beautiful. When I think of my declining body, one of my best bits is my erect penis.

I love clothes. I love the symbolism of clothes, the theatre of it, the dressing up. Deep down I think it's a bit of frippery, a bit of fun, an enjoyable way to spend your money. I think clothes are important.

I've always dressed the same. I have the same tie clip I bought for 35p 20 years ago. Without my suit I would feel naked in meetings. I'm an open person, but I do like to feel buttoned up in that most conventional of outfits, the three-piece suit. I don't think the suit makes the man, but it can't hurt. Clothes are like armour.

Normally I am in my suit and my tie clip. This is a rare opportunity to be seen as I am. A not terribly impressive lump of flesh. I think as men we are redefining ourselves.

I'm not trying to impress anyone anymore, I'm not a player. I've been with my wife for over 20 years. I am careful with younger women I know, the girlfriends of my nephews, girls in work settings. Girls are very sexualised these days. I am conscious and careful of that. I am a flirtatious person by nature and I adore women and I modify what my natural behaviour would be. A man in his 50s with a sexual appetite would seem disgusting to a younger woman, and I do have a duty of care.

I love looking at nude women, and I like a nude photograph, but I never look at porn. I have looked at it, but I don't like it. What is the line between artistic photography, erotica or porn? It's difficult to say. A female friend told me to look at this very mainstream porn website. So I looked and I was revolted. It wasn't about sexuality, it was about power. I only want to see a beautiful naked woman on her terms. I wouldn't pay some poor woman to show me her body, which is kind of what porn is about. At school I was the older-looking one and I was sent in to shops to buy the porn mags, but I consider that to be 1970s sex education!

Masculinity means different things in different cultures. I think in the US everyone probably thinks I am an effete, arty Englishman. I was troubled by people thinking I was gay in the past. Now I don't care. As I've got older I've become less obsessed with masculinity or femininity. I think we should just be who we want to be. I think we need a more accepting view of people.

What it means to be a man has changed as I have got older. I no longer compare myself to others or use their standards. There will always be someone who is buffer than you, has more hair than you, a bigger penis or a bigger bank balance.

You have to be your own hero. We all have to get by in this world. Running organisations, bringing up kids, photographing penises, whatever you do, we have to get by with good grace and humour and care and dignity. You have to look for the hero within.

Fifty-two years old

Methodology

I wanted to include and represent men of all ages (18 was the minimum age for participation), ethnicity, sexual orientation, career, life experience, shape and size. It's important to remember that *Manhood* is an art project, not an academic one. I was looking for willing participants in a sensitive project, who would have interesting tales to tell.

The participants were given information about the project and its aims, and signed a release form. Interviews were recorded, then transcribed verbatim. In the editing stage, word choices were rarely changed, although the text was shortened and rearranged to improve the flow.

The photographs were not altered in Photoshop, aside from a few identifying tattoos and birthmarks, which participants requested be removed. The photographs were shot consistently so they could be viewed comparatively and non-sexually.

I wrote a discussion guide to help me structure interviews where useful, but it was never strictly followed. Conversations were allowed to flow according to the individual man and his interests and experience. The conversation guide covered subjects such as: growing up, appearance, size, penile enhancement surgery, circumcision, erections, media, society, culture, gender, sexuality, relationships, pornography, occupation, health, ageing, compliments and harrassment. All men were asked what they think about their penis.

Acknowledgements

Thank you to all my family and friends for listening to me and encouraging me. Thank you to Martin, Maria, Zoë and Emily at Pinter & Martin for believing in *Manhood* and bringing it to life.

Thank you to Ethan and Cole, my wonderful sons – the two best men in the world. You inspire me to be the best I can be. Your boyhood has been a delight and my greatest project is watching you grow into manhood.

A huge and heartfelt thank you to the 100 men who took part in *Manhood*. Thank you for trusting me and stepping into this unusual, brave and intimate space. I hope that *Manhood* honours your courage and vulnerability in baring your bodies and stories.